Wakefield Press

Wallaby

An Aussie, A Broad

Rod Maclean always wanted to write the 'great Australian novel'. Instead he ended up as a journalist writing grabs, voice-overs and, of course, the story of the day for television news.

But in between the news, he somehow managed to traverse the world and to keep diaries about those journeys. This is his story covering 25 years of travel with his wife and (sometimes unwilling) offspring.

Rod proudly did write an Aussie novel, *Eric and Ian get a life* and a biography of Griselda Sprigg, an outback pioneer, *Dune is a four-letter word.*

Rod Maclean

Wakefield Press
1 The Parade West
Kent Town
South Australia 5067
www.wakefieldpress.com.au

First published 2004

Designed and typeset by Ryan Paine, Wakefield Press
Printed and bound by dbooks

National Library of Australia
Cataloguing-in-publication entry

Maclean, Rod, 1955–2003.
Wallaby: An Aussie, a broad.

ISBN 1 86254 653 3.

1. Maclean, Rod, 1955–2003 – Health. 2. Cancer – Patients – South Australia – Biography. I. Title.

362.1969940092

Wakefield Press thanks Fox Creek Wines and Arts South Australia for their support.

LIVORNO STATION

As the train stays its pensive passage
and waits, regaining steam,
preparing for another reel of miles and minutes,
you read and wait for me to tell you
where the journey ends.
The train will regain its resting stop,
its terminus of belching sleep,
its reconstruction; we must travel on.
In a strangeness of cities and tongues
and threadbare hours of passing through
and being gone
before all time departs
and all goals die along the road
like quickly eaten dinners,
we seek to belong to something,
perhaps afraid to find we only have each other.
The train hauls us into another country,
bearing south in sunlight.
Our journey is not past.
It will never end in Rome.

26 October, 1977

Contents

Introduction

The train pulled out of Adelaide's Keswick terminus a few minutes after its scheduled 6.40 pm departure. My wife Teddi and I were bound for Perth, 2659 long kilometres west. We had just come aboard the Indian Pacific, the transcontinental service that originates in Sydney and is often described as one of the great railway journeys of the world.

It was a foul winter night in mid-June, 2003. Rain streaked the picture window that dominated one side of our sleeper. As the train gathered momentum and racketed through the city's industrial back alleys, there was a faint clang of level crossing warning bells, a flash of blinking lights and headlight queues in blurry diagonals. Then blackness stole the view. As I stared into the gloom, I found myself reflecting that my first experience of the Indian Pacific was also likely to be my last.

'Enough of that crap!' I told myself. 'This is meant to be *fun*!' I left the window and joined Teddi's examination of the first-class cabin we'd been allocated.

Berths 7 and 8 in Gold Kangaroo Service Car J were configured for daytime travel. We had three broad seats to ourselves, lots of ingenious stowage spaces, and a tiny private bathroom in which the toilet and hand-basin folded away so you could draw a waterproof curtain over the whole works and blast away with the hot shower whenever the mood to be clean so demanded.

Before he left us to explore, Doug asked if we wanted to dine during the 7 pm sitting, or wait until the second session two hours later. These days my appetite is rather ascetic. Knowing I'm far too lazy to feed myself, Teddi is sympathetically sparing with what she serves up, in lots of smaller serves. Now, though, we both felt ravenous and we opted for the early bite.

We found the Queen Adelaide restaurant and were rewarded with an agreeably inventive menu and a wine list to suit. While we were noshing and enjoying the company of a couple from Port Macquarie, Doug transformed our cabin. The seats were turned into bunks, the upper accessible from a nifty metal ladder, both beds cozy with quilts and extra pillows – a comfortable cocoon in which to ride the rails, through this night and another to come.

We arranged ourselves on Teddi's lower bunk, me with my back to the window, Teddi's against the wood-and-chrome-trimmed wall that separated us from the corridor outside. Our legs were tangled; the quilt was warm. I tried to write my journal. She tried to read a book. Rail rhythm soon sent the both of us to sleep.

I woke about ten-thirty. The train was rolling smoothly through an opaque night. I hauled myself into the top bunk and settled and stretched and considered myself the luckiest bloke alive.

I had lived long enough to ride the famous Indian Pacific, and soon I would add Perth to my list of lifetime firsts.

From my journal: Tuesday 7 January 2003

When he came in Dr K gave me a sympathetic pat on the back and said, 'We're in trouble, my boy.'

I didn't know about him, but I sure was. The CT scan had found one tumour in a lung plus the suspicion of another, two growths in my liver, and another tumour along my spine, showing what the report described as 'significant' damage.

It was a reasonable assumption that the tumours were metastatic melanomas, secondary cancers that invaded my organs after the initial excision of two skin lesions in 1997. Both lesions proved malignant and demanded further slicing away of my skin, leaving long scars on my left bicep and in the curve between my neck and right shoulder. I had seen Dr K and one of the state's most respected skin cancer specialists on a regular basis ever since, to ensure there were no new cancers or signs of secondary growth through my lymphatic system. There had been none. I had believed I was on the cusp of being cleared for good and had no idea my recent aches and pains were cancer related. It was now horribly clear that they were.

The doctor put the films up on his light wall and explained where the lesions were. I took it all very calmly, but there was a big, big sinking feeling in my stomach.

'So basically,' I said, when he'd finished, 'I'm fucked.'

'I wouldn't want to be the first person to say that, but it's pretty diabolical.'

(Next day, Wednesday, I tried to go to work. I lasted, but towards the end lapsed into a sudden and massive fever that my doctor put down to a bodily shock reaction to the terrible news.

I was senior producer at ABC TV news in Adelaide. Somehow I had managed to compile a news rundown, sub-edit the reporters' scripts and the presenter's 'intros'. I even managed to make a brief farewell speech to a colleague who'd been poached to another newsroom. At 7 pm, news time, I sat in 'my' control-room chair and watched the show go to air, drifting in and out of consciousness.

Fortunately, the night was routine; no fast footwork was demanded of the man who had no idea he was working the last paid shift in his life, or that his 29 years in journalism were suddenly over.

I drove home with care, shaking and shivering inside a navy blue jacket I'd borrowed from the make-up room to keep me warm.

On the following Friday an eminent surgeon specializing in cancer told me that, because there were lesions in so many places, surgery was not an option. He added this: on the averages, I had four to six months to live.)

It was 11.38 pm. The train was stationary. Teddi murmured faintly in her sleep. I eased my spine carefully so I could peer out the window. The rain had stopped but all I could see was a platform bathed in wan yellow light and a couple of antique railway benches.

I found my timetable and figured we were either changing crew at Port Augusta or pulled up at Spencer Junction. I didn't much care. I had a dose of hiccups. Sometimes my recently repaired belly acts badly.

When the train rolled again, a solitary man watched us depart. He stood in a pool of golden light and didn't move a muscle.

Ward 7B, Royal Adelaide Hospital: Tuesday 21 January 2003

Four entire days have disappeared. Things have happened that I have been incapable of following. . . .

It won't be easy to reconstruct this. I'm still up to my eyeballs in morphine on demand. . . .

Exactly one week after my diagnosis I had suffered an agonizing partial spine collapse and was hospitalized for emergency pain control, urgent radiotherapy and possible surgery to put some 'metalwork' in my spine. My sister Andy flew from her home in northern New South Wales to be with me. I had had two of the proposed five radiation treatments, and—with my back pain under control with painkillers—I was lobbying to go home and have the remaining three treatments as an outpatient.

It was just after breakfast Saturday morning. I'd showered and shaved, feeling good. The phone rang. I was chatting when something gave way in my upper left stomach or bowel and I was in searing pain. In the parlance of the 'pain scale' this was a force 10 hurricane. I gasped that I couldn't talk any more, hung up, pressed the buzzer for the nurses and lay there writhing, praying they would hurry. . . .

At first the staff seemed satisfied this was constipation. My drugs (morphine and several other constipation-inducing painkillers) had gummed me up for days. I had been warned to expect it. I was written up for two suppositories that I self-administered in the toilet, shaking with pain, for little result. Then I lay back in bed, trying with zero success to ease the pain, which—every time I was asked—I described as in the high range, agony.

At various times people came to visit. I was no great company. Teddi was asking the staff if this might not be something more than constipation. She asked if it could be a bowel rupture. There was no denial that this was a possibility. There seemed an almost palpable fear that Teddi could be right. . . .

Day turned to night. The country was blazing with bushfires. I had no idea. All I could see was the full disc of yellow moon climbing ever so slowly from the lower right corner of my window up through the blackness to the upper left. By the time it reached the top I had had no change – no new ideas, new treatments; I was lying there and thinking it was possible I might die there. . . .

The fact that I lived, I put down to the night shift nurse, a no-nonsense and experienced Englishwoman named Jean. It was she who distinctly muttered that all was not well, and who calmly proceeded to galvanise the interventions that combined to save my life. I recall more doctors, more hands on my belly. I remember going for x-rays (somewhere around 2 am), flat on my back, pushed along in my bed by muscled orderlies, bumping into the lifts, grimacing always through pain. The x-ray people confirmed a perforation somewhere in my bowel and a surgical registrar was consulted. It was put to me that we had two choices:

'We operate, find the perforation, stitch it up. Or we do nothing and you die.'

I signed consent documents, including permission for a colostomy bag if it was needed. Early Sunday morning, Teddi and the girls and Andy said, 'Goodbye, good luck, love ya'. The anaesthetic brought sweet oblivion. . . .

Eventually I became aware the pain was gone. I had survived.

There is a down side to picking the 7 pm dinner sitting on the Indian Pacific. It means you get the early sitting for breakfast and lunch as well.

Doug brought us a morning cuppa at 6.15 am and we were blearily parking ourselves in the dining car at 6.45 am, still dripping from our first experience with the ingenious but cramped shower.

The rising sun gave a brilliant pink-red hue to the sandy country we were clacking through, the dunes liberally scattered with low shrubs, stunted eucalypts and desert oaks. We'd rolled through the tiny siding of Barton, where we spied the shambling ruin of some man's castle, home and fencing alike constructed entirely of rusting corrugated iron, festooned with graffiti and glaring an insolent red.

Now we were on the fringes of the Nullarbor Plain, next stop Cook, another transcontinental service town that had the misfortune to be named after a long gone Australian Prime Minister. Cook used to boast a population nearing 300, before the government-owned Australian National Railways were sold off to private companies. These days the refueling station has a population of two. One of them was a lady selling souvenir beer stubby coolers, tea towels and fridge magnets to the twice-weekly train-full of holidaying pensioners and backpackers who dutifully disgorge themselves from the first class sleepers and coach-class seats, clicking mercilessly away with their cameras. It was cloudless, windy and cold. We shuffled through the souvenir store and looked at the uniform, verandahed government-built houses and neatly paved pathways of a company town turned to a ghost town, virtually overnight. You could almost hear the kids, still playing on the swings.

I shot a photo of a water tank on which somebody had painted a large picture of the train, and the smiling, bearded face of 'Murray Sims, Cook's longest serving railway worker, 28 years, died at Cook.' Murray grinned out at us all, good-humoured eyes winking beneath his bushman's hat. Below the water tank was a jumble of old signal lamps, hand-push carts and rusting fettler's tools. This was 'Sims' Playground'. Nearby a sign said 'No food or fuel for next 862 km. Kalgoorlie.' What a lonely place to die.

Ward 7B: Australia Day 26 January 2003

Poor Teddi; poor me. We are so close yet so far away. Connected, disconnected. Together yet deeply afraid. This is the roller coaster and we're on it – the girls too. I have, through no fault of anybody's, tipped us into uncertainty. I can no longer be relied on as any kind of rock, and yet I strive to regain normalcy so things can carry on and our new lives begin.

The sooner I can get home the sooner this can be for all of us. Today is Sunday. That leaves three full days, before I march out of here. It will require all of my patience. I must get back my strength and not stress and champ at the bit to cut loose too soon.

(I spent the remainder of January in the Royal Adelaide, clawing back my independence from the battery of tubes and drugs and catheters that sustained me over those four days of near-death. Sustained for days by nothing but ice chips and intravenous fluids, I had lost 14 kilograms and looked – when I was able to stand long enough to take a shower – like a survivor from Changi.

Before I left hospital I had the final three radiotherapy treatments. When they let me go, Teddi sent a chauffeured car to collect me. A gentle and polite Japanese lady drove me home, classical music playing softly on the car's CD system. I felt blessed.

At home it was heaven. I drank a bottle of Carlsberg Elephant and cried at my luck in surviving. I was determined to get strong again, to live with a quality of life that would confound every doctor on the planet.)

By the time the Indian Pacific refueled and took aboard fresh crew at Cook, the tracks on which it rested comprise a tiny fraction of what is – at 487 km – the longest straight stretch of railway in the world.

Jackie, cheerful entertainment director, told us that Cook was 2829 kilometres from Sydney. 'Which means we've still got 1657 k's to have fun in!' She sipped at her fizzy blue cocktail and beamed at us.

Then Jackie told us what Murray Sim's two successors actually *do* at Cook, apart from selling fuel and crappy souvenirs. 'They look after the crew quarters for the engine drivers,' she said brightly, but somewhat suspiciously, as if the drivers were of another species and the people at Cook *certainly* were. 'The ones from Kalgoorlie stop at Cook and stay there in one of the houses you all saw – *didn't* you, Freddy!'

Freddy guffawed as if Jackie had just caught him pissing in the garden, and swiftly retorted, 'What about the drivers from Port Augusta?'

'That's easy, Freddy. They hitch a ride back later today with a freight train going back the other way.'

It didn't seem easy to me. This was bloody godforsaken country. What if the freight broke down? You'd be stuck with the souvenir woman for days on end!

But Jackie gave me little time to ruminate. 'It's 11.45. That means lunch for you Maroon Card holders for the early sitting. Chop-chop!'

I'd barely digested breakfast.

A letter to my family: 5 February 2003

Dear Everybody,

Let me now share with you my thoughts about how best I might deal with my future metastatic melanoma treatments, and my hopes to continue regaining strength and health as time goes by.

Believe me, I am a hoper. I am motivated by it and fired with ambitions and goals to achieve, knowing that the strength of my hope will carry me through.

I will tell you some more about these projects a little later.

But first, a situation report. My recovery so far has been a good one. The wound in my belly is healing. I've been home from the stint in the Royal Adelaide Hospital just under one week now, which means my fifth and final radiotherapy treatment happened one week ago. I have had some reflux and big hiccups but otherwise the guts are coming back strongly and my capacity to breathe deeper and more relaxed is improving all the time. I am exercising gently, eating well, keeping it moderate and balanced and healthy. I might not be up to a round of golf just yet, but don't count me out forever.

In short, I am feeling good and more optimistic each day that if I treat myself right and strive to achieve my many goals, they will one by one be reached, and I'll have a bloody good time getting there.

You have all shown keen interest in what I think about the treatment options. While I was in RAH, a team of medical oncology coats gave me the drill on chemotherapy strike rates in terms of metastatic melanoma – one in five get some palliative benefit, but often, because chemo is systemic, to the detriment of the body's own immune system.

You will understand, therefore, that I am not attracted to taking chemotherapy. I'll be further discussing this with the RAH team during outpatient clinics and an appointment with Prof. G, who I'll see next week. My stance is that I will say no to any chemotherapy for now. The option can be reviewed if circumstances dictate, but while I am feeling fit and fine I do not see the need to be meddling with an immune system that needs all its senses alert.

Now, to what we call the Brisbane option.

(This was preparatory to my addressing a suggestion by my extended family, that I consider a series of visits to Brisbane—where they mostly live—to join an experimental melanoma vaccine project that was showing 'encouraging' early results and attracting considerable attention in the media.)

For now I am going to take the same approach here as with the chemotherapy option. I plan to take one month's 'time-out' from this process. As I say, I'm feeling fine right now, and taking the month will enable Teddi and me to find our new house/apartment and move out of Guilford Avenue. (We had sold our Prospect home of 15 years to our daughter Myra's boyfriend, Andrew, a decision we had made before I fell ill; settlement was due within weeks.)

During the course of the month, as well as settling into new digs, and getting on with my various tasks, I will monitor my body's progress and will be in a position to know if it's in need of further boosting. If I feel it is, I'll be revisiting the options including Brisbane, and I'll have a CT brain done to send to the team at Mater Hospital.

Some of you may feel this is a cop-out by me. I describe it more as a workable delaying tactic.

And, realistically, what am I delaying? Prof. O's own estimate on the Melanoma Vaccine trial was an 'encouraging' 20% remission rate (with one or two four-year survivors), and an 80% failure corollary. These are exactly the same 'gambler's odds' given to me by the RAH medical oncologists. . . .

Now to speak briefly about my projects: Obviously, number one is the new digs. We are sending out a posse today and it is my intention to settle on a choice by the close of business. No need to delay; let's just do it.

Meantime, I am working strongly through my manuscript for a book I'm calling Wallaby: an Aussie, a Broad. It is my ambition to present Teddi with as many polished chapters as I can on the occasion of our 25th wedding anniversary, which we will combine with a housewarming party at our new place, on Tuesday 25 March.

We would love it if all of you could be here in Adelaide for that wonderful occasion. Please let me know if you'd like to be here, and we'll make it happen.

After we party I want to finish the book, a sort of travel book and autobiography all in one.

Other goals on my list include a good stint in Brisbane irrespective of the Option. We want to travel elsewhere in Australia–Alice Springs, Katherine, Darwin, to visit dear friends there as well. And ditto for the USA and Canada.

So you see I have a bountiful list. Now you see why I am keen to get on with it, to keep getting fitter and living healthy, and living every day to its maximum potential.

I promise you I will do this. Trust your son, your brother on this one, folks. I am not afraid of whatever lies ahead. I embrace my life, and I surround myself in hope.

The Nullarbor Plain lives up to its Latin derivation: no trees.

It stretches away north and south like a bleak brown infinity. Fleece clouds holding no rain scud across the burnished sky and the brown of the earth is harsh and blinding. You can imagine how ghastly the place could be in summer.

If you do see rare clumps of vegetation that are taller than the prevailing salt and blue bush, they're so far away the furthest one looks like a speeding car keeping pace with the train and overtaking the 'slower' one in the foreground. It's a strange illusion, akin in this vast place to the tracks that seem to meet on the horizon, but never do.

Letter to a friend in New York City: 20 February 2003

Dear Jonathan,

Greetings, as always, from the southern climes of Down Under, where it is pissing rain for the first time in several bad drought seasons, the El Nino effect moving its meteorological claws elsewhere in the Pacific. Good news for farmers, the deluge caused the usual chaos in Adelaide, where drivers galore lost the plot and generally acted like Americans on the occasion of winter's first blizzard. . . .

We've been ensconced at the above address (in Semaphore Park, a beachside suburb in northwestern Adelaide) for the past two days now, setting it up how we like it. We have a lot of large art works we'd like to hang along a gallery-like masonry corridor that links the front of the house to the two back bedrooms.

My main writing aim now is to finish Wallaby. As I move into a second draft of Chapter 5 I see the first drafts of 1–4 took a lot of working over. I know therefore that I'm not as far ahead in meeting my self-imposed deadline of 25 March as I had thought. . . .

Talking of Wallaby prompts me to get on with it. The afternoon is yet young. I confess, though, to feeling mentally pretty tired right now. I fear I might botch the job. . . .

At 4.10 pm Teddi wrote in my journal: 'Ro, you're sound asleep. The landscape has not changed. It's barren and flat. For me, train travel is really something to adjust to. Only because you begin to RELAX! You are not bored, drunk, tired; you are actually relaxed. It's an odd feeling. I think that's why you are fed so regularly and massively, so you aren't comatose for the entire journey.'

Teddi wasn't comatose; she was gone. She was in the club car with Jackie and the peripatetic pensioners, playing word games that were too complicated for my morphine-addled brain.

When the games were over, dinner was on. My food was sensational – we applauded the two chefs as Jackie introduced them, young and gleaming from their tiny, steaming kitchen – but I barely sampled it. I only mention dinner now because of its cumulative bloating effect and because we met a woman who divined I was sick.

Next morning, she was to slip me a note with the name of a religious man I could contact in Adelaide. 'Don't leave this earth without finding Jesus,' she implored.

What I pity, I thought bitterly, that Jesus hadn't bothered to find me.

From my journal: Thursday 27 January 2003

Well this caper, this carousel, this roller coaster, keeps on coming up with something new and unpredictable.

Yesterday was a tough one for me and Teddi – doing the pension planning thing right after making the arrangements for a pre-paid funeral contract. We had just, late in the day, talked things over and gotten past all that, when the scenario started changing unexpectedly and sadly with a series of phone calls from (my brother) Jamie in Brisbane.

At first it was just to say that Dad was in the Greenslopes Repatriation Hospital. He was eating nothing and was dehydrated. He'd had a minor fall and was depressed; eyes glazed over and listless. Jamie said he'd been acting depressed since he got the news about my illness.

I said I'd give Dad a call in the morning, and try to cheer him up, with the positive news of all the things we've achieved and how well we're going.

But not long afterwards, he called again to say Dad had a minor heart attack and he had fluid on the lungs making it hard for him to breathe. He was going to the hospital and would report back that evening if the situation changed drastically.

Sure enough, not a couple of hours later, the phone rang again.

My Dad was dead.

Jamie said he'd call again in the morning once he'd had a chance to get a date for the funeral. I asked if he was okay – he sounded like he was doing his best to be objective and detail-oriented so he could hold off the shock and maybe the tears. He said he was all right.

I had my share of tears last night. Teddi's were of anger, that this had happened now, and that I would blame myself. I do not. Myra was good enough to come over and sit with us for an hour or so, so we could talk about Dad and decide if everyone wants to go to Brisbane for the funeral. We're decided we will. I tried calling Sylvie but she was already asleep. When I told her this morning, she was instantly in tears. She wants to come too.

The sky might have been star-studded but it was still windy and cold outside the train, which had pulled up in Kalgoorlie, Western Australia, for a four-hour crew change and servicing.

Kalgoorlie seemed to have closed and gone home. The blocks of houses and locked-up shops surrounding the railway station seemed abandoned. Stray couples, who like us went walking, reported on their return that they had tried one or two pubs but they were full of young louts determined to get a Friday-night skin-full.

Thus the lounge car filled with Kalgoorlie explorers, like me, determined to denude the Indian Pacific of its entire stock of red wine. We would get a *genteel* skin-full.

There are benefits to being sick. You can tell the alcohol-intake moralists to leave you alone in the most emphatic terms.

(I missed my self-imposed Wallaby deadline. When our 25th anniversary came around, I gave Teddi 108 pages, still a long way from a finished book.

I presented it nevertheless, as we celebrated the big day with family and friends, and I vowed it would be finished. I also vowed that our travelling days were not over. We had decided to take a 10-day cruise to the Pacific Islands of New Caledonia and Vanuatu. The tickets were paid for. We were due to sail from Darling Harbour on the afternoon of 20 May.

Who knew? The trip could be Wallaby's *final destination.)*

From my journal: Friday 2 May 2003

For the record I suppose I should detail the developments of the day.

You could say it started a long way before I was ready for fate's ambush. I was up about 7am; we'd innocently slept a night in the brand new double sofa bed we got from a local furniture store (so Teddi could watch TV when I zonked out at night). It was comfortable and warm and I could easily have slept in. I knew I was getting picked up at 8.50 am by the Red Cross to go for what I thought was a routine affirmation of my new painkiller regime, and a sort-of 'you're no better but you're no worse' assessment of the CT scan I had from neck to pelvis last week.

Dr B, however, was full of bad news. My CT scan shows three lung lesions now, not two. The liver is even-steven: one bigger, one smaller. There are a few enlarged lymph glands in the skin-like tissue that contains the bowels. There may be something else as well; I can't recall the specifics. But still, the spine lesion is the worst. It's bigger and it's closer to involving my spinal cord, which – if it happens – could leave me paraplegic.

B warned me to get to hospital fast if there was any sudden change to sensation in the legs or around my bowels and urinary tract. He said it would cost us our house if we went cruising and I had to be evacuated to hospital by helicopter in the middle of the Pacific.

He wants me to start, next Friday, on a course of chemotherapy. It's a drug called Dacarbazine. It's given intravenously over an hour or so every three weeks. There are side effects including nausea and loss of white cell immune protection. But he says it's my best hope of getting the tumour away from my spinal cord and preventing full collapse. The odds are, as always, 20%.

I haven't decided if I will take the chemo, yet. He called a half hour or so ago, wanting to know if I'd take part in some study regarding informed consent issues, which would involve an interview for an hour or so before my first chemo session next week. I said that was okay, so long as I decided to take the chemo. He sounded surprised. I told him Teddi and I have some deep thinking to do.

So that's where we are. I'm booked in for all this shit, plus an MRI on 15 May. But whether I go through with it involves the same quality of life issues I had with the so-called 'Brisbane option.' I said then that I never wanted chemo. Why change my mind now?

(After thinking it over on the weekend, I refused the chemo. Why flood my body with chemicals that make me sick, when I feel fine and that's all I ask of life: feeling fine, not sick and sweaty and tied to the umbilicus of medicine, gambling, gambling, hoping for an impossible reprieve, like a pokies addict in so many pubs and clubs. I said I felt fine and wanted to stay that way.

We cancelled the cruise. We satisfied ourselves with short-range trips around the state – sandwiched in between energetic episodes of writing from me – until Teddi hit on the idea of riding the train to Perth.

We wouldn't even tell the doctors we were going.)

When Doug came around with our morning cuppa we told him we were skipping breakfast.

Again it was barely light. The train was humming through the back yards of a biggish town called Northam. We showered at leisure, then moved up to the lounge car: Our second dawn aboard the Indian Pacific was producing some wonderful scenery winding along the Avon River Valley and we wanted to watch it from big windows on both sides of the train.

For a few happy moments, while I slurped another coffee and got lost in the view, I forgot my predicament. A twinge in my lung soon reminded me, but I wasn't worried.

I was on holiday, and soon we'd reach our destination. The train was sharing stations and switching yards with modern little commuter trains, city-bound, workers nose-down in their newspapers, eager with after-shave and office chic.

We stepped into the clear air of Perth, and rode a taxi to our bed and breakfast, fringing the city. We passed the WACA ground where Dennis Lillee took eight wickets against Pakistan. I listened to his exploits on a transistor radio as a teenager, getting fried by the sun, on a beach on the New South Wales south coast, thrilled for the hero Dennis, unaware that the burning of my skin contained the microscopy of my potential death.

We crossed the Swan River and climbed to our destination, Victoria Park. We stepped blinking into the robust light.

It might not have been a Pacific Islands cruise, but I was a five-star happy man. Thanks to Teddi and my own pig-headed refusal to quit travelling, I'd crossed most of the country in the famous Indian Pacific. I even had a certificate to prove it. It was one in the eye for the doctors – and it looked like I'd be able to add a new chapter to *Wallaby*, after all.

Fingers crossed, I was within a whisker of beating the four to six month sentence. And, touch wood a double time, my journeying with Teddi was far from over.

Chapter 1

The feisty hitch hiker

One of the good things about our trips together is that Teddi and I are terrible planners.

We *pretend* to be the opposite, buying maps and guidebooks and moisturising facial wipes and all kinds of aids to our comfort in transit, but once we get going, the laws of chaos take over and we get swept along for the ride.

The year was 1977. Teddi and me and five-year-old Wyeth, our son, were going from Brisbane to Sydney to Singapore, then on to Copenhagen, our jumping-off point for adventure in Europe. We figured we'd be in Europe for three months, and maybe get work in Britain. Or maybe we'd go over to Teddi's homeland, the USA. We had no idea that we weren't to set foot in Australia for more than three years.

Yet we set off looking like we were taking a weekend run to the campground at Noosa Heads. Looking back on it now, I think I expected Europe to *be* Noosa Heads. You could get there by hitch-hiking. You could pitch a tent where the river let out to the sea and bathe in the ocean. You needed few clothes and if you got hungry you could get a pizza or a banana smoothie along the esplanade. I packed accordingly.

I had an English-made backpack called a Karrimor, which had pockets and pouches and flaps all over it. Inside, I jammed a pup tent and a sleeping bag, a few pairs of jeans, some Dunlop Volleys and a bunch of shirts and grungy jumpers.

For Teddi, I selected a blue Army surplus haversack, about half the capacity of mine. Into this, I expected her to cram all her clothes and all the creams and cosmetic fripperies that women insist upon. I considered Wyeth too small to lug a pack, so he got to keep the snap-fastened cardboard suitcase Teddi packed his pre-school lunches in, plus a drawstring bag made out of an old denim jeans leg, in which he kept his Lego pieces. We must have looked like the three bears of back-packing.

One of the first things I discovered about the woman who was soon to be my wife is that she carefully picks her moments to tell me things I'd rather not hear.

What she didn't tell me was that she was afraid of flying and that my hands and forearms were going to be ripped to shreds by her panicked and grasping fingernails as soon as the Brisbane to Sydney plane started down the tarmac. Had she told me before that somewhat surprising lift-off, I might have organised a mild sedative, like maybe six or seven Valium. I tried to get her pissed on Bloody Marys in Singapore. The SAS airline attendant took one look at her and gave me two little white pills.

'Whatever you do, don't give both at once.'

Teddi managed to get off the plane in Bangkok and stare at the gaggle of wooden souvenir elephants I had bought for Wyeth in Don Muang Airport's ornate transit lounge. She nodded vaguely at the smoggy air of New Delhi, where we landed to refuel. This was India, where I had fantasized that one day I might end up, a wandering Saddhu in search of Enlightenment. I was thrilled.

'That's nice,' she muttered. 'Take me back to our seats.'

But I digress. I was telling you how Teddi picks her moments. She *could* have told me before we left. She could have told me over a plate of *mee goreng* in the Singapore night markets after Wyeth fell into a metre-deep drainage ditch and Teddi sent me off in search of Dettol and bandaids. She *could* have told me on the foggy dawn ride from Kastrup airport to the Copenhagen Centrum, where we waited for the Tourist Office to open so we could get a list of cheap hotels and a decent sleep. But no, she waited until I was dozing comfortably beneath the toasty covers of a continental quilt in our room at the Hotel Ry.

'Ro,' she said innocently, snuggling up beside me. 'I *hate* camping. Can't we just stay in places like this?'

I retorted that I hadn't brought the bloody pup tent half way around the world for nothing, and furthermore insisted that *soon* the time would come when it would be erected beneath European skies. 'Maybe when we hitch up to Norway.'

'Mmm,' she said, already asleep.

As a base for seeing the sights of Copenhagen, I had to admit that the Hotel Ry was in every respect far superior to a pup tent.

The proprietor was a cheerful bloke who presided over a lobby full of maps and a breakfast nook that looked out on one of the city's many canals. It looked cold out there. Inside, the proprietor served strong coffee and a silver platter piled with crusty bread, fresh Danish butter, huge slices of Havarti cheese and homemade strawberry jam. For a toast and Vegemite lad like me, the combination of flavours was a revelation, a promise of new delights, still unknown but waiting to be discovered in this civilized city.

So the pup tent stayed stashed as we made ourselves known to

Copenhagen, window-shopping in the fashionable streets, visiting the Little Mermaid and the Christiansborg Palace and the once-rough sailors' district of bars and brothels at Nyhavn. We walked everywhere, marveling at the centuries of history, aghast at the expense of *everything*, subsisting on Carlsberg beer and hotdogs called polser, realizing that autumn in Denmark *was* cold and showing every sign of getting frigid. Teddi suggested it was time we invested in some warmer clothing.

I was born and raised in Canberra, the capital city of Australia, a town frigid come winter. I *know* what it's like to have your toes tingling from incipient frostbite. I am also a cheapskate. 'Like what?'

'Like gloves and beanies for me and Wyeth. Like a coat for you, unless you plan to freeze your ass off before we even get on the ferry to Malmo.'

Malmo is an industrial city in Sweden, across a fog-shrouded, squall-battered narrows known to the Swedes as Oresund. We planned on using it as our starting point for a hitching run north to Norway. Teddi had relatives in Norway. She thought we might look them up.

Never mind that it was the cheapest item on the rack and the fur in the hood was glued on rather than stitched, my new blue 'Canadian Airman's Jacket' cost a fortune. I was still in shock and muttering gloomily about Scandinavian Shylocks when we got on the ferry for the two-hour crossing to a city of gantries and industrial towers floodlit in the murk, the horizon obliterated by steady sheets of rain. The downpour showed no sign of relenting as we berthed near a sign that read: *Valkommen till Malmo!*

On the bus to the outskirts of town, Wyeth had fun laughing at the roadside Entry and Exit signs that read Infart and Utfart. He wasn't laughing when we had to start hitching in the persistent drizzle. Teddi covered him with her coat and they huddled on our pathetic heap of baggage. I stood apart in my new jacket, hooded and warm, waving my thumb at the traffic.

It was getting dark and still pissing rain when a guy in a battered old Saab gave us a ride fifty or sixty kilometres up the coast to a town called Helsingborg. He smoked a pipe and had a heating system that just about blew him into the back seat with Teddi and Wyeth. He dropped us off at the railway station and said something stern:

'If you have any brains that away yet have not been washed, the midnight train to Oslo you will take!'

I had secretly been hoping for the pup tent. I said so.

Teddi said something unprintably dismissive and ordered me to find a hotel.

I did so.

Next day was brighter. Slightly. We emerged blinking and stiff from our room and returned to the railway station restaurant where we had a meager breakfast of invisible fish, smeared on smorbrod with a film of onion and one-sixteenth of something that Teddi said was a caper. It looked like the end of a mouldy pickle. Wyeth looked like he'd been robbed.

But he wasn't complaining, and neither was I: Teddi had a determined look about her. Today she was taking crap from *nobody*!

The watery morning sun shone on rocky ramparts that supported Helsingborg castle. Fishing boats bobbed in Norra Hamnen. We got a bus that dropped us close to the northbound freeway called E6 and started hitching.

There was plenty of traffic – mostly the cars were empty – but nobody stopped. For half an hour we thumbed without fortune. Then along came a police patrol car, complete with a polite young officer.

'Vatt dast da,' he wanted to know, 'Utfarting im das oggbladdett?'

It soon became clear that we had no idea what he was talking about. He switched to English.

'You must move on. It is not allowed to hitch hike from here. No vehicle is permitted to stop.'

'Where *can* we hitch from?' I wanted to know.

The policeman said the road ceased to be a freeway and became a two-lane highway precisely seven kilometres further north. We would have to walk there.

'How about you giving us a ride?' suggested Teddi brightly.

The policeman declined.

'Oh come on! You're going that way anyhow!'

'It is not allowed.'

Teddi started to ask what the hell *was* allowed in Sweden, but stopped herself and tried another tack. She indicated little Wyeth, who was looking obligingly forlorn. 'He's too small to walk so far!'

The policeman looked uncomfortable at this obvious logic. But still he refused.

'Okay,' said Teddi, 'You guys can do what you want, but I'm not moving.' With that she stepped out towards the oncoming rush of traffic and started thumbing.

The cop's resolve collapsed. He ushered us inside his pristine vehicle and without a word delivered us to a place where E6 rolled pleasantly through late autumn fields. Teddi gave him a cheerful wave as he sullenly roared away.

That day, we made 240 kilometres inside eight hours. We got to Gothenberg before the Tourist Office closed. We were directed to the home of Fru Bergman, who lived in a veritable mansion on Carlbergsgatan, just a few moments out of town on the streetcar. Fru Bergman rented us a beautiful room. Wyeth and Teddi luxuriated in the spa while I went for provisions at a nearby supermarket: bread, cheese, tomatoes, fruit and milk. We ate well and slept like kings.

As for the pup tent, I confess: it was forgotten, wedged in the Karrimor, damp and neglected, its nylon expanses unexposed to the stars that blazed that night in cloudless Scandinavian skies.

So it was in Oslo, and all the way across the mountains to Bergen Fjord. On the Fred Olson Line ferry from Bergen to Newcastle, to lighten my load and score a slug or two of duty free whisky, I gave the tent to a bearded young cyclist from Wales.

Chapter 2

Jonathan Bear's battle with the bottle

Somewhere in the boxes of photos and memorabilia we've gathered over the years, there is a time-yellowed piece of paper typed with the address in Norway of the distant relatives Teddi had the notion to look up when we got to Oslo.

Had we done so, we would have ended up somewhere near Trondheim, which is about 400 kilometres north of Oslo on the other side of several forbidding mountain ranges, and only a few degrees of latitude south of the Arctic Circle. We may have got in to Trondheim, that autumn of 1977, but we might never have got out again. And we certainly would never have met Jonathan Bear.

That's the great thing about chaos, or fate, whatever you want to call it. That's why the planning caper is such a waste of time. People like Jonathan just *present* themselves, out of the blue, circumstances irrelevant, implications immense.

We didn't choose to meet Jonathan. We *chose* to do laundry, which seemed far more sensible than going to Trondheim. We found an antique-filled pension room, our hostess a genteel war widow named Fru Gystad, and we stopped a few days in Oslo.

Once, Oslo's heart must have been centuries old with medieval walls like Copenhagen, but most of it had to be built again after the city was bombed to rubble during World War Two. Freshly bathed, clothes suffused by the antiseptic odour of a Nordic version of Omo and its blue beads of bleach, we walked and walked, checking out the natural history museum and the Edvard Munch art museum where we got to see *The Shriek*, which was what I felt like doing when Wyeth complained of being hungry, sick of Polser and sick of being footsore in his red plastic gumboots.

'Why do we have to go to all these New Zealands!' he demanded.

What do you say to that? I hoisted him on my shoulders. Suddenly he was far more adventurous, pointing out places to go, like Horatio Nelson on the bridge of his first frigate. Many hours and miles later, we walked all the way to the central railway station to buy tickets on the Oslo to Bergen railway.

Here I have a confession to make. Thanks to a friend back in

Australia, we had been able to buy cheap tickets to Europe by getting faked student identification cards and booking our fares through the Australian Union of Students Travel Service. In Copenhagen, our jovial hotel proprietor had suggested we could get similar fare bargains in Scandinavia and the rest of Europe, if we had suitable student ID. Where could we get such ID? Why, it was merely a matter of hopping onto the number 16 bus to Skindergade and looking out for DIS Travel, right next to the Universitaats Kafeen. We had a beer in the latter smoky cave, to celebrate our illegal acquisition. Now the cards were to be put through their first test.

The man at the ticket window quoted a price in the low trillions. I chuckled and proffered the trumps. The man took a single dismissive glance. 'That is not a proper student card. Have you the *correct* credentials?'

'Fucking Danes,' I muttered.

'I beg your pardon,' he said.

'Bastards!' I replied, glaring at the poor bloody bureaucrat as if he was a deliberate conspirator, reaching in resignation for my vastly depleted stash of Travellers Cheques.

The man issued the tickets, regarding me as if I was a particularly noisome type of soccer hooligan. 'Enjoy your trip,' he said, shoving the three little stubs across the breach between us.

'If it's getting me out of Norway,' I wish I had replied, 'I'm sure I will.'

The train was one of those bright tubes that looked like it belonged on a movie set, all Scandinavian Space Odyssey minimalist with its own life support systems to keep out the mountain cold. It was full of tourists with parkas and cameras clicking as the train hauled out of Oslo, up hillsides of fir trees and past picture postcard farms bathed in autumn sunshine.

In case you've never been to Norway, believe me, that place has mountains. This wasn't Kosciusko National Park in New South Wales, where as a high school kid I went to study stuff like onionskin weathering and cirques and glacial moraines, where the biggest mountain in the entire continent of Australia is barely tall enough to top the tree line. This was a world in which the train climbed so high there was no warm life-colour at all, out there beyond the windows, just snowy wastes and icy-grey lakes and black barriers and tunnels to stop snowdrifts from covering the railway tracks.

When the train reached the summit, it rolled to a silent stop. The captain came on the intercom to tell us we could all Utfart to take photos. Outside it was freezing, with a bone-cutting wind straight off the North Pole. The tourists scuttled around for a while, snapping photos that might as well get developed in monochrome. It was horrible out there, true tundra, bleak as a killer's eye.

Soon we were on our way again, rolling through long black tunnels, and down into deep misted valleys.

The train arrived just after Bergen's tourist office closed. So we walked off toward the docks, past a lake called Lille Lungegardsvatnet, looking for a cheap hotel or pension room, settling for a place that looked like a sail-maker's shop. It was occupied on the lower floor by ancient twin crones who showed us up a flight of stairs to a room overlooking a narrow street.

In the morning we strolled along the crowded harbourside and found ourselves in the middle of the Saturday fish market at Torget, bustling at the calm inner end of what looked like Bergen's main harbour, Vagen. The wharves were crowded with trucks and wagons smelling of oil and fish, horns blaring, fishermen shouting, laden containers being pushed along shiny tracks embedded in tar-encrusted planking. In the market, weather-beaten old guys with caps and pipes and gumboots and fearsome knives filleted the catch for the picky housewives they haggled with.

I wandered among the Bergen fishermen's slabs, examining the dead-eyed slimy creatures, nodding happily in the weak morning sun. I actually *volunteered* to buy Teddi and Wyeth a bite to eat and some hot chocolate in a nearby café.

In the café were a couple of backpackers, immediately obvious as Australians, so we said, 'G'day' and struck up a conversation based on the usual 'Where you headed?' and 'Where you been?' They had Eurail passes and were going south to Kristiansand, where a ferry would take them to Denmark and then it was back onto a train through northern Germany to Amsterdam.

I explained we were planning to take a ferry to Newcastle in northern England. 'Yeah?' said one of our new mates, looking a little puzzled. 'When are you planning to sail?'

'As soon as possible,' said I. 'While we still have money for a ticket.'

'You better get a move on, then.'

'How come?'

'Mate, from here the Fred Olsen Line sails to Britain twice a week. The next boat's in about an hour and a half.'

See what I mean about chaos? Two hundred and twelve Kronor later we had steerage tickets for Newcastle aboard a big ship, all white painted superstructure and flags flapping on masts with whirling radar.

I'd left Teddi and Wyeth at the quayside and run back to collect our baggage and check out of our room. I hurried along, sweating inside my airman's jacket, buried beneath all our bags, running a few paces then stopping to walk and hitch everything back into place, then running again, approaching the gangplank in a lather of heat and ill temper.

The steerage section was a V-shaped upper deck in the bows of the ship, enclosed and covered with deep blue carpets, full of airline-style reclining seats. I dumped our gear and slumped in one.

Wyeth patted the Karrimor and the bulge of the pup tent. 'We can camp on the floor!' he suggested brightly.

Teddi was not listening to this unintended irony. Her attention was diverted. She tugged my sleeve. 'That guy!'

'What guy?'

'Him!' She pointed *him* out. He had longish well-styled straight black hair and a face like the currently adored American rock star Jackson Browne, which means he was *very* good looking. He wore a creamy-white v-necked cashmere sweater and blue jeans and neat white sneakers, and he was loping around looking loosely athletic with a bottle of orange soda in his hand, seeking some way to get the top off.

'What about him?'

'He has a problem with that bottle,' she whispered. 'Lend him your pen knife.'

By now I was more interested in sorting our gear. 'Why?'

'Lend him your *pen knife*!' she repeated, looking set to stab me with it.

So I crossed the expanse of blue carpet to the young man who was bracing the bottle cap against part of a metal bulkhead, and offered my knife, which instantly did the trick. I received many thanks and Teddi got herself an introduction to Jonathan Bear.

Jonathan turned out to have some major connections with Teddi's home state of Wisconsin. He'd recently graduated with a degree in literature from University of Wisconsin at Madison, which is the state capital, an hour or so west of Milwaukee. His older brother Peter was a State Representative on the Democrat side of Wisconsin politics. Jonathan had spent the summer rambling about in Britain and Norway. Now he was on the way back to New York City, where his mother Nancy had an apartment near Greenwich Village and where Jonathan was soon to commence a job as a rookie teacher.

Of course we didn't find all this out in five minutes of greetings. We had all night for that. And what a night it turned out to be, crossing the North Sea to England.

The omens were good from the moment the ship slipped its moorings and made for the mouth of Bergen Fjord. We went on deck and watched the harbour's features slide away behind us. We exited the plunging fjordlands and then there was nothing but the cold blue sky, the receding mountainscape and the wind-tossed dark grey sea.

It was Wyeth who spotted it first, a beautiful white-hulled three-masted sailing ship with ant-like people aboard swarming in the rigging, setting sail astern of us and catching up fast.

'That's the *Christiaan Radich*!' We all looked at Teddi in astonishment. She explained, yelling into the wind: 'They made this movie called *Windjammer*. My Dad took me to see it. They made it on the *Christiaan Radich*. I think if I'd been a boy he would have had me join the Norwegian Navy, just so I could learn to sail on that boat. Wow! It's gorgeous!'

The tall ship slipped abeam then surged ahead of us. The crew had her flying. We watched in awe until she disappeared and then we went below decks, shivering with the cold.

'I have just the thing to warm us up,' announced Jonathan, producing a full-sized bottle of vodka. We supplied the orange juice and, while the rest of the passengers went off to the dining room for dinner and Wyeth was comfortably wedged among our bags for a good night's sleep, the three of us proceeded to get really plastered.

Before we were too far-gone, Teddi established Jonathan's immaculate literary credentials, and the fact that he was a fan of the French existentialist Albert Camus. This led to a lengthy discussion about The Meaning of Life, about which Jonathan and Teddi were able to make many sensible offerings based on their obviously wide reading and apparently abundant common sense.

I had recently read Hermann Hesse's *Siddhartha*. I now fancied myself an antipodean incarnation of Hermann's hero and, as the ferry let out its fog-horn blasts to warn approaching shipping, and the spirit level in the vodka bottle fell with steady gulps, I expounded my theory of the Cosmic Yawn, which came to me in sickness and paranoia one New Year's Eve at Noosa, after I swilled too many magic mushrooms. In essence, we were all wandering *saddhus*, seeking Self and Enlightenment and escape from the endless curse of reincarnation.

Jonathan's dark eyes twinkled with amusement. I was encouraged. He understood! I was making sense at last!

Back from dinner, others joined the debate. A ruddy-cheeked

Cornish kid dressed up like an Italian cycle champion told me I was not even an *original* wanker. He was helping himself to liberal swigs from a bottle of whisky, owned by his mate, a Welsh student who had also been amusing himself with a holiday season of cycling. The Welshman bellowed inanely for a while, expounding theories of his own, which climaxed in his passing out on the floor, my pup tent in his arms, his whisky in my hands.

In the morning when the ferry berthed in the fog-shrouded harbour of Newcastle-upon-Tyne, we carried our brain-shrivelling hangovers aboard a southbound train.

It turned out that we had agreed to travel to London with Jonathan. He knew a cheap bed and breakfast hotel, somewhere in Knightsbridge, somewhere near Harrods, wherever *they* were. He'd be staying there for a few days until he headed for New York.

Our carriage was so full of cigarette smoke it was near impossible to breathe. Teddi fed Wyeth on fruit, and British Rail white-bread sandwiches with fillings even more invisible than the Helsingborg smorbrod. I stared out at what we could see of the passing fogbound countryside, starting to feel depressed. I hoped London would be better than this.

Edgerton House in Knightsbridge was cheap, all right. And nasty, according to Teddi, who in addition to disliking camping now turned out to abhor shared bathrooms. There was a basement kitchen and common room in which we cooked a basic dinner of items looted from a nearby Indian grocery. There was a blackout. I grumbled, but Teddi just searched the cupboards until she found a candle. When she first lived in London – when Wyeth was born into the hands of a West Indian midwife in a south London hospital on 12 April 1972 – she recalled that the entire country was gripped by recession and there was trouble galore between bosses and unions. The blackouts were long and frequent.

Eventually we got to eat, and endured a chilly night in a high-ceilinged bare room with a shilling-in-the-slot heater and iron-framed beds, sagging mattresses and a dearth of blankets.

Over the next few days we went with Jonathan for tours of the London parks, visited London Zoo with Wyeth hoisted once again upon my shoulders, fed pigeons in Trafalgar Square, trudged along King's Road in Chelsea, riding the tube, the double-decker London buses and once, for the sheer indulgence of it, in one of the ubiquitous black cabs. We also had reunions with Teddi's friends of early days. I was jealous of these people and their claims to her fond attention, their familiarity with each other – how they rubbed shoulders with famous folk like Joe Cocker and Richard Branson and other names I also knew and envied. One night I threw a petulant wobbly and threatened it all.

Teddi soothed me. It was all in the past. And Wyeth wanted me to be cool. When I raised my voice he stated it plainly: 'I want us to stay together.'

The message got through. That night we cried and cuddled.

Chapter 3

How to get a green card

Back in 1977, I reckon, you could safely have described me as a bit of an innocent.

I was just 22 years old and twice a university dropout. Now, mere months after we met and I invited myself to move in with Teddi and Wyeth in a ramshackle rental place at Daventry Street in Brisbane's West End, we were travelling the world on money we'd saved – Teddi tending bar at the National Hotel near Fortitude Valley, me a soon-to-quit clerk in the Australian Government's Department of Veterans Affairs.

In a significant way, I told myself, I was now responsible not for one life but three. I quickly had to pick up a few survival ideas.

Take Paris, for example, and the quest for a hotel room. We got there on a train-and-ferry combination from London to Dover and Calais. The train whistled and rattled across yellow mustard fields and through towns like Boulogne, Abbeville and Amiens, names to me full of history-book ghosts and the muddy insanities of the Western Front. Those things I'd learned about as a kid, examining the horribly realistic museum displays at the Australian War Memorial in Canberra.

It was close to dark when the train rolled into Gare du Nord. It was a Friday night. We had no hotel reservations. Teddi, who'd passed through Paris half a dozen years earlier, had an idea that the Latin Quarter, south of the Seine and about 15 minutes away on the Paris Metro, would prove hospitable. There we went.

Hotel after hotel bore the sign 'Complet'. We wandered in Boulevard St Germain and Boulevard de Port Royal, then Montparnasse. Eventually we tried a trio of hotels across Boulevard St Michel, around the corner from the Sorbonne University on Rue Cujas. The two decent looking places also turned out to be full. Our last hope was a dingy fleapit where it was immediately obvious the rooms were rented by the hour.

The desk clerk was a pockmarked Algerian who gave us a key so we could check out a room, which we reached by climbing a labyrinth of creaking stairs.

The room was horrid. The walls were stained, wallpaper streaked with grease and suspect moistures. A single lumpy double bed that looked dirtier than the walls would have to accommodate us all. There was no toilet or bath. To shower we had to rent a key for five francs. There was no other furniture.

'I'm not staying here,' said Teddi.

'Where else will we find a room? I'll get us a better place in the morning.'

'I'm not staying here.'

We went back downstairs and gave the key to the clerk, telling him we'd return if we had to. He shrugged indifferently. He knew we'd have to.

The only solace that night was our meal. We found a place full of carousing students and got pissed on cheap Beaujolais while we gorged on char-grilled veal with mountains of pilaf. We settled Wyeth as comfortably as we could in the middle of the bed, and spent cold sleepless hours tossing and turning on its edges. Well before 6 am, I gave up the attempt to sleep and went downstairs in search of coffee and some cigarettes.

Boulevard St Michel was deserted; the cafes – so busy and loud the night before – were empty and shuttered, wooden chairs stacked on tables. But near the lofty gates of the Sorbonne there was a cul de sac, which had a café that had either opened early or never closed. I went inside, ordered Gauloises and an espresso, and took a seat not far from a group of bleary-eyed student types – three young men and a woman – who were raving in a mixture of English and French. They seemed to be debating where to party next. I excused myself and asked if they could help: I needed to find a comfortable but inexpensive hotel.

I was told to join them. For some time their debate continued and my question was ignored. Then the woman asked for something to write on:

My love
Since I know you, I am
Just feeling great. You
Have beautiful eyes and
You are really attratiff
Man. I love you. I want a kiss.
Hotel de la Loire
20 Rue de Sommerard

To this day, Teddi does not see why I found it necessary to submit to the woman's demand, and we sure as hell didn't stay in the Hotel de la Loire. But you see what I mean about survival clues.

Even though our exchequer had been ravaged by the time we spent in Scandinavia, not to mention London pubs and Paris cafes, we decided to make a run for Rome and Brindisi, hoping against reason that our funds would hold out long enough for a splash across to Greece.

Our train was due to leave Gare du Lyon in the early evening. We already knew that French railway food was almost as bad as English, so we compensated with a little pre-travel marketing – a couple of long crusty loaves, a large and extremely ripe Camembert cheese, some Dijon mustard, a slice or two of ham for Wyeth and a couple of bottles of wine for us.

We found an empty compartment, hoping we'd be able to spread out and get some sleep on the long overnight haul to Italy but, just as the train was about to pull out, in stepped a man dressed in a business suit. He nodded civilly and took a seat in a corner where he remained silent and immobile as the train gathered speed and rattled into the night.

We produced our portable feast. It was delicious and we must have looked like we hadn't eaten for weeks as my penknife slathered out the mustard and slabbed the cheese on the bread.

Conscious that our companion had nothing to eat we offered him some of our tucker. But in the confined space of the compartment, the stench of the Camembert was noxious, and the Frenchman's gills were looking decidedly green. He declined with a terse shake of the head.

After dinner, we tried talking to him but he made no response. I gave up and dozed, awaking as the train departed Dijon. The man was gone.

'Thank God for that,' I said. 'Next time we want a compartment to ourselves, let's open the cheese *before* anyone else climbs in.'

We did get a good night's sleep. There was an interruption when uniformed Italian border guards with shining buttons and epaulettes sauntered into the compartments. Disinterested, they shone a torch on my passport, then at me. They were considerably more interested when they clapped eyes on Teddi. She got an official *benvenuto*!

After that we slept until dawn, waking to the stunning sight of villages, the whitewash and red tiled buildings lodged precariously on sea-facing cliffs, leaning towards boats on a sea an impossible white-capped blue.

At Livorno, there was a long delay, waiting for a connecting train. I sat and wrote the poem that starts this book. When we finally got away, our compartment was full of passionately noisy southbound Italians rigged in soccer colours. We found ourselves in rolling hills where the only stain on the bright blue sky was the smoke of little fires where farmers burned the cuttings from autumn vines and, in *fattorie* glimpsed among copses and orchards, enjoyed the bounties of their vintage.

In Rome, we got ourselves a pension room with cool tiled floors and shuttered windows overlooking a cluttered street close to the Spanish Steps, and we went exploring.

I discovered Teddi was a born-and-raised Catholic when she bought some rosary beads for her father at a stall near St Peter's Square at the Vatican. Being a fully fallen Protestant and self-styled proponent of The Cosmic Yawn, I was not bothered by this trifling news – even though it is the sort of information that has rent asunder entire communities. I joked about getting hit by lightning for having the sheer temerity to enter St Peter's Cathedral. Teddi looked mortified, as if she half expected I might get fried. Nothing happened: God must have been too busy counting the gold and jewels in the Vatican museum, an almost unbelievably ornate catalogue of Roman Catholic conquest and spiritual omnipotence through the Old World and the New, obscene in its fabulous wealth.

Everywhere we went, we walked. We gaped over the ancient buttressed walls of the Tiber, and more than once I wondered how some Italians could so carelessly indulge their passion for graffiti on walls and bridges that were clearly centuries older than anything that existed in the adolescent world Europeans had carved into niches of the bush in my own country, Australia. It seemed shocking vandalism. The chaotic and relentless flow of the Roman traffic surged indifferently past. Or maybe it was with an indifference born of the knowledge that this is *Roma*, the city of the seven hills, of legend and empire, nerve centre for a world-flung civilization, the Rome to which all roads lead. Romans took their piled-up ruins – like the looming marvels of the ruined, then restored, then ruined again Forum – almost entirely for granted, hurrying past without a glance, past the pastry-laden caffes and gorgeously fashionable but treacherously narrow shopping streets, horns blaring, scooters dodging cars and pedestrians alike, everyone in a rampant rush to be somewhere else.

In Australia, people had tried to warn me that it was an impracticality to be travelling with a five-year-old kid – but in Italy, young Wyeth proved to be a survival tip all on his own.

To anyone who has seen the phenomenon, this will come as no surprise. No matter where you go, children are attention-getting magnets. With his curious little eyes peering cheekily from beneath a thick swatch of strawberry blond hair, Wyeth was irresistible.

In Paris, Wyeth had made a colourful drawing and put it on display outside our hotel, like the artists did along the banks of the Seine. A girl had found him so charming she gave him five francs for the picture. He rewarded himself with a toy car from a gift shop at Gare du Lyon. Now, fingers sticky with gelato from a stall at the base of the Spanish Steps, he tried the same trick. The tourists came and went. No dice.

But these were tourists. As soon as we wandered exhausted into a *trattoria*, hoping to find affordable items on the menu, Wyeth was adopted – taken out to the kitchen for a bowl of pasta, presented with a bonus slice of veal or a piece of *pizzetta*. The little artist's pockets might have been empty, but his belly certainly wasn't.

Pretty soon, our money was getting so low that we knew were going to have to forget Greece and make some decisions about whether we were going back to Australia to earn some survival money, or making for America and doing it there. The idea of getting work in the UK had worn-off on both of us and there was something about Milwaukee that was calling Teddi home.

Teddi had not been home for nearly four years; I had never been to the USA and nothing about Australia was calling *me* home, so really the choice was simple.

The US embassy was not far from the Spanish Steps. We confronted an ornate building guarded by Marines in dress uniform and crammed with visa supplicants. I was brusquely told that the only way I'd get anything more than a tourist visa was if I was married to a US citizen or I had a job in the States that would not – by virtue of my having it – deprive an existing citizen. Even a tourist visa would take as long as a week to process.

Teddi had a hunch it would take nowhere near so long if we dealt with the bureaucracy in London. We decided to high tail it north. We did stop a couple of days in Florence, again stunned at the casual indifference with which the Italians literally rubbed shoulders with a cityscape bulging with treasures. Back then you could walk up and touch the Michelangelo statue of David. Wyeth was again spoiled with treats by the mama in the kitchen of a back alley *ristorante*, who served us double dollops of rich and hearty minestrone, fresh breads and cheeses and antipasto and a couple of glasses of local red.

Then, blink or miss it, we were rattling along the Po River Valley by train, on our way past the Leaning Tower of Pisa, then angling north towards the Alps Hannibal crossed with his Carthaginian elephants, when Rome still had not fully established its supremacy in the Mediterranean. Hannibal was intent on sacking Rome. My wallet, too, was sacked. We were down to our last few hundred bucks. We were bound for Paris and London and back to shillings-in-the-meter at Edgerton House.

Teddi's prediction proved correct. We visited the United States embassy. I concocted a convenient story that I would be travelling on to Australia from the US and my passport was trustingly stamped with a three-month tourist visa.

We flew out of Heathrow Airport on a Freddy Laker Skytrain late on a drizzly October afternoon. In a holding pattern, descending through a violent thunderstorm, the DC-10 circled JFK. My first 'Welcome to the United States, have a nice stay' came at two in the morning. I vaguely remember Teddi calling her sister Julie in Milwaukee and saying, 'Guess where we are?' I remember a bus ride and a ride in a graffiti-streaked subway train with black guys in beanies and cheap airman's jackets just like mine.

I remember we got off at one of the big avenues in Manhattan, near 42nd Street. There were huge buildings with important names. We trudged along to the YMCA. In the lobby, there were hustlers and dealers. For 14 bucks we got ourselves a room with a tiny bed and a big neon sign, advertising 7-Up from our window ledge, pumping lurid spasms into every cranny of our exhausted eyeballs.

The city that never sleeps sure didn't. Ghetto blasters rumbled and voices cursed from every doorway along our corridor. In the predawn I showered in a grey-tiled communal sink and went down to look for coffee. There was a huge cafeteria, white-lit by glaring fluorescence, like a MacDonalds for derros, crammed with toothless guys in great-coats eating hand-out hash-browns and slurping bottomless coffees. I got some coffee, and some donuts for Wyeth. Upstairs Teddi was already packing.

We walked along crowded sidewalks with steam coming out of the grates. In the Port Authority terminus there were dispossessed people of every kind. We bought Greyhound bus tickets to Milwaukee and sat among them. Wyeth got hungry again so I got him a burger and some fries for all of us. On the bus, the first guy I met when I went back for a smoke told me he was a junkie leaving New York to dry out. Out of New York the countryside was bare and blackened and the dusk fell quickly. I remember freeway lights and the flare of gasworks and gantry lights and the bus stopping in glaring truck-stop burger joints. The elevated freeway rode us out of Gary, Indiana, and rolled us in another pre-dawn among subterranean pylons into Chicago. We got to Milwaukee with 42 bucks to our names, plus the packs on our backs.

Recently, rummaging the internet not long after I came home from hospital seeking some social and historic context about Milwaukee I could add to these pages, I came upon a piece of research that suggests I might have picked a better place to seek my fortune:

'The 1970s saw a massive erosion of the city's manufacturing strength,' wrote a University of Wisconsin-Milwaukee researcher in its Graduate School Research Profile Magazine, 'as high labour costs, aging production facilities and soaring transportation costs combined to threaten the city's flagship industries. Even the breweries, so firmly linked in the national consciousness with Milwaukee, began to disappear.'

At the time though, all I knew about Milwaukee was that it was a city of about a million souls, 80 miles north of central Chicago on the Wisconsin shores of Lake Michigan. I had no way of knowing that this was where I would be living for the next three years.

Teddi's sister Julie and her husband, Greg, invited us stay. They had an attractive plant-filled apartment on Milwaukee's pleasant East Side. We were so broke we were dependent on their hospitality.

Teddi had a lawyer buddy named George from a previous foray home. George helped her find some secretarial work with a guy who sold organic fertilizers out of an office on East Capitol Drive.

Because I had no Green Card, I had to look for work that paid cash in hand, no questions asked. Answering a 'Men Wanted' ad in the newspaper, I presented myself at 7 am one chilly morning in a ramshackle warehouse by the heavily polluted Milwaukee River.

The warehouse was stacked with advertising pamphlets. There was a loading dock, at which minibus-sized delivery vans were being piled with pamphlets. Each van had a driver who was boss for half a dozen guys who climbed aboard with their cargo and left to deliver the pamphlets in mailboxes across the suburbs.

The pay was minimum wage, $2.75 an hour. A man with a greatcoat and a fat cigar gave me a cold appraisal and told me I had a job if I wanted it.

There were about forty guys, hunkered in the dark morning chill, waiting for their crew to be formed and work to start. I found a place beside two young guys who were talking intensely together about some secret deal. One of them suddenly erupted in anger.

'You fucker! You owe me that grass. You ripped me off!'

'Listen,' said the other. 'I'll tell you something. I get home last night, some dude comes out my front door carrying my deer rifle and my shotgun. I chased the mother but he got away. It don't matter, I still got one good gun right there at home. You say I ripped you off. I say bullshit.'

Some of the mini-buses loaded up and left. Then another batch of pamphlets and delivery 'boys' departed. I waited for an hour and a half before my turn came.

In Australia, the guys on the delivery teams would mostly be classed as derros. Unkempt, maybe homeless, mostly blacks and Hispanics but some hobo whites as well, they obediently trudged the long blocks, stashing flyers in the mailboxes of homes in places like Wauwatosa. Here the lawns were perfectly manicured and the Stars and Stripes flew proudly from household flagpoles, and there were signs on people's doors:

NO PEDDLERS AGENTS OR SOLICITORS
BEWARE OF THE DOG
THESE PREMISES PROTECTED – BURGLARS WATCH OUT
WE'RE PROUD OF OUR SON – HE'S A MARINE

At lunch break, the boss would take us to some nearby MacDonalds and dole out a dollar fifty to each of us for cheeseburgers and fries and maybe a Coke. They must have been as hungry as me, but most of the men hoarded their cash for the payoff at the end of the day. After the afternoon deliveries, by which time my feet were leaden and bone weary, the boss would whistle us back to the van. Mostly in silence and a fug of tobacco smoke, we'd return to the warehouse and be handed the remainder of our day's pay. A lot of the guys would disappear into a little bar nearby. It had tarpaper shingles and neon signs for Pabst Blue Ribbon beer glowing in the twilight. The light of the signs shone in their eyes as they filed inside.

Next morning, the guys would turn up again, some looking shaky, all of them hopeful that the big-cigar boss would point at them and there would be more cash for beers and shots at the end of the day. If they were not selected, they would hunch away, disgruntled but silent for fear of causing offence.

Being young, I was always called on. This was okay until the Wisconsin winter decided it was time to settle in. We were delivering in the black ghetto. There were long rows of dark brown houses and a heavy grey sky misted the tops of leafless trees. When it started snowing, at first it was pleasant, with the dirty sidewalks fresh and white and the street sounds muffled by the falling flakes and people looking out from their doorways as if it was the first time they had ever seen it snow.

Even the cold was not so bad at first. Greg had loaned me some gloves, and I had my airman's jacket. But then the wind got up, and the temperature fell fast. My thin white jeans were useless, and the slush soon soaked through my holey Dunlop Volleys and the layers of socks I had foolishly thought would keep my feet warm. Soon my toes were freezing, so cold they burned with pain. I envied the official mailmen with their natty blue Jeeps and furry hats with the drop-down earmuffs. I spent the remainder of the day in shivering misery, determined to last on the job only long enough to collect the day's pay and get myself a warming shot in that suddenly welcoming neon bar.

In the end I just took my money and walked away. Nobody gave a damn.

This first American job instilled in me an interest in junk mail, a culture in which America proudly leads the world. I always read the stuff in Greg and Julie's mailbox. One day, there came a new biweekly newspaper, distributed free, called *Cityside*.

It had a counter-cultural flavour that appealed to me. There was an article about the controversial issue of bussing white kids to schools in black neighbourhoods as well as the other way 'round; another about how big and fat everybody was in Milwaukee. In an article entitled 'I am the Copy Editor' a guy named Michael Brickley explained with fresh and youthful humour that the newspaper existed to 'help dispel some myths about Beertown USA, and to prove Milwaukee was not just a cultural wasteland that existed some place north of Chicago between New York and San Francisco'. *Cityside* was as new as I was. Then and there, I decided – I *knew* – I was going to write for it.

The *Cityside* office was within walking distance, a narrow storefront in a fashionable shopping strip, next to a corner store that sold Native American jewellery. I went in, and introduced myself to Dan Ullrich and Michael Brickley and Bill Milkowski – young graduates keen to offer an alternative view to that of the city's daily newspaper monopoly. There also was Tom Kafka, a grinning, gum chewing, semi-professional baseball player from rural Wisconsin, fresh-hired to charm local businesses into buying advertising space in the fledgling paper. Tom seemed to be living out of a suitcase and a sleeping bag in the back of the elongated office.

I chattered away at Dan and Michael about my experiences so far, in the Land of the Free. They told me later that my accent was rather opaque, reconstructing it thus:

'He *seems* to be speaking English.'

'He *needs* subtitles!'

'He wants to write us an *article*!'

I was shown to a typewriter, near Tom's camping equipment and

Bill who was sheafing through a collection of arty black and white photographs.

There, taking a couple of days to do it, I tapped out my first contribution to the gutsy little paper that would eventually make me its News Editor.

The article was called 'Greyhound to Ghost Town'. It had a photo of me standing in front of a Greyhound bus at Milwaukee's downtown depot, looking hungry and depressed. The article pretentiously attempted to contrast the haves and have-nots in Milwaukee society. For the have-nots, I described the bums on the leaflets run. For the haves I chose Teddi's aunt and her family – good people who had innocently invited Teddi and Wyeth and me to join them for Thanksgiving.

This is part of what I wrote:

> 'I happened to visit the three-storey home of a wealthy dentist, who at the time of my visit was lounging on his recliner chair, sipping Diet Pepsi and chain smoking Benson and Hedges Menthol Light 100s, watching the Bears hammering Detroit while his wife stood on a chair sanding the French windows and his kids played pool and pinball in the rumpus room below. A 30-pound turkey cooked in the kitchen range. I sipped a Michelob and thought about those guys walking up to the front door and placing a handbill on the doorknob, forever excluded from enjoying such affluence and ease; on the outside looking in. Somehow, I felt the beer go sour in my mouth and, pleading illness, I left.'

Which wasn't exactly true, I have to confess, as I reflect on my decades of otherwise honest journalism: because, you see, I now recall eating a rather sumptuous dinner in a warmly ornate dining room. The turkey was delicious. There was a feast of side dishes, including a circle of green Jello, with cold and crispy coleslaw trapped inside. I guess I must have recovered from the 'illness' that made me flee.

Very soon there came to me another clue about life. *Don't* tell the readership of any publication, no matter how small and insignificant it may be, that your girlfriend's family makes you sick.

The fact that I did not possess a Green Card did not matter to Michael and Dan, because *Cityside* in its early days had no money to pay me anyway. They wanted to, but for now we would have to take each other on faith. I submitted some poems and streetscape vignettes, and vowed to learn my lesson about writing the truth.

Meanwhile, if we were going to get us an apartment of our own, we *had* to supplement Teddi's income. I resorted to methods illegal.

Early in 1978 I spotted an ad for an office clerk with an outfit called

Tru-Feed Computer Services. The company provided a service to accountants who mailed in big batches of tax returns which were computer-processed and sent back as a fancy and professional looking printout. The job was to proof read the printouts to make sure the data matched the original inputs.

I secured an interview and borrowed some decent clothes from Greg. Before the interview I had to fill out an application form. It asked for my Social Security number – my Green Card number. I had anticipated this. Wyeth had a number from Teddi's last visit home, so I quoted his.

The interview lady asked me about my accent. 'What is that? English?'

'Australian, ma'am. I was born in California, but I grew up in Australia.'

Considering I was also using a false name to go with the fake Social Security number and was attempting to commence forbidden paid employment while visiting the United States on a Tourist Visa, this little piece of California Dreaming was a minor lie. I carried it off well. I got the job. I did it well.

Meanwhile, Teddi got a cheque account and found us a two-bedroom basement apartment in a three-storey corner block on East Webster Street for 195 bucks a month, payable to our landlord, an affable Jewish gent in a brown suit named Mr Blitstein. He gave us the keys when I said I'd shovel the snow off his building's sidewalks.

The first thing you saw when you stepped down, directly into the living room from the front door of our basement place, was a bunch of large and very ugly heater pipes criss-crossing the ceiling, the rust-stained white paint flaking away from the constant changing temperatures. Below, there was a tidy expanse of newish carpet, crossing to a bookshelf recessed into the far wall and to two doors – one on the left leading into the main bedroom, the other to the right accessing the kitchen and the smaller bedroom where Wyeth was to make his home for the next three years. On both sides of the front door were street-level sash windows set into deep bays that had to be kept clear of fallen leaves and winter snow.

At first we had nothing to put inside. Our 'curtains' were large tea towels. There was an old tea chest in the boiler room: We brushed it clear of cobwebs, covered it with patterned Indian cotton, and used it for a coffee table. We got a nice couch from a deceased estate, and a card table and some wooden chairs. Teddi found an old Japanese watercolour of two swallows angled above two hills, and an Audubon print of *Corvus Americanus*, a beautiful black crow. We have them still.

Teddi's mother Sandy gave us her old black-and-white TV, and – bless her forever – the only time it ever worked properly was when Peter Jennings reported live from the nuclear melt-down emergency at Three Mile Island, and when PBS showed the weekly episodes of *All Creatures Great and Small.* Here we were, in Wisconsin, watching a weekly dose of drama from the Yorkshire Dales. We'd watch the show in harmonious silence, savouring its humour and humanity. The good feeling transferred itself to me and Teddi and Wyeth and this new apartment in which we found ourselves. I felt like I was the king of my own little castle, and I liked it.

In this place I truly became the father of the tyro named Wyeth. His hair was the same colour as Teddi's. He had freckles too. And, like his Mom, he had a spark of fearlessness about him, a what-the-hell fearlessness. I liked it in him. I loved it in his mother.

What she saw in me, I'll leave it for Teddi to tell in her own words one day, but she agreed to marry me.

We ordered nicely embossed cards and announced the plan to the rest of the world.

Chapter 4

Among the Cheeseheads

In recent years Wisconsinites have been nicknamed Cheeseheads.

Partly this is because rural Wisconsin is so full of cows that milk products, including some of the world's blandest pasteurised cheeses, are an economic staple. But the *real* reason the concept of Cheeseheads has spread is that most Wisconsinites 'root' for a professional football team called the Green Bay Packers. In the 1990s, Packer fans started wearing large plastic cheeses on their heads when they went to root at Green Bay's home games, and the team's marketing gurus successfully flogged the big yellow heads to nationwide notoriety.

Packer home games are played in a stadium called Lambeau Field, an expanse of grassy tundra in the rural 'city' of Green Bay. Most Packer fans are 'normal' people, but the TV cameras always manage to pick up the Cheesehead exceptions – some of whom look fiercer than a Nordic Thunder God, chest-naked in the frost, fortified no doubt by some form of alcoholic anti-freeze. At Lambeau Field, the weather can get extremely bleak. They have heater pads under the turf so it doesn't turn into permafrost. These Cheeseheads defy blizzards to get to the game. One guy flew his own plane into Green Bay to see a game. He was piloting himself back home when the plane suffered engine failure and crashed. The pilot was still wearing his headpiece, and it cushioned him from the impact. He escaped completely unscathed. That guy can thank his Cheese for saving his bacon.

Teddi's Mom, Sandy, was a Cheesehead, or would have been if Cheeseheads had been invented yet. She knew every thing there was to know about America's various sporting obsessions. She and Teddi's father Tedd were long divorced, but they were still an item when it came to a love of sports.

Sandy supported herself and – until they found their independence – three daughters, working at a downtown department store called Chapman's. She lived alone in a small but comfortable apartment on East Capitol Drive and she shuttled to work and back by bus, regular as a metronome, six days every week, with two weeks annual paid vacation.

The first time I visited Sandy's apartment, I went alone. It was never said in so many words, but I figured that I was on one of those visits in which you must successfully answer an implicit quiz: 'Young man, what are your intentions with my daughter?'

We sat down with some crackers and dip and Sandy asked me a bunch of questions about Australia, my family, how Teddi and me got together, how we got to be in Milwaukee. Listening to myself and knowing how little I had to offer Teddi, I felt Sandy would be within her rights to reject me: 'Young man, you are plainly as broke as the Texas Panhandle. Why don't you go back to that university you dropped out of?'

Instead, she went into her little kitchen and came back with a couple of cans of Pabst Blue Ribbon. She popped the tops. She gave me a can and a tight little smile. 'Do you know how to play cards?'

'Yeah, some.'

'Like?'

'Oh, Five Hundred, Pontoon.'

'What about Gin Rummy? It's easy. I'll show you.'

She showed me all right. Sandy Young should have been a professional gambler. She is the only person I ever met who knew how to count the cards, no matter how many decks were in play. That day I got *skunked*.

While I was getting skunked, we drank more beers and Sandy turned on her new TV. After a blare of advertising, we were into live coverage of the Sunday Game of the Day.

'Oh gawd,' said Sandy. 'It's the Cowboys. I *hate* the Cowboys.'

Sandy slapped a bunch of cards on the table. 'Gin.'

In disbelief, I counted the cards (for penalty points against me) as Sandy racked up another colossal score.

'Want to go again?'

I went again. Pretty soon the losses caused no pain. Sandy rooked me, honestly and cheerfully, meantime keeping up a running commentary on the football game so I could get some idea of the rules of combat, and generally treating me like somebody she had known all her life.

Maybe it was just because I was an amiable easybeat at cards, but that day I passed muster.

Saturday 25 March 1978 was a bitterly cold and windy day, threatening snow.

I ran down to a neighbourhood bakery for crusty French loaves – Teddi ordered them to go with the champagne and goodies she was serving to Greg and Julie and Sandy and Teddi's middle sister Christine, who had travelled from Colorado. The weather was bad further south, so Teddi's father Tedd Young and his wife Carol couldn't make it from their place in Barrington, Illinois.

Not counting Teddi and Wyeth and me, that was the extent of our wedding party. Reserve Judge TJ Pruss, a retired magistrate, was hired to conduct the civil marriage ceremony in our apartment, preferring it to the bureaucratic anonymity of Milwaukee's colossal City Hall. He was supposed to show up at 11 am, but he didn't.

The weather was bleak. Snow flurries eddied on the black tarmac beyond the front door. Eventually I saw a bent figure in black coat and hat, undecided on the other side of Webster Street. I ran out to guide the man to shelter.

Poor old TJ was so nearly blind he almost married me to Julie. Eventually he got it right and we rewarded him with a glass of bubbly and had a few more ourselves while we witnessed the documents and the judge doled out copies for everyone to keep. I escorted him to what he thought was his bus stop, waved my thanks and ran home, where Teddi looked every bit as surprised as me. 'Wow! We're hitched! Us! How cool is this?' It demanded we polish off the bubbly.

Then we all climbed in Greg's car and went for lunch at a fancy Greek joint. We drank gallons of *retsina* and I demolished a brain-blasting lamb *burek* and beamed at the lovely young woman who had suddenly become my wife. Like Momsie, who had accepted me so well and so readily, Teddi's sisters and the wonderful Greg, my best man, had done the same.

We had a *very* enjoyable nap that afternoon, alone at Webster Street. At Greg and Julie's place, everyone was preparing for the evening's big wedding reception. We showered and dressed up again, then set off arm in arm, strolling through the East Side twilight, among twinkling lights and spangled houses on Newberry Boulevard, so rich and mellow it felt like Christmas Eve.

Suddenly the wind dropped to nothing and a bright blowzy cascade of snow came tumbling and swirling on gentle cue from above. It was beautiful. It made whorls in our footsteps all the way to Cramer Street.

One thing Greg and his three brothers know how to do, is throw a party. They had a keg of beer in the bathtub; there was wine and champagne, plus an array of drinks like Margaritas and good old Vodka slammers. With Momsie holding court in the kitchen, the entire family was well on the way to having a skinful and the record player was cranked. Things only quietened – briefly – when the actual guests arrived.

I was nervous about the mix of certain guests. The first were my new mates at *Cityside*, Dan and Michael. There were also going to be colleagues from Tru-Feed. Despite their friendship, and the fact they were juniors like me, I was paranoid they'd find out my secret plans with the newspaper; worse they'd discover I was using a fake name. I'd get exposed and prosecuted for Immigration Fraud!

Of course, my paranoia went completely unrewarded. Nobody said a word to anybody, not then, not ever.

As I said, Tedd and his Carol didn't make it up the turnpike to our wedding from Barrington, Illinois, on account of the filthy weather and reports of black ice. But Tedd had helped us raise the necessary bond money to snare the apartment – a loan I paid back immediately to prove I was a person to be relied upon. And he bought me a Zippo lighter for Christmas just as I had commenced one of my quit-smoking attempts. That was when we first met and, like Sandy before him, he had been instantly accepting of me, the antipodean interloper. He held court, handing out presents, delivering wisecracks and witty little barbs and holding forth on all matters sporting.

That Christmas, we also played cards. Tedd lacked Momsie's unrelenting drive to win every time, and I actually won some hands. I had some victories too, during a later visit to their Barrington townhouse. Tedd barbecued steaks and burgers and Carol made salads, a twilight ritual even with two feet of snow on the ground outside. One moment, he took me aside:

'You'll take care of the girl, I know,' he said, clinking his glass on mine. 'You'll do fine.'

In the morning, Tedd took us into one of Barrington's malls. He spotted a street park and manoeuvred his car into the space by nudging the cars in front and behind, forcefully enough to shunt them away without causing damage.

Wyeth was agog at his grandfather's lawlessness. On the way back, Tedd shunted a snowdrift, accidentally on purpose, and Wyeth cheered at his lunacy.

Tedd Young has survived two strokes and heaven knows what lesser ailments in his 80-plus years. These days, as you will discover, he lives in Denver, Colorado. Yet he was constantly on the phone to give Teddi his support when I got so ill early in 2003, and he organised for Christine to fly out and visit us in Australia, a precious week when my life was still in the balance and my own father was so suddenly dead.

Tedd Young cares for and protects Carol like a nurturing mother. Nothing stops him, or erodes his air of optimism. He drinks and smokes, 'What the hell!' He *always* has fun, and he doesn't feel there's time to waste on people who don't.

One man who was *definitely* giving Teddi his blessings on the occasion of our wedding was Gordy Simons. Gordy was Teddi's first long-term, live-together love match. At the wedding, Gordy had a new gal by his side, Sue Bock. Not that Sue or I ever had any cause to be jealous, but right from the start I could tell that there was still some love between the other two – perhaps a little unfinished business.

Gordy was at least a decade my senior, a marvellously accomplished photographer and guitarist and I was absolutely in awe of the man. What could Teddi see in me?

The Wisconsin winter is a rugged one. In 1978 I shovelled a lot of snow for Mr Blitstein before the first Lilies of the Valley pushed through the solid ground that bordered our basement windows.

By the time winter turned to spring, I had made many visits to the Federal Building on Wisconsin Avenue for photographs and the deposition of documents including a certification from Milwaukee Police Chief Harold Breier that I was in no way felonious. I was now the holder of my own, genuine Green Card. I had officially become a Resident Alien of the United States of America.

I wasted no time in quitting the bogus job at Tru-feed and signing on with *Cityside*.

I had made a bit under a hundred bucks a week at Tru-feed. It had been good to go into the Sentry supermarket on Downer Avenue and spend thirty bucks on a trolley full of groceries and to be a contributor to my family's finances. At first, *Cityside* could barely match that kind of cash. I could still help with the groceries and some of the rent, but Teddi – who wanted to enrol at UW-Milwaukee to do a degree in anthropology and Native American studies – had no option but *more* work. As well as the office job with the guy from Organic Compost she did a night shift in a pizza joint called Francesca's. The pay was minimum wage but most nights she did okay with tips. She'd come home at two or three in the morning, wide-awake and full of the news of her shift, me still stupid from sleep. She'd check on Wyeth, snug in his blanketed bunk. Then we'd sit together in bed, which was actually just a base and a double mattress, backs propped against pillows and the bedroom wall, chatting in the pre-dawn silence, munching pizza and making plans, determined that she would enrol in the fall semester come hell or high water.

Even if Teddi had enrolled at UW-Milwaukee that spring, we could not have afforded the campus-based child-care for Wyeth, who was still half a year too young to be starting elementary school.

Teddi's search for an alternative led us to a lady named Bessie Gray. Bessie ran a child-care centre near the intersection of 3rd and Center Streets, in what was then one of the tougher parts of Milwaukee's black ghetto. Bessie and her volunteers looked after the kids of single working mothers and unemployed women needing time out to do job interviews or go to classes. Most of the mums were young enough to need childcare themselves. Bessie said she'd find a place for Wyeth.

Even though the *Cityside* office was a mere block away from our apartment, my days began with a bus ride – getting Wyeth to the ghetto every morning on the Center Street bus.

Mostly, the riders were black. There was one old guy who got on every day at 6.25 am, a man with a broken body and a grimaced 'smile' fashioned from a lifetime of physical pain. He had no gloves to protect his arthritis-gnarled hands from the biting wind. There he was, every day. I had no idea where he was coming from, or going to. All I knew was that when he got on, we were still on the fringes of Milwaukee's affluent East Side. Wyeth and I got off at the 3rd Street intersection, where there was a Ham'n'Egger diner full of hunched guys in airman's jackets and a yellow-and-black painted store with barred windows and a sign that promised: WELFARE CHECKS CASHED HERE. The broken man would still be there as we rose to get off the bus, seated silent as reproach just a few rows back. He looked such a wreck, every day I expected him not to be there. Then, one day, he wasn't.

Bessie Gray was always there. Her childcare centre was a converted house, run down but brightly painted and scrubbed clean inside. It was crowded with donated books and toys, and at breakfast and lunch the children were given what for many was their only sustenance for the day. When Wyeth and I got there about 7 am, the rooms were already busy with feeding children, Bessie calmly issuing orders and keeping control over the threat of juvenile bedlam.

I wrote a piece about Bessie in *Cityside*, another about the old guy on the bus, and I looked at the causes of why the ghetto housing was so run down, and why – if Milwaukee had a fair housing law since the race riots of 1967 – it was still regarded as one of the most segregated cities in the United States. An outsider myself, I had no trouble identifying with Milwaukee's minorities, and *Cityside* gave me a mouthpiece already oriented towards issues of social justice. My work had meaning.

Cityside was also fun.

'When winter turns to spring,' so the saying goes, 'a young man's thoughts turn to . . . well . . . *baseball*.'

This was certainly true of Dan Ullrich and Michael Brickley, who would also have classified as Cheeseheads. Not long after Teddi and I got married, Michael and Dan started discussing an event known as Opening Day at County Stadium.

County Stadium was the Milwaukee Brewers' home ballpark. According to Michael and Dan, the entire population of Milwaukee just *had* to be there on Opening Day.

Partly, this had to do with the advent of weather you could actually go outdoors to enjoy, and it wasn't dark by 4 pm. Winters in Wisconsin are so long that there is a psychological condition colloquially called Cabin Fever: you get cooped up for such lengthy, agonising months that you end up wanting to kill somebody, preferably with an axe or a chainsaw. Opening Day is a celebration not only of sport, but also of glorious spring, and the humid, *sweaty* days of summer.

Not that I was at the game. I confess, I do not even remember if the Brewers won. They certainly didn't go to the World Series. But Milwaukee was waking up to a season of hope and possible glory. Mike and Dan started organising a *Cityside* softball team and I decided I *had* to be in it.

Mike and Dan were happy enough to have me along because I recruited Greg to play third base. Teddi and Julie packed a cooler with beers and formed a raucous cheer squad.

Pretty soon they had something to celebrate. On my first 'at bat' I took a swing at an incoming softball the size of a watermelon. It lurched away somewhere over the infield.

'Run, Ro, run!' yelled the cheer squad.

I took off, heading desperately for the safety of first base.

'Run, Ro!'

I had seen it on TV: base runners, anxious to beat the tag, slide into the safety of the base bag. I did not notice the shortstop drop the ball. I was running! Nobody warned me that base runners *never* slide into first base. Nobody warned me that the bag was attached to the ground by an iron pylon strong enough to hold up the Sydney Harbour Bridge. So I slid. It was a spectacular spray of stretching sneaker and flying dirt.

'Fucking ye-ouch!' I screamed, as my ankle got sprained black and blue.

'Ha ha-HA!' went everybody else. 'He's *safe* at first!'

When everybody got over the hilarity of witnessing such a completely unnecessary injury, I was asked if I was okay.

'Absolutely!' I insisted. I stood defiantly on the bag. 'Batter up!'

Everyone laughed again and the game went on. My ankle throbbed murderously but I stayed on the field.

Not possessing a mitt, I caught an outfield fly ball with my bare hands. This feat was vaguely impressive; there was no laughter at my expense this time around. Teddi gave me a mitt for my 23rd birthday and I became a Saturday afternoon softball regular.

As promised, when the fall semester started, Teddi was able to commence her studies at UW-Milwaukee. Wyeth was enrolled in the Milwaukee Montessori School out on the West Side past the enormous Miller Brewery. The university studies were free, but the school cost us a hundred and fifty bucks a month. But by then I was getting a decent wage from the paper, and Teddi traded pizzas and organic poo for an excellent part time job typing up social assessment reports on troubled black kids for a psychologist. We had money for movies and decorations for the apartment, which we gave a fresh coat of paint courtesy of Mr Blitstein. For Teddi and me, things were looking good.

We had settled into a pleasant domestic routine: Fridays we'd often have a steak au jus or a fish fry at one of the local eateries. Every Saturday we'd take our weekly shopping list and troop up to the big Sentry supermarket. Up and down the aisles we traipsed, stocking up on good healthy foodstuffs and cooking to recipes which included a paperback offering from the sidewalk Hare Krishna handouts. Saturday afternoon was the ballgame. Sunday I'd buy a *New York Times* and I'd browse it – and the Milwaukee *Journal* sports pages – while I did our weekly wash in the laundromat.

Every second Sunday, I'd walk to the UW-Milwaukee union building, which housed the offices of the student newspaper. There, Dan and Michael and Bill Milkowski and art director Sharon Nelson would be hard at work, sometimes until dawn the next day, designing each edition of *Cityside* and putting it to bed for the printers. It was my job to proof read all the copy, one final time. It was typeset and printed out on paste-up ready paper. I marked any 'typos' with a red wax pencil. As the work went on, there was always a TV or a radio blaring, and it was always sport.

Cityside was always going to struggle to survive. It was free, and its circulation of twenty or thirty thousand was too small to attract big-hitting advertisers. Tom Kafka worked miracles with the local small businesses and – as fall deepened towards winter – Tom persuaded Michael and Dan that they had to spend money to make it and they hired another advertising sales person. Her name was Cathy. She started the job in a blaze of energy, but soon it was obvious that no matter how hard she and Tom worked, Michael was paying a lot of the bills from a personal inheritance. The paper was going broke, and if things didn't improve through the Christmas sales splurge, the winter of 1978–79 was going to be *Cityside*'s last.

By then I was writing with a crusader's passion. One of my pieces helped prevent a pro-nuclear academic from winning an important state government position, at a time when the legislature was debating an end to the moratorium on new nuclear power plants, which then existed in Wisconsin. After two elderly women froze to death in their own homes, I campaigned against the mighty Wisconsin Gas Company to stop it cutting off the gas of customers who couldn't afford to pay their bills. I wrote a piece about how Milwaukee's city building inspectors were losing the battle to protect exploited tenants from slumlords who'd hire an arsonist to burn their buildings for insurance rather than spend the money needed to keep the tumble-down places up to code. The ghetto was a wasteland of charred framework. The houses still standing were falling apart.

The rest of the crew battled gamely on until May 1979, but Volume 3, Number 10 was *Cityside*'s final edition. Without fanfare or farewell, the brave little paper ceased to exist.

One of my last articles was a feature on the great folk singer-activist Pete Seeger who'd come to town to do a fundraising benefit for a group that was trying to stop a city jobs program that made long term unemployed people work in a sheltered workshop. By then, of course, I knew the newspaper was going down, that the city's activists had lost a voice for reform, and too few people seemed to care. I asked Pete Seeger what would keep him motivated in such circumstances.

He told me a story. 'There was a young peace worker in Times Square at midnight with a peace sign. It was New Year in the 1950s and there were revellers all over. A passer-by asked, "Do you really expect to change the world? Standing here at midnight with a sign?" And the young man replied, "Maybe not. But I'm gonna make damn sure the world doesn't change me!" '

Chapter 5

Cheesecake

While *Cityside* was dying, a new magazine called *Milwaukee* was starting up. Its parent company was a classical music and jazz radio station called WFMR, which for years had published a black-and-white monthly program guide. Now it was 'going colour' and being expanded into a glossy city magazine modelled on successful examples from metropolitan markets the nation over. The newcomer quickly attracted refugees from *Cityside*.

Bill Milkowski was so quick off the mark his name featured in Milwaukee's third issue. Sharon Nelson was picked up as Art Director and Tom Kafka went on board to sell advertising.

Michael and Dan regarded *Milwaukee* as way beneath their consideration. 'It's cheesecake,' said Dan. 'Lightweight,' said Michael. 'No insight in 90 per cent of the writing, attempting to copy the formula of all the other city mags. Trying and failing.'

'But there's room for features,' I objected. 'There's room for solid writing there even if it's not there right now.'

'Don't count on it. Bill's already having clashes . . .'

Milwaukee was prepared to publish just about anything to fill its fledgling pages. I cranked out a feature based on travels in Thailand before I met Teddi. The article's relevance to Milwaukee was zero, but they bought it for a hundred and fifty bucks.

By July, Bill Milkowski had another series of run-ins with the magazine's hierarchy. He moved to New York and became a successful jazz writer. The magazine needed a new features writer and copy editor. They made me an offer.

Teddi was pregnant. She was due sometime in November and American hospitals don't come cheap. The pay at *Milwaukee* was much better than *Cityside*, plus I'd get full medical benefits for my soon-to-be expanding family. I took the offer without a moment's hesitation.

Despite the warnings about cheesecake, I was convinced I could get *Milwaukee* staff and hierarchy sharing at least similar editorial ideals as *Cityside*. I was soon to receive a blunt lesson to the contrary.

One weekend anti-nuclear activists hired buses and rolled north along the shores of Lake Michigan to the town of Sheboygan, which had been identified as the proposed site for a 1000-megawatt nuclear power plant to be called Haven. I took Teddi and Wyeth and went along on the protest march – six hundred Rainbow Coalitionists and a naïve scribe from Down Under who planned to use the August 1979 edition of *Milwaukee* magazine to tell the entire state of Wisconsin about how their kids could end up inheriting a radiation factory and how the state's politicians should learn the lessons of the nuclear meltdown at Three Mile Island and maintain the moratorium on nuclear power plants.

The article came out as a four-page spread, complete with a Sharon Nelson drawing of five solemnly innocent children playing in the shadow of two looming, steaming cooling towers. Its publication occasioned my first – and very nearly last – face-to-face meeting with *Milwaukee*'s owner and publisher, G Douglass Cofrin.

The day the mag hit the newsstands, I was ordered to his office by my editor, Marlene Knopf, a carefully coiffed blonde.

'And, Rod,' said Marlene, as I looked puzzled at this never-before-issued instruction, 'I don't think he's very happy.'

On the way upstairs I reviewed the little I knew about the man. He was only in his middle to late thirties, but he looked a lot older. He was fat. He had a handlebar moustache. He was loaded. He bought WFMR with some of his share in the inheritance of a major Wisconsin paper-milling fortune.

According to an article he wrote, he also owned a house and land on the island of Moorea near Tahiti. The article had been in the May issue, complete with a full-page *cover* photo of himself on the shore of a gorgeously rugged tropical island, bare-chested with a sharks teeth necklace, his colossal belly barely enveloped by a sarong the size of a tablecloth.

I knocked and entered his office. Dressed in a rumpled but fine suit and silk tie, Douglass Cofrin loomed over an enormous hand-carved wooden desk. He had the magazine opened to the offending pages. He stabbed a fat finger at my copy.

'What the hell is this crap?'

I tried to tell him, but he shut me up with an imperious wave of his arm. 'I'm reading this crap and I'm looking. Know what I'm looking for? Balance. You know what that is, son? Balance?'

Again I tried to speak, to say the company proposing the plant had refused to discuss its plans. Again he waved for silence. 'This state needs power for industry and jobs and economic development. I'm looking, but I don't see you saying that in any of this crap.'

'You can read that sort of line in the *Journal*.'

His fist hit the table. 'And I won't mind reading it here, either. You write any more of this shit and you're out on your ass.'

'But . . .'

'Son, you say one more word and I'll fire you now.'

There was silence. Then mildly he indicated the door. 'Off you go, then.'

Let us taste a slice of cheesecake.

The issue after my nuclear power plant item, there was a discernible lack of controversy within *Milwaukee*'s covers. We were 'Looking at Fall Fashion,' according to the cover-page headline. There was a close-up of a brunette model with glossy red lips, looking earnestly at the reader. The cover also featured sub-headlines asking whether blacksmithing was a dying art.

I sure as heck would not have paid a dollar-fifty for an offering like that – except mine was the piece on blacksmithing. I suggested it as a harmless photo feature on a kid from Cedarburg who ran his own forge and smithy. It had great pictures shot at sunrise by Gordy Simons, and it was far less controversial than my other near complete article at the time. This examined the plight of Wisconsin's forgotten minority, the Native Americans, and no doubt contained far too much fifth-column 'crap' for the liking of the boss.

The September 1979 issue also offered a chatty new column called 'Hot Shots', a series of vignettes gleaned from press releases that came our way from well-oiled public relations operators hustling for a line. I was the column's editor. We encouraged contributors of gossip and punchy one-liners, but I ended up writing most of it myself. I also wrote the monthly calendar of events, and sub-edited every line of features copy, submitting my own stuff for clearance by Marlene herself.

Not that I was going to make the same mistake twice. I steered clear of politics, writing personality yarns instead – like a scoop on the Wisconsin speed skater Eric Heiden. Although idolized in Europe, he was unknown in his own country until he won five gold medals at the 1982 Winter Olympics. I really cracked it with the lightest and fluffiest cheesecake when I came up with an article that, with great goodwill and very little actual evidence, confidently predicted that the Milwaukee Brewers would win the 1980 World Series. The clever bit was getting some of the Brewers players to do a photo shoot with models who were hired to do a spring fashions feature. Linked by the photography, the articles ran seamlessly back-to-back. Marlene was thrilled. I got promoted to Associate Editor and we got invited out to her fancy house for cocktails.

On 25 November 1979, at 8.58 pm, my daughter Myra came into the world. Doctor Vincent Lubsey was supposed to be there but he got caught in a jam on the blizzard-hit freeway, so my pre-birth coaching came in handy. Julie was there, the two of us huffing and puffing along with Teddi once her contractions started in earnest. Greg paced the corridors with Wyeth, who got to hold his new sister just after I gave her a Leboyer bath, which was supposed to make her feel good because it was the same temperature as within the womb. She hated it. Maybe my hands were too rough, or nervous. She squalled and squirmed and was silenced only by a nurse with a big warm towel. Teddi ordered me to get her a cheese sandwich. I hurried to do my duty, thrilled at this warm new feeling that welled inside me. I had helped to make the extraordinary new life that just arrived, even if the new life wasn't acting like she was thrilled to be here.

Greg took photos of the now expanded family before the staff kicked us out and Teddi was taken to the room where she and Myra would spend their single night in hospital. He took the rest of us home via Kalt's where he ordered double Metaxas and we toasted the baby named for the song:

Myra Myra
Many boats in the harbour
Going to go down south,
Make many first dollar,
Shake up the party . . .

Greg's mom Jean owned an ancient perambulator with huge wheels and a suspension system that looked like it belonged on a 1910 roadster. We could be seen on weekends in Lake Park, squeaking along, Myra swaddled in pillows and padding, peeking over the ship-like sides, big-eyed at the wonders of the world around her.

While I was to stay clear of writing any leftist crap and to keep trowelling out the verbal cheese, the same restrictive rules did not apply to my boss. Here, freedom of speech came with *ownership*.

An article vilifying the 'flawed liberalism' of Democratic Presidential Candidate Edward Kennedy had been reprinted verbatim from a conservative political magazine, with no rebuttal or balancing copy.

I made discreet inquiries and was told the article was planted there by Doug Cofrin as part of a political campaign of his own. The boss was scheming to bid for the Wisconsin Republican Party's nomination to the United States Senate, an election that would be decided on the same day as the poll that would send ex-actor, California Governor

Ronald Reagan, to the White House at the expense of the widely ridiculed Democrat incumbent, Jimmy Carter.

A quick check of the Republicans' Wisconsin personnel indicated that if Douglass Cofrin wanted to go to Washington, he'd first have to get past the incumbent Senator Robert Kasten in the preselection 'primaries'.

It was easier for Reagan. This was 1980, the year of the Iranian Hostage Crisis, and the disastrous military mission to rescue the hostages inside the United States embassy in Tehran. Americans were furious that their citizens could be abused by the Iranians. They were furious when the mission failed. They were furious that the crisis caused an oil shortage and gasoline prices skyrocketed. There were angry demonstrations in parks and on street corners. Intersections were blocked by petrol protests. Highway speed limits were reduced. America's cherished 'freedoms' were being eroded and Jimmy Carter was doing nothing about it. Reagan swept Carter in a landslide. We watched the results on our crackly black-and-white TV. It was all over before the polls closed in California.

Douglass Cofrin was rumoured to have spent nearly a million dollars in his bid to unseat Bob Kasten. He failed, embarrassed in the end by the fact that he 'forgot' to disclose his property on Moorea when officially listing his personal assets. The word around town was that he was just about broke. There was talk the magazine and radio station were up for sale.

Wyeth had two particular neighbourhood buddies. One was a black kid named Michael who lived in a mansion with his wealthy Cadillac-driving parents. They were schoolmates at Milwaukee Montessori. Every morning I'd walk Wyeth to the school bus stop. In winter the three of us had fun throwing snowballs at a nearby lamppost, improving our arms for spring and the advent of sandlot baseball.

But Wyeth's best friend was a tow-headed eight-year-old named Fletcher, who lived with his Mom in a small apartment in the next building. The last I heard of Fletcher, he became a soldier and saw action in the 1991 Gulf War after the Iraqi invasion of Kuwait.

When he was a kid, Fletcher was adventurous. He and Wyeth were forever disappearing on unexplained missions, which usually led to Fletcher's mother coming over and asking us if we knew where the hell they were *this* time.

But they were good kids, even though we often had to mount lengthy search parties and rescue posses, they rarely got into any serious trouble. When they did, it was usually of someone else's making, like the time some ghetto thugs cruising the lakefront parks stole the bike we got Wyeth for his eighth birthday.

Then, in an alleyway just one block from our apartment, some deranged man stabbed a kid to death. The kid was the same age as Wyeth and Fletcher and Michael. We were all horrified and frightened – first stolen bikes, now knives and murder!

For the first time since we'd started our American venture, Teddi and I started wondering whether Australia might be a better place to bring up the kids. We decided it was.

We gave our cats to a lady who had a mouse-ridden barn in the country and stayed for a family Christmas at an apartment now shared by Christine, who had moved from Colorado, and Julie who had separated from Greg.

At the railway station, we hugged and cried with all the sisters and teary-eyed Momsie. Gordy and Sue were there as well. He took photos; maybe he was trying to look busy. His 'gal' was leaving again.

'You'll be back,' he said to Teddi. They hugged a long time. Sue and I shared an accepting smile.

For two nights and most of three days, Teddi, eight year-old Wyeth and baby Myra and I rode the rails. From Milwaukee we were aboard the afternoon shuttle to Chicago's Union Station, a great cavernous space, beautifully designed, where we got beers in a bar and burgers and fries for the kids. Then we sat piled on our luggage in the waiting hall. In addition to my Karrimor pack, we had an expensive crimson-coloured set of Pierre Cardin luggage. We got the bags almost gratis, on credit from a department store that went belly-up before we made more than a couple of payments. The bags made great pillows as we waited to be called aboard the Amtrak service to Denver. Our route took us westward across the Mississippi River to a morning stop in the mile-high capital of Colorado, hunkered below the snowy Rocky Mountains. After a brief crew change, it was north to Cheyenne along the face of the mountains, then west towards the continental divide, into the badlands of Wyoming and across the canyoned country of northern Utah. Wyeth got bored and amused himself by telling our fellow passengers, in a loud, outraged voice, that he was a victim of child abuse. We silenced him with Coke and fries.

In darkness we crossed Nevada and got a whistlestop glimpse of Reno, the neon flare of casino lights purpling the desert night before the train clacked us on towards the California line at Truckee, then down to the verdant fields of California. At Oakland station, my cherished portable typewriter was stolen.

We left America on New Year's Eve 1980. The Qantas cabin crew served champagne and gave out multi-hued crepe paper hats. In the morning the sun rose on blue sea with whitecaps, and glowed on the red roofs of Sydney. There was the Coathanger, and the sails of the Opera House glittering above the sun-spangles of Sydney Harbour.

It had taken more than three years, but our circumnavigation of the globe was complete. It was January the first, 1981. Teddi's hometown had welcomed me. Now we were going to see the welcome she'd get in mine.

Chapter 6

Narrabundah boy

When I was growing up, I used to think that my brother Jamie and I were the only kids living in Canberra who were actually *born* there.

All my childhood and teenaged mates came from somewhere else, big cities like Sydney and Melbourne mostly, and they had moved to Canberra because their fathers were recruited to work there for the Australian government. My best mate Bruce Robbins came from New Zealand, and there were kids in our hockey team who were Sikhs from India. The Public Service was expanding rapidly and so was Canberra, new houses mushrooming in equally new subdivisions, almost as fast as the National Capital Development Commission could plan them.

My father, Ian, was a lieutenant with a heavy-calibre anti-aircraft gun battery based in Papua New Guinea, posted to a hilltop overlooking Port Moresby harbour in the fearsome months of 1941, before Pearl Harbour. The Japanese armies were rampaging through the supposedly impregnable Far-Eastern defences of the British Empire and heading south for Australia. His orders: shoot down as many Japanese bombers as you bloody-well can. Three years later, he was plucked out of the army and dispatched to Canberra with a new set of orders: establish, operate and maintain Australia's National Archives. He set about the task with enthusiasm and, if the obituaries in nationally read newspapers like the *Age* and the *Canberra Times* are anything to go by, he did it well.

In 1955, when I was born, the broad divides of Captain Cook Crescent in the southern suburb of Narrabundah had only just been laid and my first childhood home at Number 120 only recently finished. This is where Ian and his English bride Barbara (nee Kemp, aged 29, attractive brunette, legal secretary and a former translator with the United Nations refugee repatriation unit in Germany, Paris and Geneva) brought me after I came into the world, caterwauling, in the Canberra Community Hospital. The place is now infamous as the structure that was 'imploded' with disastrous and tragic results in 1997, when stray lumps of brick and concrete cascaded into the spectator fleet crowded around on the waters of Lake Burley Griffin. Their crews had come to watch the spectacular implosion, an event that had been promoted by the local government of the Australian Capital Territory. A 12-year-old girl was killed by the flying debris.

In 1955, the lake that held that unsuspecting flotilla of sightseers did not exist. Scrivener Dam was not even under construction. Canberra was still divided into its northern and southern halves, and in those days the intervening waterway was the Molonglo River. On Saturday shopping days we drove to the northern shore at Civic, Dad at the wheel of his FJ Holden, across the big white wooden trestle bridge now replaced by the Commonwealth Avenue Bridge and its monumental twin, Kings Avenue.

The first Archives buildings were in war surplus Nissen huts, situated about half way between the two bridges, a short distance from the Kingston boat harbour. It wasn't very big because recreational motorboats were banned, and the yachties berthed elsewhere. Now the Archives are ruled from a massive building inside the pompously named Parliamentary Triangle. The wartime huts are long gone. The Canberra I grew up in was in a non-stop spiral of growth.

My family life was changing. Mum and Dad divorced. I was in my first year at Narrabundah High when Dad announced he was moving to Bangkok, to work as Head Archivist with the South East Asia Treaty Organisation. Mum announced she was remarrying; a doctor named Peter Norman who had two daughters of his own, Madeleine and Caroline.

The combination of households led to years of spiteful clan warfare between five selfish teenagers, dominated always by Madeleine the elder, who was Captain of Girls at Watson High and who split for her mother's swank London flat as soon as she matriculated.

She was just the first to leave. The entire family decamped in my matriculation year of 1973. Peter saw better opportunities in Brisbane. I got my exam results while holidaying with Dad in Thailand. When I returned to Australia I was confronted by the culture shock of Brisbane, recently ravaged by floods from biblically heavy monsoon rains. The zigzagging hilly streets, the wooden stilted architecture, the sub-tropical vegetation were all so strange! So too was my house, near Kallangur, on a rural-urban acreage infested by bugs and wildlife totally unheard of in Canberra – lurid snakes, enormous spiders, fruit bats and cane toads included. The block was bordered on one side by the main northern railway, on another by a motor racing circuit and on the third by a dairy farm that had cows which inadvertently helped produce the most potent magic mushrooms in the history of man.

Despite this latter enticement, I couldn't handle the place. After a single term 'studying' anthropology and Asian civilizations at Queensland

University, I dropped out and returned to Canberra, where Bruce's mother was kind enough to give me shelter.

Just back from a four-month stay in Kenya with his botanist father (also divorced), Bruce was working as a copy boy at the *Canberra Times*. He swung an interview for me and I too became an official editorial messenger. It was my first proper job. I cleared $79 a week and was 'invited' to join the Transport Workers Union, because we drove messages all over town, and collected copy from the newspaper's busy bureau inside the old Parliament House.

I liked the job but I nearly got sacked twice. The first time, I forgot an important packet of papers dispatched for Sydney on the last overnight flight. The second time I let the messengers' car run dry of engine oil. I'd left the car running in the parking lot at Parliament House and charged inside to pick up some urgent copy from the Press Gallery. I got the story and was skidding down stairs and corridors on my way past the Labor Party Caucus Room when I thumped into the towering figure of Gough Whitlam, Australia's Prime Minister.

Beneath solemn portraits of his luminous Labor Party predecessors, the great Gough gave me a disdainful glare, down his proud nose, as if to say, 'There's a large, red pimple on your chin, you microbe of a boy. Go away.'

I took the hint and scarpered, discovering upon my exit down those famous parliamentary steps that the newspaper's car was gently billowing an evil mixture of smoke and oil, soon to seize up unless urgently attended to. It was the copy or the car. I hurried my delivery to the chief sub-editor. The engine choked.

I didn't get sacked, but Bruce did, for neglecting to verify the authors of letters to the editor that were mildewing at the bottom of a drawer in the messengers' desk.

I liked the *Canberra Times*. I'd written book reviews, short features and a poem – all published, all earning a few extra bucks, fueling for the first time my desire to be a writer. But I was also footloose and restless. I quit in sympathy with Bruce. Cashed up with leave and severance money, we hit the road in the Toyota Crown he brought from his Mum, with a sack of dope and some camping gear – including for the first time my Karrimor backpack and a certain ill-fated pup tent.

We were in northern Queensland some months later when the money ran out. That's why we cut south again for Brisbane, determined to get on the dole but destined to find some proper paying work. Both of us took the Australian Public Service entrance exams and passed. That's where we were in 1977 when I met Teddi.

It had been sad to hit the highway and farewell Canberra. For so many outsiders, Canberra is The City Without a Soul. Some people won't even concede that it can be a nice place to visit. 'It's so arti*ficial*' they say, lumping the National Gallery and Library and Archive and Museum and institutions like Parliament and the High Court into a noisome category of things for which they, the taxpayer, have endlessly shelled out. Got a gripe? Have a whinge at Canberra!

For me, Canberra means something different. Because it's where I grew up and began to build my view of the world, the thought of the place always makes me more than a little sentimental. Returning to Canberra in 1981 was a homecoming.

As we'd done when we arrived destitute in Milwaukee, my growing family of four fell upon a temporary haven. We had friends from Brisbane, Roddo and Terry, who had moved to Canberra and rented a place in my old neighbourhood, Narrabundah. Generously they let us camp in their spare room, Wyeth sharing with their toddler, Joel.

We had never been so cramped. We had to find a place of our own, but right now we were far too broke. It was up to me to get a job.

Within the week of our arrival, I sent letters to every local media outlet, enclosing the fancy CV I had printed on expensive paper in Milwaukee. The *Canberra Times* never bothered to answer. Who cared? I had a job within a week.

By coincidence, Canberra's only commercial TV station, CTC-7, was planning an expanded half-hour of local news and was looking for an extra journo. I was invited to the station's Watson studios for an interview and screen test, cranking out a hypothetical news story from a press release and then delivering my 'script' down the barrel of a camera set up on a tripod in the parking lot.

I landed a D-grading – one step up from a lowly cadetship. Plus I got a wad of cash in hand from Doug Holden, my new boss, to go to David Jones in the Molonglo Mall and buy myself presentable clothes and a fistful of ties.

For Teddi, there was little time for celebration. She was negotiating for enrolment at the Australian National University, transferring credits from UW-Milwaukee to a degree with majors in Anthropology and Aboriginal Studies. And she had to find a school for Wyeth. Third grade was starting in a matter of weeks.

I advocated Griffith Primary School. We got him a bike and every day he cycled dutifully down the hill to school. His route took him past Rocky Knob, where Bruce and I once smoked ourselves blue on filterless Pall Mall cigarettes pilfered from my old man, and where in the spring territorial bands of magpies would swoop at our strawberry-blond son as he tried to speed past their tall gum trees.

For me, getting to work was no bike ride. It was a two-bus journey from Narrabundah to Watson, swapping routes at the Civic interchange on Northbourne Avenue. Unless I could cadge a ride home, it made for a long day, working and commuting, dawn to dusk. I yearned to get a car, but finding a house was far more important.

We scrimped and saved until I had a wad of bond and rent-in-advance cash. Then one Saturday morning I walked down to the Griffith shops for a paper, hunted through the classified ads and found a place at 11 Finniss Crescent, Narrabundah. The rent was affordable, it was still reasonably close to Wyeth's school, and it was furnished. I found a phone box and called the landlord.

After the basement apartment on East Webster Place and the cramp at Roddo and Terry's, the place seemed palatial. It featured three large bedrooms, a huge L-shaped dining and lounge area, an enormous kitchen and laundry space that let out to a set of back stairs and a yard that could almost be *heard* inviting Teddi to plant flowers and vegetables. The living room featured an open fireplace. Apart from a couple of electric radiators, this was the only source of heat.

The deal was made. My family – for the first time in its short history – was about to occupy an actual house.

Teddi wasted no time getting enrolled at the ANU. Wyeth made a new best friend named Clete. Like Fletcher, he lived alone with his mum in a flat. Like Fletcher, he enticed a willing Wyeth to disappear on daylong weekend adventures which once led to parental agonies, Clete badly breaking his arm after he fell from his bike somewhere on the steep and picturesque slopes of Black Mountain.

Meanwhile, button-nosed, brown-haired Myra started talking. To this day she has not shut up.

I started talking too, on air, learning to be a TV journalist.

Some people, mostly those who come from sheltered backgrounds where soap opera stars on the cover of TV magazines constitute hero value, think that being a TV journalist is a big deal. I don't want to deprive anybody of meaning in their lives, but I have to say, they *could* be wrong.

One of my first jobs was to go with a cameraman to a meeting of landholders in a rural town in New South Wales. I think it was Murrumbateman. It had something to do with sheep, and they were protesting (the farmers, not the sheep). Beyond that, I knew virtually nothing.

I got interviews with weather-beaten blokes in checked shirts and battered hats. I was still mystified. On the way back to the station, my cameraman gave me his interpretation of what had happened. Scribbling in a notebook on my knee, I thanked him and did my best to turn his thoughts into a script.

The first sentence of the story I presented to John Bok, Capital 7's newsreader and news editor, was apparently a long one.

'There are 54 words here,' he said, sounding mildly bemused, 'In one sentence. I think that's a new record.'

I explained that I was used to writing 9000 word features. Fifty-four words was nothing. 'You want short sentences?'

'Yes, please,' said John, politely. 'Plus it would help if I had some simple idea – right at the top – of what you're trying to say.'

'Let's have a look,' said Bill Muldrew, the bulletin producer. He scanned my script, head shaking imperceptibly. Then he grabbed a piece of copy paper, rammed it into a typewriter and hammered a few simple sentences, all in capital letters. He glanced up once or twice, fixed me with a serious look and ordered: 'Find a decent grab that supports this view.' Then he resumed, spat out a concluding sentence, ripped the paper out of the machine and thrust it into my hands.

'*That's* how you write a TV script. It's called the KISS Principle.'

'The what?'

"Keep it Simple, Stupid.' Now, go find Sonia and get her to record your voice-over. She'll know what to do.'

I went to find Sonia, the senior videotape editor. As I went, I could have sworn I heard Bill muttering to John, 'There's *got* to be more to life than this!'

Somehow I managed to keep my job. Within a few months I even got promoted to a C-grading, and I was given the title of Civic Reporter, covering the shenanigans at the Australian Capital Territory House of Assembly.

The ACT has been self-governing since 1988. In 1981, the Assembly could merely make recommendations to the Federal Government's Minister for the Capital Territory. This was Michael Hodgman, a florid Tasmanian with pomaded black hair and a carnation in his lapel.

Hodgman was a master of saying almost nothing while making it seem deep and meaningful. One of his big ideas was to turn Canberra from an economy dependent almost entirely on the Federal public service, into one which had at least some capacity for privately generated industry and employment. Hungry for publicity, he'd talk about his notions in front of my camera almost any time I asked.

His grandest scheme was for a huge American microchip manufacturer to set up a factory in Belconnen. He announced the plan at a news conference in a vacant paddock not far from the town centre.

Months went by and no building began. There were not even survey pegs. Every interview, I'd ask him about the delay and he'd make reassuring noises, assuring Canberrans the factory was definitely on the way.

One day I got up really early and called the company's head office in Silicon Valley, California. I spoke to the President of the company, who told me that world economic circumstances had put the plan indefinitely on hold.

My scoop led the bulletin that night, and it was an extremely embarrassed Minister who – the following day – conceded the bad news to the rest of the media. After that, he was a less forthcoming with his interviews.

I got myself a B-grading.

We celebrated by getting a credit rating, borrowing money to buy my first car.

It was a 1971 four-cylinder Holden Torana. Otherwise an unremarkable factory-standard, it had a blue racing stripe the length of its white body, mag wheels and a racing-style steering wheel. I liked it. I took it for a test drive. I still liked it. I looked under the bonnet and nodded knowingly. I refrained from kicking tyres. I shelled out cash. I proudly drove home in my lovely new wheels.

It wasn't long before there were mysterious, rattling sounds – one from the engine, another from one of the wheel wells. Since the car kept going, I wasn't bothered. Following the ignorance-is-bliss principle, I figured that – so long as I kept the Torana topped up with petrol and checked the oil and water and tyre pressure once in a while – all would be well.

And so it was, until we took an incident-packed road trip to Victoria during the long, hot summer holidays of 1981–82.

Chapter 7

The outdoors life

Tens of thousands of Australians, many of them footloose retirees, annually traverse the Island Continent's country regions, far beyond the big cities where the majority of them live.

These travellers are invariably experts at camping, or at least the comfortable alternative of caravanning. They take to the road equipped with all the mod cons, often with a boat on the roof or trailer, nonchalant in the knowledge that they've used all the gear before and their needs in the sometimes life-threatening Australian elements will be met.

Attentive readers will recall that my stocks of camping gear were now reduced to one large Karrimor backpack. Even if I still had the pup tent, it would not fit a family of four.

I had given up the thought of camping again, when Teddi suggested it: 'Rocklands Reservoir in western Victoria.'

'What, where?'

'Near Horsham and the Grampians Mountains. I stayed there when Wyeth was real little. It's beautiful! There's fresh water and the kids and I can swim. You could go fishing, and prove to me at last how good you are! There are kangaroos and koalas and emus all over. Plus it's grassy – you don't have to contend with boulders and rocks and sand. There's barbecues. And there's a nice shower block, too. I can only camp if there's a good shower block!'

Teddi had at last agreed to go camping! I could hardly admit we weren't equipped!

It was easy getting a map to show me where we were going and borrowing enough sleeping bags. But everybody I asked about a tent offered either a space-aged one-person tube suitable for a precarious life among yaks and trekkers, or one of those room-sized caverns that, with the addition of a few rugs, would have looked well placed on the set of *Lawrence of Arabia*. These big buggers would have been great, I knew, but they would never fit in the Torana's spatially-challenged boot, and the thought of going to some place like Paddy Pallin's camping accessories store and actually purchasing something an appropriate size never even *occurred* to me.

Eventually I borrowed a well-used and somewhat frayed affair, maybe half-metre broader than my original pup tent and a similar length. We did possess a few mail-ordered cast-iron pots and pans that would serve for preparing campfire fare. A visit to Woolies at the Manuka shops supplied us with plastic plates and cups and cutlery. We filled a box with canned food and Deb mashed potato and a jar of Vegemite. Somebody loaned us an Esky.

I had a nagging sense that we were still under-equipped, but when Teddi bought me a fishing rod for Christmas, complete with a Shakespeare spinning reel, I felt we were ready for anything.

Most people driving from Canberra to Melbourne choose to drive up to Yass and then, through Albury along the Hume Highway. We are not most people.

We wanted to briefly visit Melbourne, but had decided to go due south through Cooma, Nimmitabel and Bombala, then into Victoria on the Cann Valley Highway to Cann River. From there we'd go west through Orbost and Lakes Entrance towards Bairnsdale along the Princes Highway, then to Melbourne. The total distance was about 750 kilometres. I figured we'd do it in a day, no worries.

It all started well enough. We had a counter lunch at the Bombala pub – a mixed grill with the typical slice of canned beetroot and slice of orange so thin you'd think oranges were as rare as truffles, and a tiny spoonful of coleslaw. Outside Bombala we saw a gorgeous green valley, fringed by tall Eucalypt woodlands, with a neat little homestead and a For Sale sign. It was so romantically beautiful Teddi fantasised about living there. We even stopped and scribbled down the name and phone number of the real estate agent.

On the Victorian side of the border, the road unexpectedly turned to dirt, slippery from recent rain. We took it carefully, following the steep river road through a magnificent rainforest. When we got to Cann River, the sun came out and we turned east on the Princes Highway, cranking through Orbost in the mid afternoon, the car – I thought – performing excellently.

We were about 20 kilometres from Lakes Entrance when an evil clatter erupted from beneath the bonnet. I pulled over in panic and killed the engine. 'What the hell was that?'

'I bet the fan belt's busted,' said Wyeth.

We got out to investigate. Wyeth was right.

'You got a spare?' Teddi wanted to know. This was a rhetorical question. 'Now what?'

'I suppose I'll have to hitch into Lakes Entrance and buy one, and hope I can get the garage bloke to come out and fix it on.'

'What about us?'

I had this vague recollection that stranded travellers in the Australian bush were supposed to wait by their vehicle until help comes along. 'You can wait here.'

'Like hell! We'll come too.'

It wasn't long before we received proof that the wicked world still contains a sprinkling of Good Samaritans. A beefy young bloke in a van pulled over to see what the trouble might be. Then he ordered us into the van, drove us to Lakes Entrance, dropped Teddi and the kids off to buy an ice cream while he supervised the purchase of a new fan belt, then piled us all back into the van, drove us back to the stricken Torana, fitted the belt himself, and took off with a cheery wave.

The whole rescue operation had taken less than an hour. We made Melbourne not long after sunset.

The West Windies were a great cricket side, and they flogged Australia in the game I saw, sitting alone among gangs of raucous drunks while Teddi met some members of my extended family. She adopted my Uncle Hector as her favourite, with Aunt Bev not far behind. She was the wife of Dad's youngest brother Don, a Geelong radiologist who insisted my Torana-load of tourists take advantage of their holiday 'shack' at Anglesea near the start of the spectacular Great Ocean Road. The shack – really a solid brick home with an airy sleep-out and an enormous back yard – was located near the top of the hill that dominates Anglesea's southern exit.

My first memory of Anglesea was of one childhood summer holiday. With our cousins we played back-yard tennis and our parents played Seekers records and we body-surfed for hours, coming home salt-encrusted, arms and shoulders burned red. The calming cool of calamine lotion was a feeling I knew well from past summers. Whether I was fishing with Dad at the outlet of the Moruya River, swimming in the lagoon at Broulee, scrambling on the rocky heights of Burrewarra Point or waiting for the car to stop boiling on the ascent to Clyde Mountain, I *always* got sunburned.

In those days there was no 'slip, slap, slop', as protection from the sun's damaging ultra-violent rays. My pale Scottish-bred skin was already a mass of freckles and moles. Nobody knew then what danger I was in.

I found the place easily. Teddi took the kids to the beach while I practised erecting the borrowed tent on Don and Bev's back lawn. Teddi took one look at it when she got back, lugging wet and sandy towels to the Hills Hoist out the back.

'Very nice, I *don't* think. Tonight, we sleep indoors.'

We sunned a few days at Anglesea, swimming and keeping cool because the weather was getting hot.

By the time we hit the Great Ocean Road and motored through Lorne and Apollo Bay and crossed the beautiful Otway Ranges, emerging at the Twelve Apostles and what was then called London Bridge before it collapsed, Victoria was in a 40-degree heatwave. We swam at Port Campbell, then motored on to the historic harbour town of Port Fairy.

There were plenty of places to stay, but the local caravan park and camping ground looked reliably shady and had the necessary 'nice shower block', so Teddi agreed we'd give it a shot and do the camping thing.

There was no way she was cooking, however. So we explored the town in search of food. The streets were broad. On one corner there was a pub that proclaimed it was Victoria's oldest. The buildings were grand, imposing reminders of Port Fairy's halcyon days. Masts and superstructure bobbed on the river, behind the waterfront inns and little shipyards and slipways.

We got ourselves a slab of take-away pizza and a flagon of plonk. We noshed out, erected the tent, and for the first time seriously realised that there was definitely no room for all of us. Wyeth and I slept outside.

Next day was another scorcher. We eagerly anticipated a swim at Rocklands Reservoir, which we figured we'd reach by lunchtime, after a 140-kilometre run to Balmoral, gateway to the reservoir where we could stock up on supplies for our campfires.

The Torana had other ideas. We caught up to a slow-moving truck and when I flicked the indicator to let the truckie know we were about to overtake, the lever went limp, hanging uselessly from the steering column.

'Shit!' said I, knowing what Teddi was going to say before she said it.

'We're not going any further before we get that fixed.'

So it was that we got to spend several baking hours hanging around a filthy grease-blackened garage in Hamilton while a lone mechanic who clearly wished he was in the pub with his mates, forced himself to deal with our dilemma.

'This won't be an easy job, mate,' he said.

'It's just an indicator switch.'

'Yeah, but whoever put on this fucken fancy little steering wheel also installed a non-standard switch.'

'So?'

'So, we don't have any non-standard switches. This is fucken *Hamilton*, mate. I'll have to try and fix the busted one.'

We had a counter lunch with beetroot and an orange slice and coleslaw. When we went back to the garage, the mechanic was down to blue Stubbies and a sweat soaked blue singlet, writhing around beneath the steering wheel, grunting and cursing. 'Garn, ya fucken cunt, get *in* there!'

Four hours and many dollars later we were on our way to Balmoral, next stop Rocklands Reservoir.

At Balmoral there was a general store that sold fishing tackle as well as the food people eat when they're not eating the fresh fish soon to be caught by me.

I loaded up on line and lures and hooks and sinkers and various baits while Teddi collected more canned food, lots of it.

'What about some steak or sausages?' I wanted to know, 'For the camp fire.'

Teddi looked glumly at the pleasant-faced matron at the counter. 'Will you tell him, or will I?'

The matron took the task with relish. 'Son, it's 39 degrees today. Tomorrow the forecast is 41 degrees, plus rising northerlies. There's a total fire ban 'til further notice. I'd say that means at least three days.'

'So when I catch fish I can't cook them?'

'Unless you've got a gas stove, Sonny Jim, that just about sums it up.'

Rocklands Reservoir was a vast stretch of water backed up from the great dam wall, flanked by rolling hills and native forest and the ghostly limbs of thousands of drowned gum trees stretching away into the upstream inlets. The campground was set near the dam's wall with a boat ramp that offered the only access to the lake for miles. There was a long, pebbly beach leading towards the drowned forest. The campground was crowded, a field of caravans and impressive folds of canvas occupying the best places, close to an ablutions block that virtually sparkled with proud and magnificent maintenance.

Now, despite the heatwave and the fire ban, I optimistically chose us a camping spot close to an outdoor fireplace.

'Sloppy,' said Myra.

'You mean it has a *slope*,' corrected Wyeth. 'Rod, we'll roll downhill tonight!'

'We'll be right! You guys go have a swim and I'll set up the camp.'

Nobody needed cajoling. I emptied the car and started setting up. It didn't take long: one undersized tent pitched at a slightly discernible angle, four sleeping bags, one box canned food, one box assorted fruit and vegetables, one box utensils and plastic ware, one billy can, one set assorted frying pans, cooking facilities nil. When it came to the flame-licked fish I pined for, it looked like Spam instead.

Our camp established, I departed in search of red fin or a miracle trout, wandering the banks for hours, casting and retrieving, and didn't get a touch. The sun was setting fireball red when I finally gave up and trudged back to the campground, only to find our site lifeless. My family was missing.

I was trudging down to the dunny block to wash up when I heard my name. I peered towards the entrance of a caravan, which had a large canvas awning stretched across it, and one of those folding table-and-chair arrangements that comfortably seats four people. A gas lamp hissed on the table, illuminating a large man with a battered hat on his head, a tattered blue singlet in no way covering his enormous sun-blackened shoulders, a brimming beer glass almost invisible in one huge and meaty hand.

'G'day,' he said. 'I'm Sid. They're inside, watching telly. Wanna beer?'

Was the Pope a Catholic? 'Yes, please!'

'Rita!' he called. 'Got another glass there, love? Better bring the bottle, too.'

Instead of Rita, it was Teddi who emerged with a large bottle of Melbourne Bitter and a schooner glass. 'I see you two have met. Sid, this is Rod, in case he's lost his tongue.'

Sid's handshake fused my knuckles together for a week. 'So, how'd your fishing go?'

'Not so good. Tried worms and yabbies, with and without a sinker. Nothing.'

He nodded, not surprised. 'They're off the live bait. You might get one with the right kind of spinner. Territorial buggers, you know. They'll strike at a passing bit of colour. Jigging 'em's the best way. Got a boat?'

I shook my head sadly. He gave me a look of frank assessment. 'Can you be up and ready to go at 5.30 tomorrow?'

'No worries!'

'Meet me at the boat ramp. I'll show you how to catch a bloody Redfin.'

I think the least insulting word to describe our meal that night is 'uninspired.'

'Rod?' This was Wyeth. 'I told you. The tent is on a slope.'

'You can hardly tell.'

'*I* can tell.'

'We're sleeping outside. It doesn't matter.'

'What about us?' Teddi wanted to know. 'We get to roll into each other in the tent? Rod the Great Camper can't even pitch a tent on the flat!'

'I'll fix it in the morning.'

'Wyeth, Myra, let's fix it now.'

Feeling suitably pathetic, I helped right the listing ship, a job we completed just as the batteries in Myra's torch waned, then died. The women retired to the tent. Wyeth and I turned in beneath a bright half moon and the shimmering Milky Way.

'Ro?' called Teddi in the dark.

'Mmm,' said I grumpily.

'If we had've gone camping in Norway, I'm sure it would have been wonderful.'

In the night we heard a stampede of kangaroos in the belt of trees at the top of the hill. There was murderous grunting from fighting males. The heavy beat of their footfall came so close we could see their leaping legs and tails in the moonlight.

I was at the boat ramp ages before Sid, rod and reel and tackle box ready to go in the pre-dawn shadows.

'You won't be needing that stuff,' he said when he showed up right on 5.30, carrying a simple wooden box under one arm, and a small outboard motor under the other, like it was nothing heavier than a football. 'It's hand-lines where we're going. Help us with the tinny.'

The tinny was a small aluminium boat. We launched it, Sid wading knee deep in the water to fix the engine to the stern. Then he stowed the box and got me to hold the boat steady while he hopped aboard and pointed me to the bench seat in the bows.

'What about my gear?'

'Bring it anyway. We might try some trolling on the way back.'

'You bet!'

He fired the engine first time, and soon we were puttering across the glass-smooth waters, heading away from the dam face towards the forest of dead gums. 'Plenty of snags in there,' said Sid, 'But that's where the big buggers are.'

Now we were among the trees, dead white trunks looming like monstrous hands and broken fingers from the still, black water. Sid cut the motor and we drifted in silence towards a cluster of jagged limbs. He roped the boat to a branch and whispered that he'd show me the technique. He took a hand-line and gently plopped the lure over the side, the line running through his powerful fingers until it stopped in what seemed like seven or eight metres of water. Then he reeled the line back in so it was taut, and starting jigging.

After a moment something bit the hooks down below and I got all excited, thinking he'd had a strike. But Sid just cursed. 'You wouldn't read about it. Bloody snag, first up! Pass me one of those spirally bits of lead from the box.'

'Happens all the time,' he said, calmly wrapping the lead spiral around the line and flipping the lure back into the water. 'Now you know what to do. Give it a go yourself.'

My first cast also produced a snag, and by the end of the morning's excursion I had perfected the lead spiral technique. But I was also thrilled: I'd caught a brace of mid-sized Redfin, and Sid half a dozen beauties. I'd barely noticed the sun was well up and the day was starting to swelter.

'They'll go quiet now,' said Sid, as if this was an incontrovertible fact. 'Besides, I'd say we've got more than enough for a feed. I reckon it's time for a coldie.' I looked at my watch. It was 8.30 am. By nine we had the top off another large bottle of Melbourne Bitter and we were getting to know each other.

Sid was a self-employed truck driver. He and Rita lived in nearby Horsham, and they came to Rocklands for their annual holidays. With its TV already tuned to a re-run of some kid's show (that my kids were watching *again*), their caravan was a home away from home. There was even an old washing machine attached by an umbilical extension cord. It had one of those roller-wringer gadgets on top and there was a clothesline strung between the caravan and a nearby tree.

Rita stuck her head out the door. She looked like a slightly more feminine version of Sid. 'I told Teddi she could use the washer if you need to do any clothes. See she does, now. And what about those fish? How d'you plan to keep them cool?'

I said I had an Esky cooler. 'I'll get some ice in Balmoral.'

'And it'll last about five minutes. Sid, you fillet 'em up and we'll all have lunch together.'

Sid nodded calmly, as if this was a plan of his own hatching. I'll never forget my first taste of the wonderful Redfin fillet, pan fried in butter and sprinkled with pepper and lemon juice.

We stayed a week at Rocklands Reservoir, Teddi and the kids doted on by Rita, Sid and me off fishing every dawn, my family shown the friendship and hospitality you'll invariably find in the Australian bush. Despite the mishaps en-route, it turned out to be a most enjoyable holiday.

Alas, the Torana had no intention of letting it end that way.

We camped a few nights at Hall's Gap, bushwalking in the Grampian Mountains by day and listening to the koalas grunting amorously in the trees above us at night. Then we hit the road for the long run back to Canberra.

All went well until we were just south of Gundagai and the four-cylinder engine started missing. We nursed the car into Gundagai, where we were told repairs could take days. So we just pressed on, driving very slowly, up to Yass and back home to Canberra, blowing increasing volumes of smoke.

That was the Torana's last trip. The engine was completely shot. A used car dealer in Fyshwick gave me a few hundred dollars for the mag wheels and traded me an olive green HR Holden with bench seats and a standard steering wheel.

That Victorian holiday was significant for reasons greater than mere motoring.

Teddi was pregnant again – about three months along – at the time we found ourselves hopping up and down steep rocky paths and bathing in mountain rock pools in the Grampians. The life growing inside her had survived the exertions of the first trimester quite happily.

Teddi continued her normal physical activities as she had done in Milwaukee, where she had ridden her bike to work and university classes despite the steady swelling of her belly and breasts. Now she caught a bus into Civic and then pushing Myra in her stroller she walked the mile or so to the ANU crèche where she'd leave the little chatterbox and hoof it all the way to classes. Come late afternoon she repeated the effort in reverse, all in time to see some dinner onto the table for Wyeth and me and 'Minnie.'

She had a gynaeocologist rather unhappily named Doctor Cutter. When Myra was born in Teddi's hometown, the doctor was caught in a blizzard and missed the party. When Sylvie Barbara Mary Maclean arrived in *my* hometown, in a delivery theatre at the Woden Valley Hospital on 6 July 1982, Doc Cutter missed out too, and Teddi did the work with the help of a couple of midwives and me. I did a pretty spectacular job of catching my new daughter as she shot out of Teddi's birth canal so fast she nearly slid off the end of the bed.

As soon as Teddi and Sylvie were allowed to leave the hospital, Teddi had to resume classes. She was starting the last semester of her final year of studies. So I took two weeks off work to look after the infant. Teddi would express breast milk into sterilized baby bottles and she showed me how to cradle the baby so her neck was well supported. Was everything okay? No worries, I assured her. And off she'd go to uni with Myra and the stroller and the big bag of books.

By late November, the classes and essays and exams were finished. Teddi had her degree! Now, what to do with it?

One thing about having qualifications in Anthropology and

Aboriginal Studies was that, unless you wanted to become a perpetual academic making field trips, in a place like Canberra there were no opportunities to apply the theoretical skills. The only Aborigine we knew was the courageous and often controversial bureaucrat and civil rights leader Charlie Perkins, and the only reason we knew him was because I ran him out in a social cricket match just as he was starting to amass a decent score. Teddi was offered the chance to do honours, but the wanderlust was rising; her eyes were looking north.

So it was for me. Being Civic Reporter in a town where the Legislative Assembly had no political power was like trying to tell the people of the ancient world that General Pyrrhus had won a great victory.

When I told Doug Holden that I'd applied for and won a job at the Australian Broadcasting Corporation, he said, 'Congratulations. Where?'

'Darwin.'

'Darwin!' Doug was genuinely aghast. In Australian TV journalism, Canberra and Sydney are where it's at, where you go en route to overseas assignments and postings. With its exponential population growth and proximity to Asia, Darwin these days is considered by many to be a desirable destination, but in 1982 it was considered a hardship post. You got tax rebates and special allowances for living there. Doug apparently knew this. 'I hope to Christ they're giving you an A grading!'

Actually, it was still a B, but I wasn't admitting that. I made much of the fact that we'd be housed in an air-conditioned four-bedroom ABC-owned home in the better-known suburb of Fannie Bay, for a mere forty bucks a week.

'Well, good luck is all I can say,' said Doug. 'I'd better hold you here as long as I can and hope common sense prevails and you change your mind before it's too late.'

Chapter 8

Green cans, green ants

Darwin's history is not especially auspicious.

Australia's colonial rulers – the Brits – were paranoid the French or the Dutch might try to grab some of 'their' unsettled antipodean turf. So during the 1820s they established forts in the future Northern Territory, one on Melville Island and another on the Cobourg Peninsula. Conditions were so harsh and isolated, neither of them lasted the decade. By the 1840s, European explorers were penetrating the region overland in the expectation that pastoralists and squatters would not be far behind. But it took decades. In 1863 the Territory was ceded to the colony of South Australia. Six years after that the site of the future city was selected, on a harbour named for Charles Darwin by a shipmate from the *Beagle*.

Like other doomed attempts at settlement, Darwin's may also have faltered, but gold was discovered at Pine Creek in 1871, bringing prospectors in their thousands – among them many Chinese – and the inevitable service and supply businesses that support a gold rush. By the time the fever subsided, Darwin had become a support base for the growing Top End cattle industry.

So it settled, for years to come, into a frontier place forgotten by those in the South, wild and barely civilised. The NT's Aborigines were steadily dispossessed and shovelled into reserves, Christian missions or onto vast cattle stations – to help in the kitchens or ride there as stockmen for scandalously discriminatory rates of pay.

World War II gave Darwin another reason to exist – it became a hub for allied airbases scattered all over the Top End, and it became a target for Japanese bombers, more than sixty raids officially killing 243 people, old timer locals adamant the toll was many more.

History shows that Darwin cops its fair share of battering. Cyclone Tracy hit Darwin late on Christmas Eve 1974. The Northern Territory's official statistics tell the story: 'By about 10 pm the winds were causing physical damage. By midnight the damage was becoming serious, and it was apparent that Cyclone Tracy was about to pass across the city. Over the next six hours Tracy substantially destroyed Darwin and killed 65 people – 49 on land and 16 at sea.'

As the first images of a ruined city reached the country's TV screens, all but essential personnel were being evacuated, on every plane that could be brought to Darwin with incoming medical personnel and other disaster relief workers on board. Soon afterwards, with bureaucratic *and* military precision, a massive rebuild of the city was commenced.

By the time the Maclean contingent arrived less than ten years later, there were still some blocks of land with twisted steel, but most of Darwin had been transformed into a tropical suburbia with streets laid out by urban planners dragooned from Canberra's National Capital Development Commission. Darwin's new hospital bore an extraordinary resemblance to Sylvie's birthplace in the Woden Valley. The suburbs all had their own shopping centres, and larger retail hubs too, just like Canberra. The streets curved and circled. It was the National Capital with palm trees and riotous bougainvillea.

The ABC in Darwin must have been used to its personnel coming and going at regular intervals. Its busiest staffer was a property officer named John.

'We'd like to get into our house soon as possible,' I told him.

He sounded a little surprised. 'There's no Survival Kit there. The only one still available I left with the Cronshaws. I could try and get it back.'

'What's a Survival Kit?'

'You'll need it, until your pots and pans and plates and cutlery turn up with the movers. There's toilet paper and such.'

I conceded we could use a Survival Kit. He said he'd get hold of it as soon as possible, and have us into our new home in a jiffy. Meanwhile, he suggested, with the generosity of someone who's not paying the bill: 'If I were you I'd enjoy a few more nights at the Don. You know you're reimbursed for everything.'

We compromised by a day. Our new address was 10 Wickham Street, Fannie Bay, and it was a radical contrast to the solid brick edifice we'd so recently left in Canberra.

Where Finniss Crescent had an open fireplace, Wickham Street featured ceiling fans and two enormous, roaring air conditioners. Finniss Crescent was closed to the elements, just a few sliding windows to open on fresh and sunny days. Wickham Street had wall-to-wall louvres. Finniss was squat and low. Wickham's elongated form sat high on metal stilts and a framework so strong that the house had survived Cyclone Tracy. Finniss had lawn and cottage garden flowers and, thanks to Teddi, a nice vegetable garden. Wickham had mango trees festooned with nests of fierce green ants looming over the stairway that climbed four or five metres to the front door. There were papaya trees by the back stairs. There were two coconut palms, from which the fruit would crash in a high wind. There was a custard apple plant lurking in the semi shade below the house. The lock-up housed some rudimentary gardening tools and a large washing machine frequently populated – like the dunny upstairs – by various sizes of green tree frogs.

To make an understatement, we had entered a different world.

Not only that, we had arrived at what is possibly the worst time of year. The Yolngu Aborigines of Arnhem Land describe a multitude of seasons, but whitefellas can really only grasp a couple: Wet and Dry. Wet is when it's *pissing* rain, day after relentless day. Dry is when the scrub crackles and the lightning-lit bush fires send ribbons of smoke into the parched-blue sky, eagles and kites circling in the thermals, looking for prey. Wet is when the roads are impassable and you can't swim in the ocean for fear of being killed by a lethal box jellyfish. Dry is when you *can* swim, at beach or billabong, so long as you're prepared to take your chances meeting up with a bad-tempered territorial salt-water crocodile.

There is a semi-official third season called the build-up. It is a time when the dragonflies come out in droves to signal climbing humidity, unbearable to all but natives and drunks. Enormous thunderheads build up in the sunset and explode with furious lightning as dark sets in. The thunder sets every dog barking and the ground shakes as if there's been an earthquake. Then it rains – a tantalising, tumultuous squall. You think it might keep on, you *pray* it might keep on, that the Wet has broken and it will rain for days. But no, the rain ceases and the thunder rumbles away into the distance. You are left with nothing but the heat and the humidity.

It's the humidity that gets you. It's like you're raining inside yourself, sweating incessantly. The air conditioners and fans are useless as you toss and turn and try to sleep in a night that chirrups with insect monsters and crawling ticks and the fecund infestations that want to eat your house and return it to the rotted jungle floor.

Teddi would climb out of her morning shower and weep because she was sweating again.

In psychological terms, the build-up is not unlike the time of Cabin Fever in Milwaukee, when people crave the end of the snow and yearn for the sight and feel of sunshine. It is a time of depression, murder and suicide, statistically proven in both hemispherical extremes. *This* is when we arrived at Fannie Bay.

The suburb, to its credit and despite its proximity to the infamous Fannie Bay Gaol, did much to lift any such dark thoughts and deeds. The gaol, for example, is now an interesting museum. On Saturdays when I had to work, Teddi went to race meetings at the Darwin Turf Club at Fannie Bay. She was good at picking the neddies. She'd have her little punt while the girls chased each other in the beautifully landscaped gardens and lawns. In the Dry, if we didn't fancy the races, or a run to Berry Springs for a swim and a close-up encounter with the generally harmless fresh water crocodiles, we could spread our towels on Fannie Bay Beach. We'd probably stop at the take-out pizza place on the way home, too sunstruck and relaxed from a day in the water to even contemplate cooking a meal.

Ross Smith Avenue also featured a large fresh-water public pool, and the Parap Primary School, where Wyeth was captain of the school cricket team and a powerful left-handed baseball pitcher; he was destined to represent the Northern Territory in both sports. The street also gave access to the Parap shops, where we found our weekly groceries, haggling for fruit and vegetables and Vietnamese herbs and colourful clothes, and browsing and hunting for bargains at the weekend markets. A short walk down to the mini-mart where we bought our basics and beer would offer the chance to jump up and grab a few fists full of the beautiful yellow-green star fruit from a bountiful tree conveniently overhanging the footpath. Our own garden produced its fair share of fruit, and Teddi had me fence a little area and build a (rickety) hut for half a dozen chickens that for some time provided a regular supply of eggs. Eventually they became too much work so we gave the chooks to the inhabitants of an Aboriginal town camp hidden away on the swampy side of Dick Ward Drive.

We had a neighbour who rates a mention here, because he was Teddi's boss. Bob and Julie Ellis had a gorgeously decorated house, with pool and a beautiful tropical garden. We became good friends. The bearded, gentle giant Bob often regaled us with fascinating, off-the-record insights into the way Aboriginal Territorians were dealt with by their government.

Like Teddi, Bob was an anthropologist. He was in charge of the Northern Territory's Aboriginal Sacred Sites Protection Authority, set up under force of the Federal Government's Indigenous land rights laws. Its job was to work with Aboriginal traditional owners to identify and catalogue landmarks, called sacred sites, which were of vast spiritual importance to Aborigines because they were part of their Dreaming. Major developments and small – all had to be cleared of sacred sites significance before the construction work could commence.

It was into this interesting political climate that Teddi started work as a consultant at the Sacred Sites Authority. At first, she did research and archival work, hunting sources in the Authority's excellent library.

She met some of the traditional owners for whom she was putting in much of the research, and officials of the Northern Land Council, and got familiar with the issues that were relevant among the Top End tribes. She was teamed up with a male anthropologist and sent into the field, south to the Jawoyn people near Katherine. Here she was involved in detailing sites of significance to tribal elders.

I never got to meet any of Teddi's Katherine mob, but one night we were invited to a feast at the Bagot Reserve. We tasted shellfish chucked briefly in the glowing ashes of a fire that lit a dozen dark and eager faces. The girls gnawed happily on chunks of kangaroo flesh. Teddi chatted to the people like she'd known them all her life.

She really had a great job. I once fantasised about being an anthropologist. Now Teddi *was* one! I had to content myself with covering the politics of a Territory in which the Chief Minister described himself as 'the king of the kids.'

We hadn't been in Darwin long before my chief of staff, Bill Fletcher, started sending me off on assignments elsewhere in the Northern Territory.

The first took me to the courthouse in Katherine, 325 kilometres south of Darwin, to cover the opening of a legal claim by the Jawoyn people, to traditional lands surrounding the town of Katherine. It was passed by the Federal Parliament and over-rode any legislation of the Northern Territory, which was self-governing but not constitutionally a State of the Commonwealth. It could in fact be 'ruled' from Canberra.

The concept of land rights might have been popular to the majority of voters down south but in the rural areas where some landholders thought – or were taught to fear – that their properties were at risk, it was about as palatable as rat poison. Already, large swathes of the Territory were legally in Aboriginal hands. The traditional owners of Arnhem Land were now collecting millions in royalties from the Ranger Uranium Mine – an unpalatable fact for rednecks and political conservatives who preferred the paternal view that *they* knew what was best for the Abos.

The hullabaloo about Jawoyn was intensified by the fact that the spectacular Katherine Gorge was central to the claim, and it was alleged by some opponents that the Aborigines would prevent increasing numbers of tourists from seeing the sights, or worse, that *they* might get the profits.

There I was at the Katherine courthouse in early '83, scribbling notes and watching the posturing of lawyers, representing the Northern Land Council, the NT and Federal governments, and sundry other interest groups. I've little recollection of the stories I filed for ABC radio news bulletins and programs like *The World Today*, but I do remember observing that the case was not going to be settled in a matter of days or weeks.

How right I was. It wasn't until October 1987 that the Aboriginal Land Commissioner, Justice Kearney, provided his report on the case, and it was almost two years later when the area was granted to the Jawoyn Land Trust.

These days the land is managed in a partnership of the Jawoyn people and the NT government, as Nitmiluk National Park – a result that might – with a little more good will and a lot less legal wrangling – have been achieved much earlier.

My next assignment was far less complicated and a hell of a lot more fun.

The job was in the town of Tennant Creek, which is a lot further down the track from Katherine – 679 kilometres along the lonely Stuart Highway.

Bill had compiled a list of eleven yarns he wanted me to develop for the TV news. I'd have two days to gather the stories, the last of which was to be a colour feature on the annual Australia Day Regatta at the Mary Ann Dam, not far outside town.

I was issued a ticket on the so-called Milk Run, an Airlines of Northern Australia Fokker F-28 that hopped daily from Darwin to Katherine to Tennant Creek then on to Alice Springs. It was a one-way ticket.

Not unreasonably, I wanted to know how I was going to get back.

'No worries,' said Bill. 'I've had a word with the Administrator.' The Administrator was a genial ex-Navy chap named Commodore Eric Johnson, a vice-regal appointment to Darwin, as the Governor-General was to Canberra and the Federal Government.

'Yes?'

'He's going to Tennant for the regatta . . .'

'And?'

'He flies his own plane. It's a Super King Air. He's going to give you a ride. You'll get back much faster in that!'

It took me a moment to absorb the news that I would have a personal pilot who was also Queen Elizabeth's official representative in the Northern Territory. Then we returned to practical matters. 'What about wheels when I get there?'

'No worries. I've had a chat with Bruce McRae. He's the Town Clerk. He's going to lend you one of his trucks. He'll meet you at the airport.' Bill leaned back in his chair and gazed serenely over the newsroom with the look of a man who has thought of everything. 'Anything else?'

'Um, yes. What about a camera crew?'

'Not from here.'

'From where, then?'

'Alice. His name is Erwin Chlanda.

'Who?'

'Erwin Chlanda – Austrian bloke. Been in the centre for a million years. He's a freelance.' I later learned that, after an ABC cameraman named Keith Bushnell, Erwin was the first to get pictures out of Darwin after Cyclone Tracy. He'd flown up from the Alice with Australia's Deputy Prime Minister Jim Cairns, on the first flight allowed into the debris-strewn airport.

'He flies his own plane too,' Bill continued. 'He'll meet you at sparrow fart the morning after you arrive. You come back to Darwin with the tapes; he flies back to Alice. When you return you do the regatta story first, and spread the rest over the next few weeks.'

The Milk Run took so long the cream went sour, but Bruce McRae was there on cue, a friendly bloke the size of a Barkly Tableland steer, with a handshake that nearly mashed my city-boy bones to chicken-meal. He had a battered dust-covered F-100 truck with a bull bar on the front and a windscreen splattered with insects. He chucked my bag in the back and tossed me the keys. 'This'll be yours for the weekend. We better see if you know how to drive it!'

It was mid-afternoon. I fumbled with the enormous gear stick and negotiated the beast of a vehicle out of the aerodrome gates, Bruce giving directions. 'This is Irvine Street. Just up there's Paterson Street. That's the Stuart Highway to you, north to Darwin, south to Port Augusta. Go right and we're nearly there.'

'Where? The Eldorado?' That was my motel.

'No, the pub. We'll introduce you to some of the locals.'

I may only have been living in the Territory for a month or so, but I had already found out that with the oppressive heat and humidity it is not difficult to drink much more beer than physicians would recommend. Common lunch-hour consumption at the Press Club would be four, sometimes five Green Cans, and the ABC social club lads *always* kept the fridge well stocked for refreshment after an arduous game of table tennis. I have no idea how many glasses of draught I knocked back that afternoon in the pub at Tennant Creek, but Bruce and his many mates – slab-girthed giants the colour of a dusty sunset – got me into round after round of shouts. They downed their glasses like their bellies had no sides. I am no tiny tick. I am six-foot-two inches tall and had *some* practise at the Press Club, but pretty soon I was pissed stupid.

I may or may not have had dinner. Somehow I found my room at the Eldorado, where I promptly passed out. I woke up to the sound of impatient hammering on my motel room's door.

I squinted into the merciless morning glare and perceived a nuggety, tanned man of medium height, with a taller, dark-haired youngster standing behind.

'Rod Maclean?'

Was I? 'Mmm.'

'I'm Erwin. This is my son Laurie. He's learning the ropes. Let's get to work!'

Bill Fletcher got his eleven stories, but don't ask me how. In ghastly heat, with flies antagonising us whether we were inside the F-100 or out of it, we tracked around the town and its outskirts, me driving, Erwin getting tracking shots and explaining everything he was doing to Laurie. He shot overlay of the gold battery on Peko Road and recorded half a dozen interviews and as many pieces to camera, busy checking off the items on Bill's infernal list.

That night, there was an Australia Day Ball at the pub. I might have been an outsider, but in true Outback manner I was made welcome as an honoured guest. Erwin and Laurie knew a lot of the locals and were set to party on, but when the rounds of shouts got earnest I was so stuffed I made my excuses and made tracks for the Eldorado, determined to be ready bright and early for the culmination of my main assignment, the big regatta.

Mary Ann Dam is Tennant Creek's primary source of water. Not only do they drink it, they play in it. It's located in a desert dustbowl, or at least it was back then: a sere set of low hillsides sloping down towards acres and acres of cool, clean-looking water. Hundreds of people came out with their barbecues and eskies. Many of them had formed teams and come up with a colourful flotilla of boats home made from milk-cartons, beer-cans and sundry pieces of flotsam and jetsam. These were raced up and down close to the foreshore, the increasingly drunken crews attempting to get their craft to the finish line before they sank, simultaneously attempting to scuttle the competition by fair means or foul. I got some interviews amid the hilarity, trying to stay at least partially dry, then parked on one of Bruce's coolers and consumed more than a few of his beers. Erwin and Laurie chased up and down the banks, getting pictures and sound grabs and earning every cent of whatever it was Bill Fletcher was paying for their gig.

Guess what? That night, back in town, we had a few beers.

I reckon the Commodore himself might have had a beer or two that weekend. He was big enough, tanned dark beneath his Navy whites, to absorb a jar or two without even noticing. He welcomed me aboard, showed me to a chair behind the little cabin of his aircraft, and expertly worked through the pre-flight checks.

We took off in a perfect sky, the morning quite still, the red rocks and earth of the Barkly falling away below us. It was my first flight in a light aircraft, and I was soon absorbed with the view.

Home in Darwin, my car had four parking tickets on the windshield. I left them there. I rolled into work, cranked out a yarn on the regatta, and went home to sleep for a very long time.

Chapter 9

Red Centre assignment

David Moncrieff, the journalist-in-charge of the ABC's Alice Springs bureau was due for six weeks' holiday. Bill decided to send me south to keep the office running while 'Monty' was away.

As a bonus, the Sacred Sites Protection Authority had some research and library work to be done at their Alice Springs office. It was agreed that Teddi would do the job, timing her work to coincide with mine.

Wyeth, then eleven and into his final year at Parap Primary School, would stay in Darwin with the family of one of his friends. Which left the rest of us, me and Teddi, four-year-old Myra and Sylvie, who was not yet two.

As you know, Teddi *hates* flying. She declared she was getting to Alice Springs by bus. 'I'll take Myra with me.'

'That's a two-day trip. What about Sylvie?'

'She goes with you.'

'What!'

'Don't worry. I'll organise day care. All you'll have to do is drop her off in the morning, pick her up after work and look after her at night. Two days at the most, until we catch up.'

For some reason I agreed to this plan. And so it was that my Alice Springs assignment commenced late on a bright Thursday morning with me lugging a baby, barely out of her bassinet, as well as my bags.

Monty picked us up from the airport, more than slightly puzzled, and took us on a quick tour of town, winding up at the ABC's offices in Parsons Street, where I was introduced to Lyn Conway, the office manager who would save my ignorant bacon on a daily basis for the next six weeks. After that Monty gave up on trying to teach a bloke with a baby anything of value and drove us to our quarters.

In early 1984, the Alice might not have had as many of the up-market hotels it boasts today, but there were a few around. They were also frighteningly expensive, so Teddi had selected a place called Toddy's Cabins, then as now a popular backpackers' hostel, situated on Gap Road about half way between the town centre and the famous Heavitree Gap. It was actually charming, the gum trees in the river bed glowing red-gold in the westering sun, the sandy expanse interspersed with shady areas where you could see the silhouettes of aborigines gathered in little groups, taking no notice of the tourists who walked along the grassy banks, marvelling at the red ramparts of the ranges across the river. There and then I knew, Alice Springs was going to be a great assignment.

The work was hardly demanding, cranking out a five-minute bulletin of local news that got read on air in the evening and rehashed in the morning, with some fresh yarns I left behind before I knocked off for the day. Some mornings I'd team up again with Erwin Chlanda to do a TV yarn. We'd send the tape for editing to Darwin on the lunchtime TAA flight while I hustled back to the office and tapped out a script to send north by telex.

On the weekends, I'd 'liberate' the ABC Datsun and take Teddi and the kids exploring the waterholes and chasms along the western MacDonnell Ranges, places like Simpson's Gap, Standley Chasm – with its tame dingo perched territorially upon one of the kiosk's picnic tables – and the Ellery Creek Big Hole, where the sandy beach tips so steeply away into the surprisingly frigid water that we had to keep an eagle eye on tiny Sylvie, for fear she'd topple in and drown.

One of the most memorable weekends we spent was at the launch of a new tourist venture called Kings Canyon Resort. Lyn Conway's husband Ian was the brains behind the plan, and he'd invested huge effort and a lot of money building an hospitable campground and a valuable bush petrol station on an acreage of Kings Creek Station.

Getting to Kings Canyon was far from easy. There were 130 kilometres of tarred road on the Stuart Highway south from the Alice, followed by nearly 200 kilometres of often-treacherous dirt and sand winding west. After a morning shopping for vast piles of supplies, Ian Conway led our convoy.

Mid-afternoon, we stopped for cool drinks at an isolated homestead-roadhouse near a dirt road junction, one branch of which led south towards the Lasseter Highway and Ayers Rock.

The place was called Wallara Ranch and it was situated on Angus Downs Station. The man who welcomed and served us was a bloke named Jim Cotterill, but Ian and Lyn called him Javed.

'Why's that?' I wanted to know.

'Well,' said Ian, a sunburned and laconic bushman if ever there was one. 'You know there's a Pakistani cricketer, Javed Miandad? You know, pronounced "me and Dad?"'

Javed Miandad was the Pakistan team captain, a great batsman too. We nodded.

'Well, Javed and his mob have been pioneers in this country. His Dad was Jack Cotterill, who built the road through to Kings Canyon from here. That was in about 1960. Jim helped as a lad – it was a bloody big effort. Anyway, Javed's always going on about it: "Me and Dad did this, me and Dad did that." So it just sort of stuck. Javed.'

It was getting late when we got to Kings Creek Station. There was work to be done, first of all, filling the trestles with breads and salads and paper plates while the coals barbecued freshly butchered beef. A lot of people had come in from Alice and the various stations all around, and everyone clapped when the old NT political warhorse Bernie Kilgariff smacked a bottle of champagne against a desert oak and unveiled the plaque that commemorates the opening of Ian and Lyn's Kings Canyon Resort.

Ian's blind old dad Mort was there too, that opening night, telling his stories of camel catching and mustering days with the Kidman cattle empire. Aboriginal teenagers sat apart, hiding cadged beers in the lee of the barbecue pits. They didn't listen to Mort. Maybe they already knew his stories. Maybe they also knew the stories of the Luritja peoples' sacred sites in the canyon hills: maybe not. Mort only hinted at those – *they* were for initiates and men only.

For the first time in our lives, Teddi and I slept in swags – stars blazing above, rustling night sounds among adjacent desert oaks. We marvelled at the wonders of the luck that had brought us – through the accidental vagaries of chaos – to this wonderful and peaceful place.

In the morning, Ian took us for a tour of the canyon itself, which was over 30 kilometres away. These days – with the advent of the Kings Canyon resort – access is easier and safer, but in 1984 it was rugged going. We bumped along in Ian's four-wheel drive, only vaguely mindful of the fact that the Luritja people managed to traverse the country successfully for the past 20,000 years or so. When we eventually got there, we hiked into the spring-fed Garden of Eden. It was so wild and empty of obvious human touch that for us – seeing the hundred-metre canyon walls and the ancient umbrella bush acacias that give the place its botanical value – it was like whitefella eyes were seeing the place for the very first time.

Another weekend, we met up with Erwin, at the annual Mount Ebenezer 24-hour race, a motorcycle endurance event that attracted young and foolish competitors from all over Australia, as well as a sprinkling of Americans, Canadians and Kiwis.

Mount Ebenezer Roadhouse is about 260 kilometres southwest from Alice Springs. Even in those days it was bitumen road all the way, and as we discussed the logistics of the job Erwin suggested that I'd be mad if I didn't cover the start of the race, get a few interviews and do a piece to camera, then leave him to shoot the action while I continued on with Teddi and the kids for our first-ever visit to the famous Rock. We could return to Mt Ebenezer in the morning, interview the winners and return to the Alice in the afternoon, via the Henbury Meteorite Crater.

For a cameraman, Erwin was certainly an excellent tour organiser. We made a booking at a place called the Inland Motel, and set off in the ABC Datsun early on a cloudless autumn Saturday – the weather a perfect compromise between the unbearable heat of summer and the bleak windy chill of winter – country music on the radio, passing southbound road trains, tourist caravans and utilities loaded with trail bikes.

The roadhouse at Mt Ebenezer, focal point for what is now an Aboriginal-owned station, was made of hand-hewn logs of desert oak, and it looked old, certainly older than the excellent highway that ribboned past it, spearing westwards towards Uluru.

We caught up with Erwin and went to work for a couple of hours; then we set off for Uluru.

It is more than 400 kilometres from the Alice to Uluru, the road traversing sandy spinifex country, the dunes glaring red, and now and then passing stands of mulga trees and desert oaks. It is magnificent country, the ancient heart of an ancient land. Long before you reach it, you see the huge tabletop mesa called Mount Conner, rising hundreds of metres from the desert floor, and which a lot of people mistake for Uluru itself. That is, until they continue on past Curtin Springs and – 85 kilometres later – they find themselves confronted by the world's largest monolith.

It's impossible to take a bad photograph of Ayers Rock, especially at sunset when the arkose sandstone keeps changing colours and becomes almost luminous. I liked ours, anyway. Teddi got one of the kids and me, sitting on the bonnet of the ABC's Datsun, all of us bare-footed, the girls in their nightgowns, the Rock looming on the right like a huge orange lollipop.

We were starving by the time we got to the Inland Motel. But before we got ourselves a plate of steaks and salad we had to have a beer or three in the bar at the Inland, with its sense of dusty Outback history. There were old pioneering relics mixed with badges and insignia and foreign bank notes, all displayed like a museum of international curios that somehow got confused with the original Aussie artifacts. Teddi and I loved the place immediately. Out in the beer garden, it was full of caravan-and-camping enthusiasts and backpackers barbecuing and yarning. We joined in and it was like having a wonderful globe-full of people in your own back yard.

It was sometime during the next year that bulldozers demolished the Inland Motel. The huge new tourist resort at Yulara would soon be open for business. The land surrounding Uluru and Kata Tjuta was returned to Aboriginal freehold title, with a 99-year lease to the Federal government's National Parks mob and a joint management arrangement. The white supremacists in the Territory government might not have liked it, but a new era had arrived.

That night at the Inland Motel, we knew that new era was coming soon. All the hotels at the base of the Rock would go – only some of the buildings would survive for use of the Mutitjulu community. Pioneering days of Australian Outback tourism were coming to a close.

In the morning, we returned to Mt Ebenezer to wrap up the bike race. Driving back to the Alice, I vowed we'd return to the Rock one day. We had no idea what would happen when we did!

Back in the Top End and reunited with Wyeth, we discovered a little more of the Territory, thanks to Sue Bock. This time we were off to Kakadu National Park.

You'll recall Sue as the better half of Gordy Simons, Teddi's original Milwaukee love interest. Gordy refused to travel anywhere he didn't have to. Sue was more adventurous, having gone on safari in Africa, and she had come to visit for a few days before she too flew south to see Uluru, then on to Sydney.

I think Sue might have preferred the new facilities of Yulara at Uluru to her brief foray into Kakadu, because the Kakadu adventure included one night's camping – with *me* once again in charge of the tents.

To say we were ill equipped is to get tautological. I had not learned from previous experience. I vaguely recall borrowing someone's canvas shelter and scrounging up some sleeping bags and maybe one or two folding chairs. I generously forked out for some plastic plates and cups and cutlery, possibly even a cheap foam esky.

Sensibly, Sue had arrived during the Dry, when days are hot but not suicidally humid, and nights are pleasantly cool. We had a civilized welcome lunch at the Darwin museum, where Sue got to see the enormous stuffed crocodile called Sweetheart and the dreaded box jellyfish.

When Saturday came around, the five of us Macleans jammed Sue into the HR Holden, wound down the windows, and took off down the track, then east on the Arnhem Highway towards Kakadu.

Along the way we saw smoke from numerous scrub fires, started by random lightning hits, the hot air providing thermals for hawks and kites hunting for prey flushed out and sometimes disabled by the flames. The air was clear and crackling blue. There were stands of enormous termite hills and groves of pandanus in the dried up creekbeds.

Our campsite destination was Cooinda, described as a 'holiday village'situated near a billabong along the South Alligator River, 200 kilometres from Darwin. The further we went, the less likely it seemed that there could be a village of *any* description. This, in the famous Australian parlance, was *Woop Woop*.

Cooinda turned out to be quite pleasant, or at least its main complex was – a modern motel with a cool blue pool and a restaurant and some well-tended lawns sweeping towards the bush and the adjacent billabong. Teddi and Sue looked quite hopeful – until we pulled off the highway and were confronted by the nearby camping grounds.

These were an undulating barren wilderness with nothing to prevent evil animals emerging from the bush and devouring the lot of us at any time convenient to them.

Only fifty or so metres away, across the highway, there was a boggy hole with a large water buffalo wallowing like a malevolent and territorial pit bull terrier. Nearby, buffalo turds crusted in the sun, gathering a horde of flies, pretty much where we'd have to select our campsite.

I am an optimist of some note. But even I cannot claim that I looked forward to making camp in this god-awful place. My doubts increased as I looked across to a path leading towards the billabong, and saw a sign warning people against swimming. The place was infested with saltwater crocodiles.

'Can we stay in the motel? Please, Roddy, please!'

'Yeah, pa! Can we?'

Here, my camping incompetence once again clashed with the fact that I was still a cheapskate. 'No. We came to camp and that's what we'll be doing.'

I started unloading. Everybody abandoned me and went to the motel pool.

We ate a joyless meal that night. Once again, I slept under the stars with Wyeth. The water buffalo grunted and passed our way with slothful crushing footfalls, followed by numerous of its babies. Teddi says it was hideous just *listening* to them from inside the tent with a cringing sleepless Sue and the little girls held close for her scant protection.

Teddi says it was lucky for me that our marriage did not break up then and there.

Poor Sue slept not one wink. Her hands trembled as she applied her morning makeup.

We took a boat cruise on the South Alligator River and got a close-up look at the huge crocs that might have murdered us that night. The water was a baby-shit yellow, the tidal riverbanks channeled with the muddy slides the crocs use to launch themselves into the opacity of their murky hunting grounds.

Jabiru storks hunkered on spindly treetops. Cameras clicked. Teddi and Sue slowly emerged from their catatonic stupors, though Sue still had the haunted look of someone who fears there's nowhere to run if suddenly hunted.

We headed deeper into Kakadu National Park, destination Ubirr, a place of amazing Aboriginal rock paintings to be found in caves and overhangs fringing the East Alligator River. The road took us past the uranium-mining town of Jabiru and into a wilderness of still soggy floodplains over-run with spectacular bird life. Ubirr in 1984 was still accessible to people prepared to do some legwork. But this is sacred ground. Some people show no respect. Now the access is much more restricted.

Beyond the East Alligator River is Arnhem Land, and to travel there in Aboriginal freehold country you need a permit from the Northern Land Council. We had none. It was time to take the long ride back to Darwin.

As we backtracked past Cooinda, I suggested that the sights we saw that day easily made up for the privations of the night before.

I received a brain-drilling pair of stony stares. Even little Sylvie looked accusing.

Teddi's contacts with the Aboriginal women were paying off. These women still lived in traditional ways, preferring their outstations to Darwin's town camps. When in town they'd often get together and go in mini-buses to places like Fogg Dam, and up among the mangroves and mudflats bordering Shoal Bay.

Teddi had asked them if it was okay for her and Sue to go. They were invited but the trip was strictly women and children only.

'We went to Fogg Dam,' said Teddi, 'crammed into a mini bus with no air conditioning. It was hot and several of them were smoking. When we got to the dam, Sue and I couldn't care less about the water lilies in the billabong, we just desperately wanted a swim. We were swimming happily in the billabong when one of the women suddenly speared a file snake, right where we'd just been!'

Soon after, a goanna was killed with a single blow. 'The women started up a campfire and the goanna and snake were chucked on the coals. I *kind* of liked the food, but not as much as the shellfish we got near Shoal Bay. The mud crabs and the barramundi fish, those women weren't sharing, but they did show me how to get honey ants with a stick.'

Poor Sue's delicate constitution was mortified. Normally well tanned, Sue came back to Fannie Bay looking like she'd seen a ghost and was in dire need of a drink.

She looked just as terrified in a photo she sent us later, of herself perched precariously atop a camel in Noel Fullarton's camel yards south of the Alice.

There was also a snap of Sue with the Sydney Harbour Bridge in the background. The sun sparkled on the harbour's blue waters. Her tan had returned, and so had her smile. Now this place was *civilized*!

Chapter 10

Bali high

One of the best things about Darwin is its cosmopolitan atmosphere. Apart from the large Aboriginal population, there is a Chinese community that traces back to the Pine Creek gold rush. When we were there, the city's mayor was Alec Fong Lim and Chinese businesses almost dominated the shops in the Smith Street Mall. For a few dollars we bought a kitten we named April from a Vietnamese woman, one of many former boat people who ran little stalls at the Nightcliff and Parap markets. There were dynasties of Greeks who made a fortune from pearling and prawns. Especially in the Dry Season, the streets were full of tourists and transients. And refugees, too: not just the Vietnamese and Cambodians, but also a growing enclave of East Timorese.

Historically, xenophobic Australians have been threatened by Asia's proximity. Anglophiles all, our earliest Federal politicians saw fit to enshrine a White Australia Policy in law – policies only repealed during a sweep of reforms generated by the social and political sea change of the 1960s and 70s. Recently the tide has swept the other way. Conservative Federal governments now jealously protect Australia's shores from boat people: Afghans or Iraqis, fleeing regimes so vile that our leaders are prepared to war against them, have been denounced as 'queue jumpers' and kept for years in barbed wire enclosures known as Detention Centres.

When we lived in Darwin during the early 80s, Darwinites seemed to feel no xenophobia towards Asia. Some Territorians may have been blatantly biased against the 'Abos' but it seemed to me that most Darwinites felt a pull towards our exotic northern neighbours.

Just as the Southern winter brings Australian holidaymakers to the warmer climes 'up North', so the Dry Season tends to send Northern Territorians into the archipelago and beyond. Almost everybody I knew who didn't have kids planned a shopping splurge in Singapore or Hong Kong. Those who did have kids planned to spend the mid-year school holidays in Bali.

We got there on a Garuda flight from Darwin to Denpasar distinguished only by the fact that little Sylvie dumped a cup of orange juice all over my pants just after takeoff. When we landed, my bum still damp and sticky, Teddi, in what I thought was a revealing dress, got the eye from James Reyne, lead singer of one of Australia's hottest rock bands, Australian Crawl. He gave her a wink as he and a guy with a guitar hopped into a taxi and headed for the surf and rowdy nightclubs of Kuta Beach.

Our own destination was Sanur, northeast of Kuta, not far from the million souls of Denpasar, on the quieter, 'family friendly' eastern side of the fertile peninsula that floods with the outwash from the volcanic interior mountains to the north. There we planned to stay for nearly a week, before a two-night trip up north for some snorkeling at Lovina Beach, another two nights near the Monkey Forest at Ubud, then back to Sanur to wind down for another few days.

Soon the five of us were on our way, our driver with his hand perpetually on the horn as he sped through a tangle of cyclists, motorcyclists, open-backed mini-buses called *bemos*, larger tour buses, delivery vans and trucks laden with everything from sacks of rice to hand-carved wooden furniture.

The air was thick and warm. For much of the trip we were in a chaotic urban clog that surrounded the airport, the fringes of Kuta and the southern outskirts of Denpasar. But between Denpasar and Sanur we were in flat, fertile paddy country, a hundred shades of green among the crops of rice and corn and banana trees in neat rows along the fringes of the dykes, coconut palms everywhere providing a roof to the view, no centimetre of space left uncultivated. Here and there were tiny wood-thatch shelters; field labourers covered head to toe in shapeless rags and wide conical headwear paused there to straighten their backs and watch the parade of passing traffic.

A few miles more and we were in a beachside fishing village, Sanur. The driver left us at a reception area of cool tiles and shady thatch and a pair of young, welcoming Balinese standing behind a carved wooden desk. An old woman was sweeping fallen frangipani flowers from the manicured grass beside our steps. There was a shrine with offerings of rice and fruit in a banana-leaf tray. Banners of many colours flapped from poles in a stiff sea breeze that carried the delighted voices of kids flying kites on the beach. Already the place had the feel of paradise.

I know there are conflicting views about the extent to which the 'living culture' of the Balinese has been warped by the hordes of international tourists who – even after the bombing atrocities of 12 October 2002 – make Bali such a dominant contributor to Indonesia's national income.

One authority, the Australian academic Adrian Vickers, has written a readable history called *Bali – A Paradise Created*, in which he argues that visitors' conceptions of Bali have been so pre-determined by generations of gushing cultural propaganda and advertising hype that, upon arrival, they wouldn't be able to genuinely see much of the 'real' Bali, anyway.

That may be true. A lot of Aussies almost apologise for having been there, the words of the song *'I've been to Bali, too'* a self-deprecating anthem. It's as if it's deplorably unadventurous of them to have set foot on such cushy, touristy shores. They really should have been living on yak butter tea among saffron-robed ascetics in Buddhist Tibet, or thirstily stomping the sands of the Kalahari.

Worse, if you're from Darwin, every time you turn around, you see families you know. In the Hotel Segara, a few doors north, were our friends Ken and Fiona Newman, with their kids. There, first afternoon, was the Sundbye family, strolling along Jalan Tanjung Sari, young David insisting that Wyeth go body surfing with him one day, over at Kuta.

Yes, there were times when you got the distinct feeling there were more tourists in Bali than Balinese – and there were three *million* of them. The hawkers of cheap sarongs and fake ebony carvings were among the world's most street-wise opportunists. Get used to it. They're part of the scenery, like the beautifully robed women swaying elegantly on hillside paths, laden with temple offerings of fruit and flowers. They too live in the shadow of towering Mount Agung home of the Hindu gods, brooding on when it might erupt and rain lava once again on this earthly paradise.

The kids were an instant hit wherever we went. The blonde-haired, fair-skinned, blue-eyed Sylvie was especially popular. Japanese tourist girls demanded that she be included in their holiday snaps. She was always disappearing into the back of sidewalk stalls and restaurants on the hip of some matron or another, emerging beaming with little treats. She scored so much fruit we nicknamed her the Banana Queen.

One afternoon we took a drive to Denpasar market with a guy called Jingo who drove an ancient but gleaming red Chevrolet. The teeming *pasar badung* was on three levels: clothing and fabrics on top, household effects in the middle, foodstuffs on the bottom. We spotted mountains of pineapples, orderly rows of fruits, vegetables, fresh fish and dried, unidentifiable jellies, noodles of every type, huge sacks of rice, spices, sweets, and pastries all offered in a Babel of strident bargaining. At one stage Sylvie disappeared. We just waited where we were. Sure enough, about five minutes later she was back, in the arms of a beaming Balinese woman, her small arms loaded up with a bag containing dozens of small mysterious fruit.

'What's this?' we wanted to know.

'Selak,' said the woman. 'You try!'

It had dark, scaly skin, like a snake. The woman broke one open to reveal the off-white flesh. She took a bite. '*Bagus!*' she said. 'Good!'

We had to agree. It was chewy, with the flavour of a tangy type of apple. We asked how much to pay, but the woman shook her head. The selak were a gift for the beautiful baby.

The baby had turned two while we were in Sanur. The hotel staff ordered a cake from the kitchens at the Penida View Hotel. It was a magnificently iced layer cake with a red marzipan rose and the words Happy Birthday Miss Sylvie Maclean 1984 piped perfectly in pink.

As you climb away from the coastal towns and villages, the scenery becomes almost impossibly gorgeous. Bali just explodes with fertility and fabulous colours. Every turn on the narrow, winding road offers an opportunity to photograph the terraced hillside paddies, and every opportunity produces postcard results.

We stopped at Tampaksiring, where there is a large temple kept specifically to capture and contain the waters of a pure and holy spring, its waters so sacred no man was permitted to drink. Yet the local villagers were allowed to bathe there, and they did so, unashamedly naked, taking no notice of the passing tourists.

On the way back to our driver Dewa's van, we noticed that a more modern structure dominated a hillside overlooking the temple. Set in lush grounds it was nothing less than a palace.

'This is the summer palace of Suharto,' said Dewa, sounding a little indignant.

'The President?'

He nodded. 'It is not good to build there. Above the temple is above the Gods.'

'Did Suharto build it?'

'No. The Dutch were first, then Sukarno.' He shrugged, as if to ask, 'Where are *they* now?' In this place where the ruins are many centuries older than anything the Dutch served up, the question was surely rhetorical.

Beyond Tampaksiring the going got steeper by the yard, Dewa revving the little engine hard in low gear, the road – still busy with traffic, pedestrians and animals – clinging to a ridgetop that fell steeply away through tall stands of bamboo to rivers far below. Off to the west we got occasional glimpses of Mount Batukau, which according to my map was a relative dwarf at 2276 metres, far lower than Agung looming to the east, a giant 3142 metres, and far taller than *any* of Australia's mountain peaks.

If Mount Batur hadn't literally blown its top – which it frequently does and often with fatal consequences – it would probably be the biggest of the three volcanos. Its crater is almost 10 kilometres wide. Smoking drifts of lava blackened the hillside.

We gazed in amazement from a roadside ledge at Kintamani, firing off a quick panorama of photographs across the crater's lake far below, where the ancient village of Terunyan nestles on the distant shore. We were hurrying because a sharp-eyed posse of hawkers had spotted us and was descending with all their wares.

Our return to Sanur was via several large towns. One was Bangli, which used to be the capital of the Balinese king of the central mountains, a ruler who collaborated on occasion with the would-be Dutch colonists while other kings violently fought against them. In Gianyar we made Dewa's day by scoring two wonderful batik paintings. With a Garuda statuette, they held pride of place in our homes for years to come, constant reminders of a day during which history, culture and geography combined with artistry and nature to form a sort of wonderland blur.

We idled a few sunny days on the beach, cooking ourselves with coconut oil. I was so tanned I felt I was turning Balinese.

A day or so later we were heading north again, this time with Yoman, another tour guide, who was taking us for two nights at Lovina, via the central mountains and down to the northern coast at Singaraja, capital of the Buleleng District.

It was a bright morning and festive too. It was a holiday, *puning-an*. Women in their finery were carrying heaped offerings on their heads. Crowds gathered at every temple, many of the men dressed in black and white checked sarongs, another visual symbol of good and evil. There were big crowds watching volleyball competitions. Hundreds of kites fluttered in the sky.

Soon we were climbing hard once more, the little van yawing around hairpin bends, its nervous passengers looking back on the distant plains towards the sea, then suddenly up at stone and forest and mountains looming in the thickening mountain mist. We stopped in a village called Bedugul, where it was clammy, almost cold, despite the tropical latitude. There was a market with friendly vendors selling fruit and vegetables and mountain flowers. We bought corn, peanuts and drinks.

We came upon it without warning – around a corner, there it was: a big grey lake surrounded by high hills, and along the shore a large and beautiful temple wharfing into the water, its dark stone tiers silhouetted by wreaths of mist. This was Lake Bratan, and the famous *pura* of Candi Kuning. Yoman stopped so we could take photos. And for some time after the shutters stopped clicking, we stood transfixed.

This, I thought, was a place you could come to die, and you could do so with serenity, knowing you'd be resting in perfection, high above the world and all its sinners.

Then commenced the descent to Singaraja. Compared with the luxuries of Sanur, our room at the Banyualit Beach Inn, was primitive. Not that we cared; it was clean and in any case we had no intention of spending much time there. It was early afternoon and there was exploring to be done.

Ours was one of only two hotels in the immediate area. Both were built just above the beach among coconut groves and paddy fields. There was a thatched bar set on rickety wood pylons, right on the high water mark. From this vantagepoint you could look along the coast in both directions.

The beach was extraordinary. It was comprised entirely of black sand, fine grains of minutely eroded volcanic rock, flecked here and there by little pieces of bleached and broken white coral. The beach curved away in little bays, broken by occasional rocky black protrusions and the mouths of many little creeks rushing mountain water to the sea.

We took a swim in the calm, clear water, and lazed about in the sun as the curious village kids came out to say hello, especially to Sylvie, who was soon surrounded by admirers tugging at her long wisps of blonde hair. The children played together for hours, Myra racing them up and down the beach and Wyeth snorkelling in the shallows. We sipped on Anchor Beer and gazed on indulgently, immobile until hunger called us up for dinner in the hotel's open-sided eatery, which also served as bar and reception.

Eating out at Sanur we had discovered that the portions were often as small as the prices were large. Tonight we were hungry, so we ordered no less than eight dishes, including a baked whole fish. The 'waitress', a young member of the family that operated our hotel, seemed a little puzzled. But she took our order anyway and stood back silently, but looking very interested when the enormous platters of food emerged from the kitchen. Then she smiled and made her eyes bulge, as if to say, 'Okay, let's see you eat all this!'

Well, the fish would have fed us by itself. We could have fed the whole bloody village! Fortunately, there was a Balinese man playing chess with a blonde antipodean woman at the next table. We asked them if they'd care to help us out. They agreed and offered tequila in return, which is how we got to meet Benju and Patrina.

Patrina was a New Zealander, fluent in Balinese and Bahasa. She and Benju had been married four years. They were on holiday from Kuta where both ran businesses. Benju's involved the manufacture and retailing of pirate music cassettes. Patrina employed seamstresses and shoemakers and ran a shop on Jalan Legian.

After dinner, the girls playing with the children of the hotel family, we enjoyed a well-lubricated game of blackjack. Teddi cleaned up half the cost of our feast and left it as a tip.

Next morning Wyeth and I hired outriggers from the village and went snorkelling on a nearby reef, while Teddi remained at the hotel with the girls. The family had a monkey that kept Myra amused as it careered around even though shackled, while Teddi kept a lazy eye on her daughters.

What an experience for Wyeth and me! The water was clear and the morning sun lit up a rainbow of coloured corals, anemones and huge starfish, waving in the wash of a gentle tide. We were out there for hours, waterlogged, wonderstruck.

The rest of the day was what holidays are supposed to be about: utterly, wonderfully idle, we sunbaked and read our paperbacks, nodding off, drunk on sun.

A day or so later, in Ubud, Wyeth and Myra insisted I see the Monkey Forest, which actually meant *they* wanted to go again. Teddi said there was no way she or Sylvie was going back.

To get to the Monkey Forest we walked out of Ubud on a sunlit dirt path, with paddy fields replacing a last straggle of little cafes and guesthouses hung with artwork and woodcarvings. It was a beautiful morning, warm rather than hot, and the forest ahead looked cool and inviting.

There was a hut where visitors were required to stop, pay a small entry fee, and buy packets of peanuts to feed the monkeys.

'What if we just go in and *look* at the monkeys,' I suggested, ever the cheapskate.

'No hope!' said Wyeth. 'You wait! You *have* to have peanuts!'

This proved to be true. The minute we arrived in the forest, following well-swept paths leading towards a series of temples, we were accosted by the monkeys. They *knew* we had peanuts and they wanted them. They snatched at our outstretched fingers. They climbed up our legs, stuck their soft little hands in our pockets, searched my camera bag like a customs agent looking for drugs. They were rude, aggressive and insistent. Even when it was obvious there were no peanuts left, we were still followed by a whole troop of males, adolescents, mothers and babies.

According to the Balinese, who give people from the traditional village of Padangtegal the thankless task of feeding and cleaning up after them, these monkeys are sacred. Maybe so, but maybe they could be taught some manners.

Patrina and Benju had asked us to visit them in Kuta before we flew home. We got a *bemo* and found ourselves in bustling Jalan Legian, searching up and down among all the other clothing and cassette stores.

As soon as we arrived, they closed up, loaded us into a battered Datsun and – Benju at the wheel – took us down the coast past the airport to a place called Nusa Dua, which Patrina explained was to be the site of a brand new, high-class resort district. Already, one hotel had been completed and several others were under construction.

We waded on the low tide out to a reef. On the shore to our right, tanned tourists lounged in the sun. In front of us, Balinese fishermen waded, fully clothed, protected from the blazing sun by wide straw hats. The surf roared on the reef, ignoring the blatant human contrast of traditional poor, indolent rich.

Which were we? That's easy: we had a farewell meal with Benju and Patrina, in a Kuta restaurant where we selected live seafood from big holding tanks and into the wok they went with sensational soupy sauces and came to the table with piles of steaming rice. It was a feast that would have fed the Nusa Dua fisherfolk for weeks.

No matter: we, too, had become part of the scenery.

Next day, once a prickly Garuda official acknowledged the legitimacy of our tickets on an as usual overbooked flight, we returned to Darwin. Ken and Fiona and Jesse and Shauna were already home in Katherine but, sure enough, there was David Sundbye and his folks, the Pashes too, all aboard our plane.

We were all relaxed. We'd been to Bali, too.

Chapter 11

Bound for South Australia

I don't think I was in danger of becoming a Territory 'lifer', but we were having a great time living in Australia's Top End. The informality of the place suited us all.

Wyeth was nearing high school age, however, and what we had observed of the NT school system convinced us that he would get a better education almost anywhere else in Australia.

Towards the end of '84, as we entered our third build-up in Darwin, the ABC decided to launch a news and current affairs show from the start of 1985. It was to be called *The National*, and it had the ambitious aim of combining the two elements of hard, breaking news and more thought-out analytical current affairs into a seamless, unified hour. I applied for reporting positions in Adelaide and Hobart. Adelaide came through first. In January of 1985, we moved to the City of Churches.

Teddi and I were instantly charmed. The Saturday morning drive past the historic Adelaide Oval, across the River Torrens, past the Festival Centre, through the King William Street business district past Victoria Square and the Hilton Hotel to the bustling, multi-lingual Central Market was a regular pleasure. The bounty and variety of the produce was incredible, made doubly pleasurable after years of haggling for fresh Asian vegetables or putting up with a Darwin supermarket that stocked only the produce that could be cold stored and freighted from the south at considerable expense to the consumer.

The natural world too, was friendlier than the Territory. You could safely swim at any one of the mile-upon-mile of sandy suburban beaches – though further south it was necessary to consider the possibility of encountering a Great White Pointer shark of the *Jaws* variety. You could go for spectacular bush-walks in the Mount Lofty Ranges. You could visit shows in pretty hills towns like Uraidla and Summertown and Lenswood where the apples grow. There were countless wineries and weekend getaway spots in the McLaren Vale and the Barossa Valley. Above all, there was an ambience of careful cultivation, of countryside tamed and shaped by cleverness and great artifice. It was bountiful and it was civilized and it seemed a perfect place to 'grow up' the kids.

We rented a neat little 1920s cottage in the inner northern suburb of Nailsworth, installed Wyeth in the nearby high school, got Myra into a Montessori School close to the River Torrens at Felixstow and Sylvie into a kindergarten in Broadview. Teddi went shopping for a new TV, a washing machine and some decent furniture.

She also got me some shirts and ties, clothing necessities that had become somewhat scarce in recent years. I looked quite the part when I climbed into the nifty blue 1976 Saab I'd bought off a Darwin colleague for a mere $5000 and presented myself at the ABC's colossal (and appallingly ugly) suburban headquarters at Collinswood. I was all enthusiasm and naivety, with no idea that I'd tolerate less than a year in the job.

In Darwin, the ABC had been a loose and carefree place to work, so I had the illusion that the rest of the organisation was similar. Also, I *believed* the ABC's PR about itself and fully expected *The National* to live up to its pre-publicity.

It took me about a week to discover the place was uptight and hopelessly split by factions. *The National* was going to be a disaster. The news division and the current affairs division hated each other's guts, and the rivals were fighting for turf as if it was a battle for their very survival. The news team used videotape. The current affairs mob used film. News reporters refused to do current affairs. The same dysfunction went the other way. Within a few months the pretence was abandoned and the 'unified' program was carved into the two, distinct halves that remain today.

I got bounced from one side to the other, nobody sure what to do with me. I did a stint on the production desk, helping sub-edit and produce the overseas news. I did some news. I did some current affairs, which I hated, mainly because some of the film crews I was assigned turned out to be surly, unhelpful and inept bastards.

One time I was sent 230 kilometres north to the lead and zinc smelter town of Port Pirie to do a story about how they were cleaning lead contamination out of the city's houses to stop the kids from getting their brains poisoned. The cameraman shot 400 feet of film 'overlay' to help illustrate the story. Or he would have, if he hadn't forgotten to thread the film into his camera.

One day I was asked to get a local angle on a story that broke the previous night in Melbourne: an elite athlete had become a quadriplegic in an accident and now wanted to die. My executive producer had asked me to find an Adelaide person who had also become quadriplegic, but instead of wanting to die had a positive attitude to life.

At the Julia Farr Centre, once known as The Home for Incurables, they had such a patient, a man so positive the staff used him to counsel the newer patients. He was reluctant to talk on camera, but eventually I persuaded him.

I was assigned a film crew and we went to the hospital, spending hours on the interview and overlay, only to find – after the film was processed – that there was a base-line scratch right through the man's face. The film gate had not been cleaned. The critical interview was unusable.

I called the man at Julia Farr and told him about my problem. He didn't believe me. He thought he'd been terrible 'talent' and that was why we'd ditched the story.

'No way,' I said. 'It was the scratch on the film!' I begged him to give me another interview, tomorrow. Eventually he agreed.

Meanwhile, the Melbourne version of the *National* had filmed an interview with the athlete who wanted to die. By some fluke, Adelaide's Videotapes Department had recorded the item. Next day I persuaded the Chief of Staff to let me hire a freelance video crew to shoot the Adelaide interview over again, so I could marry the two angles together, two sides of the existential dilemma, yin and yang, and edit the whole item on videotape.

The COS agreed to my plan, so I went and did the interview on tape, profusely thanking the guy at Julia Farr for giving me an even better interview the second time around.

I got back to Collinswood, picked out my best 'grabs' and started writing. Then, as I was about to start editing the piece for that night's show, the chief tape editor shook his head and told me the story had been 'black-banned' by the ABC Staff Association.

'Why?'

'Because,' he said, calmly but firmly, 'you used a freelancer when there was a film crew available.'

'But the rest of the yarn was already on video. I wanted to edit in the same medium!' I did not add that the ABC's Adelaide telecine chain was so old that it killed the colour in the best work our camera operators could come up with and made it look the colour of faded Ektachrome from 1963. I stuck to the issue. 'What the hell is wrong with shooting *and* cutting on video?'

'There was a film crew available.'

'Are you *listening*? Half the yarn was already on tape!'

'It doesn't matter. The Industrial Agreement between the Staff Association and the ABC is clear. You don't use freelancers if there's a film crew available.'

There was no point arguing with the editor. So I went and hit the roof at my boss, who tried to soothe me by saying the ABC would pay for it if I wanted to send my again-to-be-disappointed interviewee a case of beer.

'A case of beer!' I railed. 'Big fucking deal! He's going to think he's fucked it up again, and you think he'll feel better if he can drown his sorrows. What's he going to drink it with? A straw? He gets around by steering his wheelchair with his fucking chin!'

On and on I yelled. And when I had finally calmed down, I silently vowed to quit the ABC and its bureaucratic battle with union power at the first chance I got.

The freelancer I had used was a guy called Bob Perry. A few months after my bitter eruption at the boss, Bob and I did another job together and I told him what had happened the first time around.

'Mate,' he said, 'At the ABC, you don't break the rules. Not the union ones, anyway.'

I knew that Bob's main work was with Channel 9, so I asked him if there happened to be any work going there.

'Matter of fact, there is. Senior job, too. Give Peter MacDonald a ring. And be quick about it.'

Mac interviewed me and made an offer on the spot. I had to give the ABC a month's notice, which meant I missed being there when Channel 9 covered Adelaide's biggest-ever sporting event, the first Australian Formula One Grand Prix, in November 1985. I missed it by a single day. I heard the scream of the engines and watched the air force Hornet fighters vertical climbs in a few moments of petrolhead exhilaration from the newsroom's third floor offices at Collinswood. Channel 9's cameras had exclusive access to the track!

When I reported for work at Channel 9's North Adelaide studios, the buzz was that the Labor Premier of the day, John Bannon, was so buoyed by the success of the race (give the people bread and circuses) that he was about to call a state election and would probably win hands down.

The Chief of Staff, Len Skinner, eyed me warily. 'Know anything about politics?'

'A bit.'

'Good. You're covering the election. Welcome aboard.'

I stayed aboard for the next 13 years.

At least I had a job. The anthropology school at the University of Adelaide was as badly factionalised as the ABC and was threatened with closure. The South Australian museum had no openings. The local Aboriginal organizations needed social workers, not field workers. Teddi started looking elsewhere for work. She found it, thanks to AIDS.

Not long after I started at Channel 9, Teddi spotted a newspaper ad from the local Gay Counselling Service, seeking an office manager for what was to become the AIDS Council of South Australia.

The state's first death from AIDS had happened this same year, and the epidemic was frequently headline news. One journalist, waiting for an interview with a government minister, jokingly suggested AIDS sufferers had a 'severe case of the Rock Hudsons'. Everybody laughed. Many Australians perceived AIDS in terms of the TV advertisement that showed a terrible Death's Head rolling bowling balls down the alley at a doomed family of innocents. The media did little to eliminate the general ignorance and paranoia, or the perception that people who became HIV-positive through blood transfusions were 'innocent victims' while – by implication – gay men and intravenous drug users had to be anything *but* innocent.

Despite this, and to their credit, the federal and state governments were mobilising fast, funding education and prevention campaigns, and using organisations like ACSA for the vital work ahead.

Teddi applied for the office manager position. She was successful, and started a job that transformed our lives. Not only did she run the office, she volunteered to be a carer for people living with AIDS, people who needed the support of those who knew something about the syndrome and weren't going to be judgmental about how it was acquired.

She asked me if I wanted to volunteer as well, so both of us took an ACSA-development training course. We were assigned our 'cases' – mine a young man wasting away from constant bouts of pneumocystis in the Daw Park Hospice, Teddi an older man suffering Kaposi's sarcoma, who found himself in and out of the Queen Elizabeth Hospital and eventually, blind, in a hospice at Largs Bay.

Both were tough and intelligent men; both frightened and brave at the same time, sometimes angry, eventually resigned and accepting of their fate. Both sadly died.

As well as 'clients', we lost friends. One of Teddi's best mates was a co-worker at ACSA. He had a steady boyfriend and two adopted children. They lived in an immaculate house with an imaginative back garden surrounding an above ground pool. They lived like there was always going to be a tomorrow, making improvements, buying new gadgets, homemaking. Eventually the symptoms intensified and our wonderful friend Steve started wasting.

When he moved with Michael and the kids to a place that was easier to maintain, they gave us their pool. I helped dismantle it one blistering summer afternoon, and with Wyeth's help re-erected it in our back yard. For one blissful summer, the water was sparkling blue. But then, not long after Steve died surrounded by his family and many friends, the pump stopped working.

We have other friends who are what the doctors describe as 'long-term survivors'. They have baffled the doomsayers who figured that HIV infection inevitably leads to the cemetery. To this day, even though Teddi no longer works at ACSA, we celebrate their survival and their strength. Sometimes, it is their strength that keeps *us* going.

ACSA's first Chairman was Ted Dudzinski. A cartographer and computer specialist employed by South Australia's Lands Department, he volunteered countless hours, offering himself as a spokesman, helping subdue the public hysteria and helping to develop a network of people prepared to give their own time to the prevention programs and the caring tasks of ensuring that the people who got sick – and too frequently died – did not suffer alone.

Before I too became a volunteer, I had heard about Ted from Teddi, but for some time we had not actually met. All that changed, one weekend afternoon. I was out in the back yard of our house on Newbon Street, Nailsworth, when the suburban tranquility was shattered by the noise of a chainsaw.

In the back of an adjacent yard, high in a tree, was a man lopping branches. It was a big tree and so were the falling branches. The noise was enormous, accompanied by a cacophony of classical music, and soon Teddi came out to see what the racket was.

'That's Ted,' she exclaimed, pointing with astonishment at the person in the tree. 'We're *neighbours*!' She waved a delighted greeting, and Ted – equally amazed – nearly toppled from his perch.

I could not begin to detail all the things we've been through together in the nearly two decades since the day of the tree. There've been plenty of tears and tough times to go with all the laughs. Sylvie and Myra regard Ted as a favourite uncle. They will never forgive us for our tortured drunken versions of *Sloop John B*, or understand what the hell Ted sees in *Star Trek*. The girls *do* know why Ted and Russell are first on the list any time we plan a party.

And Ted was first on the list when I decided I needed an executor to a will I had not yet written. If Greg Walker was my best man in Milwaukee when Teddi and I got hitched, Ted was my best man now that my wife and I were half a world away and nearly 25 years married. Ted agreed immediately.

I wrote the document at a downtown lawyers' office, and signed it on Tuesday 14 January 2003, less than an hour before I was admitted to hospital and nearly killed by the melanoma that ruptured my bowels, just four days later.

While I was helpless in hospital, Ted and his brilliant partner Russell helped to hold Teddi's life together. Their kind of friendship is the only kind of love: unconditional.

Despite that, Russell was *far* from impressed that we named our butchest big white cat after him. I don't know why he's so disgruntled: we named our *weediest* cat Ted!

Our association with the AIDS Council also led us to Kangaroo Island. Two guys from the Gay Counselling Service owned a holiday house at American Beach, not far from Penneshaw on the island's bulbous eastern tip. They rented us the place for a week one summer.

To explore Kangaroo Island properly, you must have wheels. To get your wheels onto the island, you take the ferry from Cape Jervis at the tip of the mainland's Fleurieu Peninsula, across to Penneshaw. The first time we took the hour-long passage, it was nighttime and there was a fierce storm with force-nine winds and a huge swell that made the ferry pitch and yaw unpredictably, its hull smashing into the wave troughs so that the boat juddered with every impact.

The passengers were forced to sit below decks. Soon there was a stench of vomit. Sylvie sensibly fell asleep but Myra puked too. Teddi sat stoic. I stared out a porthole, at what I hoped was the horizon, belly heaving horribly.

At last we made landfall at Penneshaw. Our friends were there to meet and guide us in our overloaded Saab through the waning storm to their place at American Beach, where the kettle was on. We'd co-exist for one night so we could be shown the ropes before they hopped back to Adelaide the next day.

The house itself was an unremarkable pre-fabricated two-bedroom affair with a large living area divided from the kitchen by a long bench. The house was full of dusty furniture that had either been purchased at second-hand stores or reprieved from being sent there. Beyond the kitchen was a laundry area that had no washing machine, and a sign that informed us that the house relied entirely on rainwater and would we PLEASE SAVE WATER.

When it comes to taking a leak blokes can help. It had now stopped raining, so I stepped outside and discovered a garden that seemed to consist of white rocks glowing in the patches of moonlight revealed through holes in the scudding cloud. The rocks corralled shriveled plants that seemed even in the darkness to be desperate for a little WATER, but possibly too far gone to benefit from the day's deluge. I pissed on one –

anything for the environment! On my way back into the house I spied two enormous rainwater tanks. I tapped their sides. Both were nearly full.

Inside, over coffee, we were admonished about SAVING WATER. Teddi was convinced the place was in perpetual drought and promised the kids would bathe and wash their hair in the sea.

In the morning I was given further stern instructions – where to find the fuse wire, how to turn the power off, how to turn the gas *on* without causing a mighty explosion, what to do if we encountered any of the locally profuse Brown and Tiger snakes: 'Don't panic. Stare it down and back away.' (I am now 48 years old. I *still* haven't the faintest idea whether or not this was actually correct.)

Then they were gone, thank God, my rental cheque safely stashed in their wallet. Now we got to explore at leisure. The picture windows opened out onto, well, no decking and nothing much else. For some reason, our landlords had bought an unfinished house that was nearly a kilometre from the beach. It sat on a rise, overlooking dry paddocks that sloped down to the water, which was a richly inviting but rather distant blue.

Bush turkeys wandered calmly past, pecking and foraging, dawn and dusk. The constant raucous din of crows and magpies and parrots in nearby treetops was the extent of the wildlife. The kids saw a Brown snake while they were exploring a nearby gully with a dead cow at the bottom of it. They turned tail and ran like buggery.

You may think, well, this was the start of a holiday from hell. But we soon learned that the trick was to ignore the shortcomings of the house and to use it as a base for operations further afield. We spent our days at the surf-swept beach at Pennington Bay; in Penneshaw watching penguins at sunset, as they launched their fishing excursions from the rookery near Frenchman's Rock; on picnics at the perfectly arched Antechamber Bay where one year a dead Southern Right Whale washed up and the TV news choppers were everywhere; at American River where in the early 1800s, sealers laid up to repair their ships and raid the mainland for Aboriginal concubines; to Seal Bay itself, where the once-endangered Australian Sea Lions bask now in safety, and breed among the rocks and dunes.

I kept rods and reels and bait in the car's now evil-smelling boot, dropping a line at every opportunity, sometimes lucky, mostly not.

The poor little Saab, designed for the temperate smoothness of European autobahns, copped a thrashing on the corrugations of the island's dirt roads. It was the beginning of the end for its suspension and cooling systems, but we ended up having so much fun we drove her back to the house at American Beach the next year for two weeks, then three the next.

It was during our third trip that we almost did some *successful* family camping.

So far, rather than subject the Saab to the island's worst roads – those on its wild western end, more than 150 kilometres distant – we had avoided a visit to the Flinders Chase National Park.

Ever the optimist, I suggested we hire a camper van. Teddi looked at me sternly. 'Need I remind you how recently I was nearly trampled in the night by a herd of water buffalo?'

It all began well. We knew the way to Seal Bay like the backs of our hands, so we stopped there first, to pay our respects.

In the late 1980s, you could still climb out of your car and walk down to the beach, and walk among the sea-lions, the Rangers keeping a relaxed eye on you in case you ventured too close to a pup and risked getting clobbered by over-protective parents. I have photos of the girls laughing on the sand, so close to a cow they could just about put their arms around it.

These days you pay a fee for a permit and a guide and you can't get within cooee of the animals. That's progress, I suppose. Tourist numbers are so much higher now that, if the sea-lions are to get any peace, the human visitors have to be kept at bay.

Kangaroo Island's South Coast is full of fascinating and wild places to visit. Nowadays the road is paved all the way to the Flinders Chase National Park, so the beautifully named D'Estrees and Vivonne Bays are more accessible. You can cruise right up to the Kelly Hill Caves and the extraordinary contortions of Remarkable Rocks and Admirals Arch, two prized features of any visit to the Chase. Fees are charged, but it's worth every cent. The rocks are remarkable, all right.

For a few dollars extra you can camp near the park headquarters at Rocky River. There you'll be in the company of big grey kangaroos, enormous Cape Barren Geese, koalas in the trees, and – if you're lucky and quiet – shy little platypuses in the river ponds at twilight.

The park headquarters is now a gleaming, modernized Outback style structure surrounded by hundreds of yet-to-mature native trees and acres of parking spaces for caravan-toting 4x4s and tour buses. When first we visited Rocky River, the visitor centre was a log cabin with faded maps on the walls and signs pegged out in the dirt asking people not to feed the animals.

We got ourselves a permit and kept on going, into the wilderness to a remote camping site called Snake Lagoon, which should have been called Possum Lagoon. The bloody things were everywhere.

At first, as I fumbled to set up the tent annexe and Teddi got chops and sausages sizzling and spuds in foil baking in a nice twilight fire, we thought they were charming. They sat at the edge of the firelight as the darkness deepened, their beady little eyes reflecting the flames, watching us hungrily as we ate.

After an active day in the sunshine, we were starving, so there were few leftovers. We were also exhausted. Without a thought, we tossed the scraps into the fire and turned in. Wyeth and the girls were in the van, Teddi and myself spread out on blow-up mattresses in the annexe. Sleep came quickly.

The possums started scrabbling in the embers of the fire, squabbling when they pawed a morsel missed by the competition. Then, not satisfied with this first foray, they started emptying the tucker box, which I had innocently left beneath the van. I had to shoo them away and lock the box in the van, where the girls were now sitting up, wide-eyed with fright. I told them it was okay, go back to sleep. Wyeth stirred them up, making spooky noises.

Soon the bloody possums were on the roof of the van, trying to work their paws between it and the tent annexe so they could pay us a visit in person. Teddi and I both bellowed at them to piss off. They scattered, then brazenly returned. Our next lungful of abuse was accompanied by rock throwing by me. One found its mark and there was a disgruntled yelp. After that we were left in peace.

Next morning I was up at dawn, fishing gear in hand, following a rough trail to where the Rocky River lets out to the Southern Ocean. There were snake tracks in the sand and I startled a couple of grazing kangaroos – no worse than they scared me when they hopped away ahead, thrashing through the bush.

The sun came up on a beautiful sight. Huge breakers were smashing onto the rocks on either side of the sandy river mouth. The surge of the waves swept furiously up the sand, sucking violently away again. There was nothing between this place and Antarctica. No wonder Kangaroo Island was a shipwreck coast. I tried but even my heaviest sinker was never going to keep a hook and bait out there long enough for a fish to swim by and chomp it. I gave up and just watched it all in awe.

Being at the western end of Kangaroo Island in those days bestowed on us another benefit denied to today's visitors. Beyond Snake Lagoon is an excuse for a road called the West Bay Track, which ends at a place called Vennachar Point, after one of dozens of wood-hulled sailing ships that came to grief on the reefs and rocks of Kangaroo Island, the *Loch Vennachar* doing so in 1905 with the loss of all 27 crew.

Then the track turns north and snakes towards the Cape Borda

Lighthouse via Ravine Des Casoars, a gorgeous forested wilderness. By 2003, this track was forbidden to regular tourist traffic. The road is genuinely dangerous – I don't know how we made it round some of the turns or across the steep wash-aways. I was relieved to see the Cape Borda lighthouse, looming like a square stone blockhouse through the scrub.

The Cape Borda light has been operating on the island's north-western tip since 1858. Sixteen headstones in the graveyard not far from where stores were winched up the cliff face at Harvey's Return tell silently of children falling ill too far from medical help. One keeper died a slow and agonizing death after his eye was pierced during a fall. By what? Perhaps a stick or a sharpened tool? The silent stones did not say.

Kangaroo Island's north coast looks more hospitable than the south. It's more settled country; farmland tamed by the soldier settlers who moved onto the island after World War II, each of them allocated 1200 acres, materials to build a basic home, and implements to get on with farming. Between 1947 and 1954, the soldiers and their families nearly doubled KI's population to an official 2522. Most of the inhabitants lived in Kingscote or the island's central plateau, which plunges through erosion-rounded hills to the more sheltered waters along the north coast.

There were delightful spots like Western River Cove and Snelling Beach, almost deserted, where we could have set up for our second night's camping, but we pressed on to a place called Stokes Bay, which turned out to be a big mistake.

We had discovered during our earlier holidays that a lot of the locals despise tourists. The camping area at Stokes Bay, it turned out, was a favourite place for the locals to vacation after the harvest was over.

The harvest was over. The campground was packed with tents and trailers and boats, and ranks of hatted men with farmers' tans sitting in their folding chairs, beer in hand, staring stonily at us as we arrived and claimed one of the few remaining sites. The unfriendliness was so palpable, it felt like we'd blundered into a village full of dangerous half-wits.

'God,' said Teddi. 'I'm not sure I want to stay here.'

'We'll be right,' said I doubtfully. 'You guys go have a swim. I'll set up the tent, then I'll come and join you.'

They needed no prompting. I was left alone. It was still blazing hot, but the wind had turned westerly and there was a suggestion of impending change.

The wind was so strong it impeded the setting up of the tent annexe. I'd no sooner insert poles into the eyelets in the canvas than a wind gust would blow the fabric clear again. I'd repeat the process and would be just about to stabilize the flimsy structure with guy ropes when another gust would frustrate me and I'd be back where I started.

The half-wits watched my 'progress'. From behind me I could hear their sniggering. I turned and glared. The cowardly bastards looked away, pretending it wasn't them. Not one of them offered to help.

Furiously I moved the van to make more of a windbreak, then assembled the annexe once again, raising it gently corner by corner, until I had triumphed at last. I grabbed my fishing gear, gave the half-wits a fuck-you glare, and stalked off down to the beach.

There, I was instantly able to relax. Teddi and the kids played in the shallows among other mums and kids, board riders and body surfers paddled further out and the faces of the waves flashed in the late afternoon sun.

I took a sluicing, cleansing swim. Then I tried my luck with the rod and almost without trying I landed an enormous flathead. Come dinnertime it tasted terrific, fresh filleted and panfried in butter and lemon juice.

In the night the wind changed to a roaring southwesterly. The windbreak afforded by the van was useless. The tent blew down again.

The guys who hired the van to us were Peter Walker and Malcolm Kleemann, and they came to be great friends.

An accomplished fisherman, Peter knew where to look for the tiny crabs that the big bream in the Chapman River find so irresistible. He'd take us to secluded rivers, inlets and wild south coast beaches, Teddi and Malcolm gossiping beneath an umbrella while Peter and I plied the beach for salmon or sweep in the turbulent, surf-frothed rock pools.

A recent visit with Peter and Malcolm came in the winter of 2002, just as they celebrated their 19th year on the island, and not long after KI celebrated the 200th anniversary of the encounters between the English navigator and explorer Matthew Flinders and his French counterpart Nicholas Baudin.

Peter and Malcolm selected a block ten kilometres east of Penneshaw that offers a sensational view to the mainland. They surrounded their house with a stunning garden. In recent years they added luxurious quarters and began to share their getaway with visitors. Now, whether it's for bed-and-breakfast and fully catered four-wheel-drive island tours, or self-catered independent visitors, The Lookout attracts international tourists, mostly through internet bookings. The place is a gem. Peter and Malcolm lodged us there when we turned up to say g'day, and it's where I'd happily *still* be if the matter of earning a living hadn't called us on.

We spent an afternoon visiting some of the old haunts: the wild surf beach at Pennington Bay; the old mulberry tree at American River where the girls' fingers were once stained red by the succulent fruits picked and eaten straight from the bough; the re-named Baudin Beach. To Teddi and me it will *always* be called American Beach.

I reckon we got some nice photos that day, until next morning when I went out to get some dawn shots.

I got beauties of The Lookout's gardens, and the silver-gold mainland pointing like a sunlit finger through ranks of boiling cloud and the grey-green ocean. Another angle I liked was an avenue of trees, lining the dirt road that ran past the Chapman River swamp. The light was beautiful. I finished the roll and reached for more film.

It was then I realized that while the camera's shot counter had been obediently advancing, one-by-one up to number 36, when I went to rewind it, the lack of resistance clearly suggested there was actually no film inside.

Teddi was not impressed.

Like Ted Dudzinski, Peter and Malcolm have experienced the death and dying issues thrown up by AIDS. They too have lost friends. In March 2003, just a few days after my father's funeral and just ahead of my official invalided-out farewell from the ABC, Teddi and I and visited Peter and Malcolm once again.

Also with us was Teddi's sister Christine, who'd come from the US to support us. Malcolm took her touring in The Lookout's four-wheel drive while Peter, Teddi and I lounged in their garden and talked about life, the universe and everything. It was the first day I felt relaxed and trouble free for months.

During one of our KI holidays in 1987, we noticed that some new beehive-style houses had been built at American Beach and were up for sale. The price was reasonable. We vowed to chase it up with the agents back in Adelaide. We called the bank and made an appointment.

The manager was puzzled. 'You want to buy a holiday house before you buy an actual house to *live* in?'

'Yes.'

'People don't do things that way. Usually.' The inference was that rich people could do what they want; plebes like us were under *his* orders.

'We're not usual people.'

The manager nodded as if that was self-evident, and politely declined to help us.

Chapter 12

Suburbia

Early in 1988, Peter MacDonald promoted me to the exalted rank of senior news producer and gave me a fat salary rise to go with the title. Armed with this extra income, and dealing with a new and more sympathetic bank, Teddi and I began to look for a house to call our own.

We found it at 18 Guilford Avenue in the inner northern suburb of Prospect. It had four bedrooms, cedar sash windows and an enormous Bird of Paradise bush in the front yard. We moved in on the Fourth of July, American Independence Day. We had recently celebrated our tenth wedding anniversary. Wyeth was 16, Myra nearly nine, Sylvie a few days from turning six. The bank's important figure was 12.5% per annum, but it wasn't staying that 'low' for long.

The brick house was built on a corner block in the late forties, not far from the then-bustling railway workshops at Islington, when construction materials were in scarce supply and people built furniture out of former ammunition and explosives boxes. Most of our neighbours lived in houses with similar stories. The men had been soldiers who'd moved into the area after demobilization. They married and raised kids, and stayed there.

And so it was for Teddi and me and the kids. The late eighties and early nineties were sedentary and suburban ones, laced with the daily lives and dramas of three fast-maturing 'younger people' – Wyeth contending with his final years of high school then branching out for forays into Melbourne, Sylvie and Myra prospering at St Aloysius College. The Sisters of Mercy nurtured them sensitively through respective Year 12 careers.

Teddi was busy with the AIDS Council. 'Business' was at its peak. There was money coming from the federal and state governments then, and various factions lobbying hard for their share of the pie. Politics seemed to sometimes outweigh the interests of the 'clients'.

Meanwhile, I was learning an irresponsible streak at Channel 9. For several years before the construction of a multi-million dollar new edifice, Mac's newsroom occupied an old cottage facing Tynte Street, part of its North Adelaide studio complex. It was the shabbiest place I ever worked.

When I started, you could still smoke inside the workplace. The decrepit desks had burn scars because there were no ashtrays, and were piled with graying old newspapers and stacks of notebooks and forgotten press releases. The air was foul and blue-gray. In these pre-computer days, the typewriters were decades-old portables with ribbons worn through. There was one expensive IBM with golf ball heads – only the boss's secretary and the girl who typed the scripts for the six o'clock news on-air talent were allowed to use it. (By contrast, my personal 'workstation' at the ABC had its own ergonomically correct L-shaped desk and swivel chair, *plus* a brand new IBM. Dear Taxpayer, if anyone at the ABC claims they have crappy gear and resources, they're bullshitting you.)

If Sue Garrard or Steve 'Cumma' Cropper were presenting a live newsbreak, a football might sail past in the background. Unaware of the lobbing orb, they would innocently deliver the latest gossip on Princess Di or some other royal for the benefit of the mums at home watching *Days of our Lives*.

Invariably, the culprit was either Tony Agars (son of SA footballing legend Merv Agars, himself an excellent athlete and as of 2003 the boss in his own right) or the urbane John Riddell, who's now a famous face on TV sets across the state with Channel 7. 'Jack' was also known to sneak up behind the newsbreak presenter, usually a female, and nudge her in the ribs.

Agars and Riddell were gun reporters who got the best yarns. They both wanted the assignment when a pair of rich young bastards broke into the children's zoo one night and slaughtered a bunch of sheep, deer and other kids' favourites. When Shirley Durdin, a 33-year-old mother of four was chomped in half by a Great White Shark while diving for scallops near Port Lincoln, Agars was the first person in the chopper.

One Good Friday, though, I scored what appeared to be *the* plumb job. We received reports from the far north of South Australia that the police were mounting a search for two injured German tourists. They had radioed that their solo vehicle had rolled somewhere in the Great Victoria Desert, east of Marla. I got the job.

My cameraman, Mark Himsworth, and I would stay at Coober Pedy overnight, in time to join the aerial search, being mounted from a command base at the Marla cop shop, soon after first light on Easter Saturday.

I mention it was Easter because – in our haste to get airborne – I had left Adelaide without a change of clothes and I had not had time to take home the Saab, the keys, or any money for Teddi to see her way through the long weekend. This would usually include a big Saturday shop so the kids could eat real food, let alone their yet-to-be-purchased Easter eggs!

I had merely had time to call home from the General Aviation office and tell Teddi what was happening. 'Gotta go,' I pleaded. 'I'll call you from Coober Pedy!'

From the air, Coober Pedy appears as a vast scattering of conical mullock heaps, from ash-white to a stained orange-red in colour, dotting the flat desert landscape for miles around. The town itself is pretty bloody ugly – what you can see of it, anyway. I recall a strip of cruddy low-slung buildings, including our hotel/motel and, next door, a pub full of drunks. There are signs asking the miners not to bring explosives inside with them.

Teddi couldn't believe I was leaving her with no cash, nothing for Easter, let alone food. She decided to make it her personal mission to extract money from Channel 9 to compensate for this insane and unexpected mission. After I was dismissed, she began a series of calls chasing every name she knew who was connected with the station in those days before mobile phones. Mac eventually came good. After much angst, Wyeth and his bike were dispatched on a mercy dash for cash.

Bob McKenzie was a real estate agent when not flying his beloved plane. Like Mac – who was also a passionate aviator and to become a qualified commercial pilot – Bob had a meaty appetite and a liking for good wine. At his suggestion we packed away two bottles of Petaluma Riesling with dinner, and he didn't say no to a few cold beers in the pub afterwards, either. We did, however, head for bed before the fights started. We had an early start in the morning, and when it came Bob was first up, dressed bright as a pin in his dazzling epaulletted white shirt, and ready to get back to the plane, which he'd tied down in last night's strong winds.

The official newsroom plan was for the three of us to fly to Marla and get an interview and some shots of the search HQ. Then we'd get airborne again and get aerials of the search area; the maze of seismic tracks criss-crossing the desert that make it so plausible that a stranger could get lost and in trouble. With any luck we'd find the missing tourists first, guide the rescuers in, and get the full yarn in time to fly far to the former Rocket Range at Woomera, where there was a terrestrial 'bearer' that could take our pictures and grabs and a voice-over I'd record on location. It was a big ask, and we were expected to cover many hundreds of air miles. We would only make the feed deadline if the Germans were found pretty damn quick.

They weren't. We got the interview at Marla okay, and the HQ shots, while Bob refuelled. Then we were dragooned into the search – quite willingly becoming a part of the grid pattern. It might have been near winter, but the scrubby dune country of the desert was no place for a picnic, and these people were hurt. How badly nobody knew, because their radio transmission had been short and garbled, and they had not been heard from since.

With Bob at the controls, chattering in strict and formal jargon on the cans with the other aircraft involved in the hunt, and Himmy working aerials with his heavy Sony BVU, I was the chief spotter. One time I thought I'd worked a miracle when I zeroed in on the body of a vehicle, partly obscured by a ribbon of stunted gums in a dry creek bed. Bob banked the plane sharply when I pointed it out, and we went in for a closer look, Himmy blazing away with the camera.

Alas, it was a trashed old Holden.

Near Emu Junction, we spotted a police four-wheel-drive and dived again, Himmy happy to be shooting something other than bloody sand dunes and spinifex. The vehicle started up and drove some distance to an impressively broad and well-made airstrip.

'That's the strip the Brits and air force bods landed at for the Emu atomic test,' Bob told us through the cans. We were close to Australia's very first Ground Zero.

We landed there, as smooth as the tarmac at Adelaide Airport. We taxied in swirls of dust to the waiting police car, past rusted and abandoned fuel drums and other airfield paraphernalia.

The policeman gave us some sandwiches and more water. We learned that the entire search so far had been a failure, and there was beginning to be a suspicion at HQ that the whole scenario was a hoax. This was vast country, but there were several other aircraft involved, including a gaggle of mustering choppers, and a lot of ground had been covered. Nobody on the ground had spotted fresh vehicle tracks.

In the end that's what I had to report, when Bob got permission to land at Woomera, which is restricted territory in these paranoid times, just as it was then. I barely noticed the country, or the faraway vista of Lake Eyre as we flew southeast that afternoon. I was scribbling my yarn. A car was waiting to take us to the feed point, and there was a Telecom bloke standing by to let us in. While Himmy fed his pictures out, I called the newsroom to confirm I was running with the hoax angle and having a swipe at the sort of bastards who'd stretch the resources of the willing-to-help local station people and the cops, costing thousands, all for the fun of a bloody stupid gag.

Back in Coober Pedy that night, I called home, hoping they were managing a happy Easter. They were. The Easter Bunny had been to visit.

On Wednesday afternoons, in the newsroom, a tall fellow who coached amateur football would visit with two baskets loaded with chocolates and sweets. We'd buy packets of jellybeans and Jaffas and Fru'Chocs and eat about half, getting revved up on the sugar and the food colouring. Then we'd wage the weekly Lolly War.

The Lolly War consisted of tossing candies at anyone who was trying to work, until at last they reached for some of the spent ammo on the filthy carpet and retaliated. You'd have to keep alert, or you might lose an eye. I invented the cluster bomb, which sounded spectacular when hurled at the newsbreak set at the rear of the newsroom, a staccato rat-a-tat of explosions against the backdrop. Eventually, Mac would get fed up and charge into the newsroom from his office, threatening dismissal to anyone caught in the act of waging a jellybean *jihad*.

The Wars erupted week after week – until one day an edit machine refused to accept videotape. The engineers were called. They investigated for five or ten minutes. And then, eureka! They found a jellybean wedged deep in the tape slot.

Mac went berserk.

Mac was Australia's longest-serving news director, survivor of ruthless TV ratings wars, a cigar-smoking, steak-chomping tactician with a pepper-and-salt beard and eyes that calmly measured the distance between himself and his prey. He was an expert marksman, and he was rumoured to keep some long barreled antique pistols in his office locker. Mac also had a decent temper.

The Lolly Man was banished.

We found other diversions. Tim Parker kidnapped a stuffed toy Ray McGhee had bought for his son Bradley's birthday. Tim and Tony Morabito videotaped a ransom message and gave Ray instructions he had to follow if he wanted to see Bradley's little buddy alive again. A desperate Ray encouraged further terrorism by paying up.

We played indoor cricket in the narrow corridor between the desks – me and Agars, Riddell, Morabito, Parker and Paul Roberts, making Georgina McGuinness and Deanna Cronin duck as the tennis balls sailed just over their heads. One time, Paul played an uppish cover drive and smashed a neat hole in the heritage leadlight above one of the doors. We also managed to smash Mac's office window in a weekend mishap, but the two Tonys clubbed together and called in a glazier.

Mac found out anyway, but Agars always was his pet galoot, so there were no repercussions. Agars thought so, anyway. Mac had other ideas. He proved the newsroom rumour about pistols to be completely correct, when he loaded them with blanks at a Channel 9 Christmas party and drilled the unsuspecting galoot twice, at close range.

In those days we were winning the ratings by a mile. TV was a license to print money. We could *afford* to have fun.

Then, to borrow the words of the then-Treasurer Paul Keating, along came 'the recession we had to have'. It came in the late 1980s. In addition to sending our mortgage rate to a crippling 17.5% the economic downturn cut deeply into TV advertising revenues and for the first time in my experience there was talk of austerity measures.

Consultants were hired. Mac nicknamed them 'toe-cutters' and thwarted them at every turn, aggressively protecting his territory and the people he'd hired. One consultant was sent to see how we covered a major bushfire. He returned stinking of smoke and ashen with fear. The station made some minor redundancies but the newsroom escaped completely. New consultants were hired. These were full of jargon about paradigm attitude shifts and something called a multi-tiered responsibility matrix. They took us on bonding sessions at Mount Lofty House. 'You guys team up and use this piece of wood and those bricks to safely cross that pond of radioactive sludge.' If we survived the sludge, we'd get to overcome our fears by abseiling from cliffs at Morialta.

They might have been innocently touchy-feely in their modus operandi but this second mob of consultants was still-toe cutting: there came steeper staff cuts. The newsroom wouldn't survive much longer.

Not that I was worried about keeping my job. Things were changing, that's all. The fun was going out of the place.

I remember the day in 1990 that Iraq, not satisfied with nearly a decade of war against Iran, invaded Kuwait.I was producing the 6 pm news and I was on the lookout for a lead story – something more inspiring than the crappy local offerings.

I got on the phone to Sydney. 'Yeah, there'll be a package,' said my counterpart there. 'Probably Robert Penfold reporting. If we can get him out of bed.'

Great! I had a lead story. Oddly, the other stations went local, but for some reason I felt the invasion was going to have global impact. Alas, how right I was.

The first Gulf War impacted on Myra and Sylvie. Then 14 and not quite 12, they had been lobbying for a trip to America to visit – for the first time, in Sylvie's case – Teddi's family. But with every spare cent going onto our crippling mortgage, we could not afford it. I tried to quit making my voluntary contributions to Channel 9's superannuation scheme. In retrospect I'm *very* glad the company secretary forbade it because it is helping me and Teddi keep the wolves from the door while I write this book, as fast as I can, knowing that every new dawn might be my last.

Teddi's father came to the rescue. By now Tedd and Carol had moved to a bungalow in Denver, Colorado. They kept themselves amused in semi-retirement by running the Rocky Mountains franchise for a company called Windjammer Cruises, which packaged tall ship ventures in the Caribbean. They had close relationships with several Denver travel agencies, and a good buddy named Dwight. Somehow Tedd and Dwight conspired to get the girls a freebie package to Denver and Milwaukee. They were set to travel during the long Australian school holidays, including Christmas and most of January '91.

The United States was gearing up for war with Iraq, and there were genuine fears that Saddam Hussein's terrorist mates might strike against America or any of the other nations pledging their support to the International Coalition that was preparing to go to war in the Persian Gulf. As with the so-called War against Terror, Australia was a willing partner.

Airports all over the world were on high alert. It was our daughters' first solo venture anywhere, and they were going half way around the world, into global paranoia.

As it turned out, the most dramatic thing that happened to them was at a ski hotel in Breckenridge, Colorado, when the girls swam together in the heated pool. They sent a photo. The girls were surrounded by clouds of steam, and heavily falling snow.

We wished we were there, and a year or so later, we were, foolishly thinking that the threat of airline terror was over. Tedd and Dwight came up with the same freebie deal for all of us – Thanksgiving in Milwaukee and a few days in Denver with him and Carol.

Things had changed for Momsie. She lost her job at Chapman's department store. The place had closed, but the company was still represented at a suburban shopping mall. If she wanted work, she had to ride several buses to get there. The ride took ninety minutes each way.

She had moved out of her Shorewood apartment. She now had a small place, with city-subsidized rental. She was proud of the place, and cooked us wonderful roast pork with mashed potatoes and buttered green beans to celebrate how well she was getting along. Then we shared a six-pack of Pabst and she skunked us at cards.

I'm glad we got to make that trip. It was the last time we saw Momsie. She died the next year with no warning. Teddi never got the chance to say goodbye.

Chapter 13

En route to doom and gloom

The AIDS Council, meantime, entertained its own toe-cutters. They commissioned a report recommending the place be reorganized. It was suggested that all paid staff positions be advertised. We weren't concerned. Teddi had become a respected institution at ACSA and was due for pro-rata long service leave, pretty rare in the AIDS caper.

We didn't count on political correctness. Her job went to a lesbian from Alice Springs.

With mortgage interest rates only just coming off their record high of 17.5%, getting by on a single salary was hard. We tried growing vegetables. The kids' school uniforms were second-hand but their fees were fully paid.

Then, independently of me, Teddi also landed work at Channel 9. At first it was tenuous duty in the publicity department. Then the Community Relations boss, Barry Ellson, took a shine to my bride and hired her over to his department. Soon after that, she was taken on by Banksia Productions, the station's production arm, as a researcher and segment producer with programs like *Guess What, Hot Science* and *Here's Humphrey*.

When Banksia was in production everybody worked twelve-hour shifts with little time for breaks. People got worn out and bitchy. Teddi had no time for her family. She wrote to Channel 10. In a matter of weeks she was hired by their newsroom to be a part-time researcher and videotape librarian. Teddi had joined the competition! It was a job she'd hold until the cusp of the new millennium.

Not long after she got that job, I cashed in ten years worth of long service leave at Channel 9. Part of it sent Myra on a two-month student exchange to Sicily, living in a tiny hamlet called Mirabella Imbacari. The rest of us prevailed on Wyeth to look after the house and the menagerie while we took a six-week trip to the USA.

Just before we left, the old Saab gave up the ghost. I had to borrow thousands to buy a second-hand Commodore. I prayed we'd have sufficient cash to carry on the most ambitious part of our holiday plan, a Maclean-as-Kerouac road trip from Denver to LA, via the American southwest and Route 66.

It was nearly dark when the JAL Flight 772 lobbed into Tokyo-Narita. This is an airport so vast it makes Sydney look dowdy and provincial. We swam with the flood of passengers aboard a shuttle train that took us to baggage collection and the immigration counters. We had a shore pass slipped inside our passports and made for the exits, where hotel shuttle buses were loading and heading off into the thickly polluted and cloyingly humid night air, tightly packed with flight-zonked travellers.

Hotel Nikko Narita was one of at least four giant airport hotels we could see in the area; high-rise citadels dominating the skyline, all of them dedicated to housing transit passengers like us, offering a night's sleep before the long haul next day. In my usual pre-travel ignorance, I had feared one of those tube-type rooms offered in some Tokyo hotels.

We discovered my paranoia was unfounded when we flopped our overnight bags and our flight-wobbly bodies into our room.

We wandered upstairs to the Sky Lounge for a taste of Sapporo beer. We only had one each: including a ginger ale for Sylvie the price was 25 Aussie dollars! We retreated to our own floor, where we found an affordable vending machine dispensing chilled sake and, among other exotic Japanese concoctions, a product called Post Water, which 'rapidly moistens your body and gently softens your soul. Post Water is life water for us all.' Ah, so!

The good thing about going east across the International Date Line is that you arrive before you leave.

JAL Flight 10 was far from full. We were able to stretch out in the upstairs lounge as the 12-hour flight took us northwest along the Russian coastline, across the dateline at the tip end of the Aleutian Islands, then across Alaska and Canada towards the Great Lakes and Chicago. Between the dawn and the setting-in of a vast gray blanket of horizon-to-horizon cloud, there were glimpses of a crazy network of lakes and waterways, scoured out of the Canadian prairie by advancing ice sheets millennia earlier, and lights winking in towns far below.

We spent three enjoyable weeks in Milwaukee, partying through the holiday season. Gordy Simons insisted on a day taking photos of beautiful Sylvie in his loft studio in the South Side warehouse district; Dan Ullrich insisted on throwing a football with us even though he'd just had a knee reconstruction from playing basketball; all of us were enthusiastic about the Green Bay Packers' chances of making it to, and winning the Super Bowl.

We stayed our last night in Milwaukee with my best man Greg

Walker and his second wife Pat, Sylvie deep in teen secrecy with their daughter Courtney. Greg cooked a barbecue, as he'd done so many times twenty years before, except this time he was being helped by his twin sons, Eric and Justin. We got plastered on Retsina, again.

In the morning, the family drove us in an enormous commuter van complete with armchair-like seats and a TV and stereo and dozens of large drink holders to Union Station in downtown Chicago. Here we boarded the 3.05 pm Desert Wind for the thousand-mile overnight run, over the Mississippi River and across the Great Plains to Denver.

We'd been this way before, but I could never get enough of looking out across Chicago's darkening western suburbs, rattling through the rural-urban sprawl of a mighty city, then into the rolling expanse of moonlit cornfields. We crossed the Mississippi River deep in the night. It seemed to take ten minutes to cross that colossal bridge, the lights of a nearby town flickering in river mist.

We spent a week in Denver, recovering from *three* weeks of excesses in Milwaukee. The most exciting sightseeing we did was to board the new light railway that runs north and south through the downtown area, supposedly helping to reduce commuter time for city workers. We rode that railway to its terminus on the North Side, quite a contrast to Tedd Young's neighbourhood. In socio-economic terms, his street – appropriately called Gaylord – spoke for itself. The houses were large and well tended, worth half-a-million Greenbacks. On the North Side, we saw graffiti-slathered walls and fences, abandoned businesses and boarded up homes. Class segregation was clearly a factor in Denver too.

This experience of the city was too scant to form a judgment. It was big and seemed to vibrate with careerist opportunities. As with Milwaukee, where I had visited one of the major TV newsrooms, I was checking out the US media; looking back on it now, it seems I was already feeling it was time to move on from Channel 9.

But in Denver my eyes were drawn to the massive ramparts of the Rocky Mountains. Considering the mineral wealth they contain, and the modern-day skiing opportunities, it's hardly surprising a metropolis grew up to help support the prospectors and the snow freaks in them thar hills.

Tedd took us up to the Continental Divide, beyond Loveland Pass. Interstate 70 carved smoothly through what once must have been an agonizingly slow climb for man and beast. Off the freeway a two-lane highway led us more slowly into a landscape of peaks and circques. Below us we could see the ski fields paradise of Arapahoe Basin, and across the valley, Mount Evans.

It was New Year's Eve. Tedd's favourite liquor store was on University Boulevard. He reminded me that they had Australian wines. So I scored a few bottles of Eden Valley Riesling for the ladies and a six-pack of Fosters for me while Tedd corralled a jug-sized bottle of Canadian Club. Then we went a few doors down to a joint called Cucina Leone. They made wood oven breads and pizzas and roasted beef and chicken and sensational Caesar salads the traditional way. We got the beef and the salad and feasted on it, Sylvie, and Rod and Teddi, and Tedd and Carol, raucously seeing in the New Year of 1996.

A day or so later we watched live as the Green Bay Packers rolled San Francisco 35-14 to go to the NFC Championship game next weekend. It was during this game that Tedd decided to take me for my first American driving lesson. I drove us to the Cherry Creek Mall where we did some shopping for on-the-road provisions. Every staff station in every store had radios keeping the workers up to date with the football scores.

Next day we went to Denver's new international airport to pick up the silver Ford Taurus we'd rented for our drive to Los Angeles. It had enormous luggage space in the trunk. Sylvie, and Tedd's two granddaughters, Mari and Brooke, fitted in there easily.

The visit to Los Angeles was supposed to be the climax of our vacation – a couple of days at Disneyland for Sylvie, one final splurge on fun and souvenirs before it was time to catch the plane for Australia and get back to work.

As it turned out, the real climax happened back in a bed and breakfast called the Old Trails Inn, a jumble of wagon wheels and palm trees and old railway workers' cabins on the edge of the Mojave Desert in a little town called Needles, California.

We'd followed the Colorado River to Needles, fresh from witnessing the magnificent enormity of the Grand Canyon. In the Old Trails Inn garden we sat in the wintry afternoon sunlight and drank Budweiser beer. Later we had beans and enchiladas in a down-at-heels Mexican joint called Lisa's. After our meal we were cheerfully waved goodbye: 'Good luck, you're getting *out* of Needles.'

We lay awake late in one of the cabins, listening to freight trains as they rattled and whistled through the lonely darkness of the desert night. In the morning I got a photo of a throbbing orange sun rising between oasis-like palm trees, the railway tracks gleaming away to a flat and hazy horizon.

We had breakfast cereal and fruit and toast and eggs and hash browns and bottomless cups of coffee with our elderly hosts, Hank and Edna Wilde. The dining area was hung with photos and badges, every polished surface covered with model cars and time-tarnished bits of memorabilia from days when Needles was a thriving stop along Route 66, the Mother Road that guided decades of seekers and destitutes to California and the dream of a better life.

These days, Route 66 exists only in long and rutted ribbons of tar, no longer connected in any meaningful way. Needles is by-passed by Interstate 40. The highway lifeblood roars past incessantly, across the hill above town.

We tarried late that Sunday morning, and watched on TV as the Green Bay Packers beat the Carolina Panthers. The Pack was going to the Super Bowl.

During the game our hosts pressed even more food on us, and as we munched they told us something about their families – all their grandchildren growing up on local ranches, learning like their elders to pray for rain on the arid fringes of the Mojave Desert. Hank and Edna had family close; their own lives of semi-retirement were mild and contented. They seemed fulfilled.

I loved all this. This *was* the climax of our trip. We were on the road, you see. We were on a journey of unpredictable discoveries in America's back yard, taking our chances with the people we met along the way.

Needles was no more or less special than any of the small-town pit stops we made since we said goodbye to Tedd and Carol in a Denver snowstorm and began our zigzagging journey towards LA.

The three of us were wearing the brand new James Dean-style Wayfarer sunglasses we got for Christmas in Milwaukee from Chris and Kurt. I was a 40-year-old teenager with his first set of wheels.

Our destination was the famous town of Taos, New Mexico. We got there in the twilight. A Native American checkout chick in a food mart on the edge of town tipped us we'd find a good room in the Sun God Lodge. The room was good and the price moderate. We switched on the telly and we discovered from a newscast out of Albuquerque that by sheer luck we had that very day *just* skirted to the north of a blizzard so severe that freeway traffic around that city, on Interstates 25 and 40, was still completely blocked. We easily could have gone that way, but for the lure of the back roads. We were charmed. We *felt* lucky. We were free!

Coyotes sang lonely songs to us in the starry night, and in the morning the sky was a brilliant cloudless blue.

Taos is an attractive place. Most American towns get ruined by mile after mile of ghastly rural-urban strip malls that over the past twenty or thirty years have tended to strangle small businesses that were the heritage of the original town and the pioneers it served. Taos has a strip too, but somehow it is not quite so blighted and devoid of architectural unity as most. The town fathers reportedly decided that all building projects – even the local MacDonalds – had to be done in something resembling the mud-brick adobe style traditional in the Southwest. Our own motel was finished in a mud-coloured stucco with carved pine banisters and rough-hewn blonde aspen poles palisaded together to form a boundary fence. The total effect, in the brilliant frosty sunlight, was blinding and beautiful.

We made our way to the old town square and the Hotel la Fonda de Taos, where there was a permanent exhibition of controversial watercolors by the novelist DH Lawrence. There was an exhibition of lurid and bestial images that had been banned amid scandal and uproar in London in 1929. Lawrence had lived in Taos, mesmerized no doubt by the mountains and the living Indian culture, and he sold the collection to the hotel's innkeeper for $11,000.

Across the square was the former county jail and courthouse, which has been turned into a trendy arts centre full of galleries flogging superb examples of Native American art and crafts – all of it fabulously expensive. One of the jail cells was the very one made famous by Dennis Hopper and Peter Fonda in *Easy Rider*.

Then – in a nearby jewelry shop – Teddi bought me a Zuni ring. It was a simple band of silver inlaid with turquoise and coral, and almost identical to the recently broken original wedding ring she got me in Milwaukee. It had a garnet too, but the chip must not have been properly set. No matter, I love it still.

A few miles north of the modern town is Taos pueblo. The Spanish explorers who turned up in 1540 found the pueblo much as it looks today, and similar to how it must have looked when its first lodgings were built a thousand years ago. The Spaniards thought it was one of the fabled golden cities of Cibola. The two pyramid-shaped miracles of mud and aspen apartments and storehouses *look* like they contain a million fables. And they do, for the *Hlauuma*, or North House, and *Hlaukwima*, South House, are the oldest continuously inhabited structures in the United States. There are layers upon layers of individual homes, side by side and on top of each other, the higher levels reached by long aspen ladders and walkways formed from the rooftops of the units below. The whole affair was framed by towering ranks of snow-clogged mountains, glaring brilliantly in the sunlight.

A frozen stream sparkled and meandered across the earthen central courtyard. An old lady with graveyard teeth sold us pumpkin bread hot from a big clay oven, one of many dome-like furnaces arranged close to the Houses, but well away from the scaffolding-like aspen drying racks, which completed the courtyard's architecture.

A friendly mutt tagged up to us, hoping for a morsel. The pueblo dog tried to climb into the car when it was time to get back on the road. We were so charmed by Taos, we nearly took him with us.

In the event, we left him standing, looking a bit dejected. Already nostalgic, we vowed one day to return and maybe live here ourselves, close to people who know the continuity and the value of history told for a thousand years. Maybe that station in Albuquerque was looking for producers.

We followed Route 68 south towards Santa Fe. On our left were some mostly snow-free low hills. To the right the land sloped away towards a deep scar winding its way closer to the road on an otherwise flat, desert landscape. This was the canyon valley of the famous Rio Grande. Soon the road started taking us down towards the river itself. It turned out to be a new ecosystem, with the river flowing clear and strong with snowmelt. The flood plain was snow-covered but looked fertile enough to support the small-time ranchers who lived along this beautiful valley with their horses and dogs and the occasional cow. The mountainous valley walls loomed high above us.

Just north of where the Rio Grande has its confluence with the Rio Chama is the pueblo called San Juan, one of eight 'active' pueblo communities in this northern part of New Mexico. Native Americans live there but at first glimpse the continuity and sense of past was missing.

Not far along the road there was a large and prosperous-looking Navajo casino. There was another in Espanola, a scruffy, down-at-heels town. Down towards Santa Fe there's another huge casino called Cities of Gold. The casinos are owned by individual Native American tribal organisations, and they generate substantial income for the communities they 'serve'.

Outside Espanola, we got on Route 84 and drove through the wide Rio Chama valley to Abiquiu, looking for the home of the artist Georgia O'Keefe. Rancho de los Burros was her summer studio in the 1930s and 40s, but after the death of her husband, the photographer Alfred Stieglitz in 1946, Georgia lived there permanently. Unfortunately the ranch was closed, and in the nearby small pueblo there was a sign that asked visitors to take no photographs.

The afternoon was wearing late. We had not decided on a place to spend the night. But suddenly it seemed important for me to see another place.

'Let's go to Los Alamos! We can stay there.'

'Why Los Alamos?'

'I'd love to see the place that was able to bring so much evil to the planet, in the midst of so much beauty.'

I didn't really say that. I think I probably just said, 'It's where they made the Bomb.'

'Okay,' said Teddi. 'Whatever turns you on.'

So we hustled back to Espanola and got on Highway 30 for a while. Then we joined Route 502, the main drag between the laboratories of Los Alamos and Santa Fe, up-market base for most of the scientists and spooks who still inhabit the mountain-top fastness that housed the Manhattan Project.

Don't expect Los Alamos itself to be especially welcoming. We couldn't find a visitors centre. Asking around, we were told of only one bed and breakfast. We drove there, slipping about in the snow-slushy streets. It was nice, but it was also full. A lady told us the name of what she said was just about the only affordable motel in town. It looked like a dour, sixties-style convention centre, where the delegates workshopped how to paint an entire hospitality establishment the drabbest grey. They succeeded. Even the prints framed on the wall were grey.

We had dinner in a restaurant that deliberately avoided dishes from anywhere in the world except the good old USA. Wholesome families sat well behaved at nearby tables. Nobody drank booze. The Stars and Stripes offered a patriotic splash of colour. Maybe Los Alamos *was* like any other American town.

Let's face it, though, it's not. Los Alamos is the home of the Atomic Bomb.

In the morning I took us on a beeline to the Bradbury Science Museum, and one of the first things I discovered was that the Manhattan Project was not the team's original name. The wartime code name was Project Y.

'On 16 July 1945, the atomic genie burst from its vessel and lit up the desert sky with a flash of blinding brilliance.' So writes a special 1995 issue of *Dateline Los Alamos*, a monthly journal of today's Laboratory. 'The explosion equaled 20,000 tons of TNT. The scientists who observed the world's first nuclear blast reacted with a mixture of awe, relief, solemnity, pride, and later, for many, the realization that their 'gadget' might change the world forever – and it did.'

Depressingly so. I got Sylvie to snap a few pix of me standing beside a replica of the original Bomb. Then we got out of town.

Interstate 25 roars a few discreet miles south of Santa Fe, and that's where we picked it up, joining I-40 and barreling through the extremities of Albuquerque, then heading westwards in search of Route 66. We found the legendary tarmac outside a place called Grants. We got off the freeway and onto Route 66.

I'm glad we went that way in winter, and not just because there was no tourist traffic. The bare limbs of the trees somehow connected organically with the way the ruined roadhouses and gas stations and motels were returning to nature – several of them with the aid of an arsonist's torch. The ruts in the road would never be repaired.

For many travellers rambling through hamlets like Budville, where the only functioning artifact in the whole place seemed to be a gentling turning windmill, the remnant ribbons of Route 66 would be a waste of their valuable time. But the enduring popularity of the Mother Road as a tourist magnet and as a piece of *almost* living history suggested to me that the US, despite its throwaway attitude to almost everything in material existence, has at least *some* connection with the past.

And for the hurried traveller Gallup, New Mexico, would be much like Needles, California – a pit stop along the Interstate. Over 100 miles west of Albuquerque, Gallup was just another oasis of cheap eats, truckers' motels and plentiful gas. But Teddi knew better. She had deliberately picked Gallup to stop overnight.

In Milwaukee she bought a guidebook called *Hidden Southwest*. It mentioned a unique old hotel called the El Rancho, built in 1937 by the brother of the pioneering filmmaker DW Griffith.

'Listen to this!' she said, as we rolled once again onto westbound I-40, the crumbling bitumen of Route 66 run out once more, dead-ended by Road Closed signs and redevelopments. 'Listen: "This is where movie stars stayed while shooting Westerns in the surrounding red-rock canyon country. Ronald Reagan checked in here half a century ago."' She added a bunch of other names too: John Wayne, Humphrey Bogart, Spencer Tracy, Katharine Hepburn and Kirk Douglas, to name but a few. Then the coup de grace: 'Rates in the old hotel are moderate.' That was good enough for me. We had to stop and stay.

The El Rancho had a large dark lobby with stone floors covered by intricately patterned Navajo rugs and beautiful wooden furniture. A double staircase framed a huge stone fireplace. The upper floor featured a balcony walkway of the same polished dark wood as the furniture. Everywhere the walls were festooned with framed, autographed publicity photographs of all the stars Teddi mentioned.

A plaque above the door to our room announced that this was the John Wayne Room. Inside there were few reminders of the man. It was merely a comfortable room.

The guidebook said the El Rancho also offered the best Mexican tucker in town, so we ate there and afterwards we drank margaritas, spread out in huge armchairs in front of the blazing fire in the lobby. We fell into conversation with some of the other guests. One was a woman who was going to a new job in Flagstaff, Arizona. She and her cat were traveling together, and they'd been delayed by the blizzard. 'I mean, there we were, haulin' balls out of Tucumcari and we hit that goddamn snowstorm. Thank the Lord my cat got constipation!'

Then there was a local laundromat owner named Cheryl, who was having a night out with her boyfriend Pedro. 'Gallup has maybe 25,000 people,' she said. 'Except on weekends when it gets to be eight times more. The Navajo come to town to sell their jewelry and blankets. Buyers get good stuff and make big profits, but the Navajo get maybe the cash for a night of drinking or some money down on a second-hand car.'

We all reflected on this – the implication was that big profits were being made by buyers and other middlemen, while the creators of the jewelry got virtually nothing.

A drunken Navajo man came wobbling into the lobby. Without a word to any of us he lay down and tried to sleep on the fire hearth. He was wet and shivering from the icy night outside. But the security guard spotted him and kicked him out before he could get comfortable. Then the guard came back and apologized for the disturbance.

The guard's name was Armando. He looked maybe sixty. He came to Gallup on vacation from California thirty years back, and never left. He said he went for walks on his days off, looking for shards of Navajo pottery and other artifacts. Teddi the anthropologist and part-Native American fell into a long discussion with him. Next morning, as we were about to drive off, Armando gave her some of his finds. She treasures them still.

Chinle, Arizona, is gateway to the famous Canyon de Chelly. What we had been driving on may have been flat and featureless, but it was in fact a huge plateau-like roof that hid from general view the jagged canyon habitat of the Anasazi – village-dwelling, crop-growing people who inhabited the fertile canyon floors, 800 to one thousand years ago.

The canyon begs superlatives, sheer red walls plunging to the valley floor, a frozen stream pooling here and there as it meanders across the snow-strewn fields of fallow corn. In the niches between ground level and cliff overhangs are the remains of settlements, from small-scale villages to one or two isolated apartments. We saw two of them. Altogether, there are 700 ruin sites, petroglyphs and cliff dwellings in the Canyon de Chelly National Monument. You could take an age to explore this place.

But don't think you can just drive up and get a close-up. Navajo people still farm the valley floors, and park rangers make sure the rubbernecks don't get out of hand. Most places in the valleys, you need to be in the company of a ranger or official guide.

Next stop was Hopi Country.We backtracked through Chinle and Ganado, Neil Young's *After the Gold Rush* harmonising away as we passed pinto ponies and trucks full of folk and farm gear. Then we got on Route 264 and went west through Steamboat and Jadito to Keams Canyon, headquarters of the impoverished Hopi people and also regional headquarters for the Bureau of Indian Affairs. Keams Canyon offered the only motel for many miles. We motored past.

The Hopi prefer to live on the easily defended tops of the mesas so prolific in their high desert landscape. The first of them is called Hano Sichomovi Walpi. We detoured to check it out, and found ourselves climbing steeply up a narrow mountainside road crammed with switchbacks. On the mesa top the view was of seemingly uninhabited expanses, low hills of scrub mottled by the snow that got dumped there during the blizzard, presenting the incongruous sight of frozen water covering a desert landscape.

At ground level in the mesa village itself it was easy to appreciate why people don't want rubbernecks shooting photos of everything. It would have been intrusive, not only because the poverty of the people at First Mesa was sadly palpable, but also because it's where they live. We obeyed the laws, though my fingers sorely itched.

Second Mesa is the only other place on Hopi land where you can rent a motel room. It's an unattractive block-like place, its squared edges softened by an attempt at the adobe look. But the rooms were perfectly clean, modern and comfortable, and we got a TV news service. There was also a restaurant that served American-style tucker or the Hopi variety. Teddi and I tried some of it, and decided that while the Hopi were great at making Kachina Dolls and silverware, they sure as hell couldn't cook.

Why they were bad cooks remained a mystery, because the only specific information on the Hopi lands I could find while rummaging about in the lobby was a single photocopied sheet of paper. This informed me that the 10,365 inhabitants of the 911,000 acre Hopi lands were taxed at $6.57 per $100 assessed valuation, that total annual precipitation was 7.89 inches and the July average maxima 91.8 degrees Farenheit. The depth of winter measured 43.3 degrees.

It was certainly chilly next cloudless morning as we ventured on, picking up munchies at a roadhouse outside a little place called Kykotsmovi, and some locally made earrings for Teddi at Old Oirabi. Photography is forbidden here, too, alas. Apart from the jewelry display rooms, all fully equipped with credit card facilities (this in a community with no cable TV), the image overwhelmingly remains one of cracked mud-brick and no tap water type poverty. This is tough country, no doubt ceded without qualm to its original inhabitants because nobody else, cattleman or miner, wanted the blighted place.

As we had been travelling west, we were approaching the valley of the Grand Canyon, which was our target for the night. The highway took us past a sign advertising dinosaur tracks, and for a few bucks a weather-beaten Navajo man showed us where, in mud turned to stone, the tracks of a raptor-like creature were laid down millions of years ago. Our guide wasn't sure how many, but he was confident about other matters.

'That's a T-Rex print, right there. And this is what's left after dinosaur crap turns to stone.'

To get to the Grand Canyon National Park we followed State Highway 64. There were mountain and canyon views and everywhere there was a view, there was a little complex of wooden stalls flying the Navajo flag but deserted of people flogging Indian jewelry, in this wintry season when tourists stayed at home.

Even as you get glimpses through the trees and rocky ramparts along the road, you realize that this is not your common or garden-variety canyon. At viewing points along the canyon rim you marvel every time you look down towards the layers of sedimentary rock that tell the geological story of an entire continent. Like Uluru, no photo you take will be the same as the next. Like Uluru, it cannot produce a bad photo, but nothing you shoot can ever contain and encompass it. Unlike Uluru, the Grand Canyon is 260 miles long. It is a soul humbling sight.

We got ourselves a room in the Bright Angel Lodge, one of the original hotels, built in 1935 right on the Canyon Rim. The joint was a haven for backpackers and rowdy school groups – one from New York insisting Sylvie join them in their room for a game of poker.

Chapter 14

Doom and gloom (LA poor)

Alas we had to go. We spent our last night in the American back blocks in Needles, on the edge of the Mojave, where the Colorado River flattens out from the Mountains and flows in a gentle meander towards Baja California.

After the Packer game was finished, we paid our bill, said goodbye to Hank and Edna and got on the road, westbound on Interstate 40, arrow straight across the Mojave Desert to Interstate 15 then on towards LA, next stop Anaheim and Disneyland.

Somehow I succeeded in navigating LA's labyrinth of freeways and got the Taurus into the network of ugly concrete boulevards that provide arterial access to the hundreds of hotels and motels and restaurants and convention centres and other theme parks that exist in Anaheim only because Disneyland does. In a smoggy rose-pink sunset, we picked a motel just across Harbor Boulevard from Disneyland's main gates and the biggest car park I've ever seen.

The motel was called the Saga Inn. It had a Budget Rent-a-Car depot in the forecourt of its own parking lot. If I returned the Taurus by 8 pm, I'd avoid an extra day's rental fee. That was a good thing, because after a week on the road from Denver, we were low on holiday cash and we wanted to show Sylvie a good time with Mickey Mouse and his mates across the street. We got ourselves a room for three nights.

It was next day that things went wrong. The plan was to enjoy the day at Disneyland, but we never got there.

I'm an early riser, so while the other two slumbered on, I dressed and went out to find a bank with an automatic teller machine so we'd be cashed up for the big day out.

I walked half a mile before I found a bank. When I got there I reached in my wallet, fished out my Visa card, slotted it into the machine, punched in my PIN and requested a couple of hundred bucks. There was the bad news: 'Insufficient Funds for Withdrawal.'

This wasn't possible. Okay, we were down on funds, but not *that* badly. By my reckoning there still had to be almost a thousand

Australian dollars available to me, even with the American transaction fees and the crappy exchange rate. I tried for an account balance and got a terrible response: 'Available credit: $0.00.' Fuck! What was wrong?

I walked back to the motel, racking my brains for any expenditure I hadn't accounted for on our six-week journey – something that might explain this sudden and complete emptying of our bank account. I couldn't think of anything. Back in our room I immediately rummaged in my overnight bag for the journal in which I chronicled our travels and noted all our costs. I grabbed a piece of motel letterhead and started working through all the figures.

'What's the matter?' mumbled Teddi, half asleep but as usual aware of any change in my personal vibrations.

'There's no money in our bank account.' I gave her a sideways look to see how she liked the news.

She was sitting up, unconsciously shaping her sleep-tousled hair. 'Are you *sure*?'

'Of course I'm bloody sure. Zero. *Nada.* Nothing.'

Now she was looking alarmed. Sylvie was awake now and listening too. 'Have you checked?' Teddi asked.

I waved my journal at her. 'What does it look like I'm *doing*?'

'No. I mean the bank.'

'Teddi,' I said, switching my anger from the ATM that delivered the bad news to Teddi who was now receiving it, 'It's not even 8 am. God knows what time that makes it in Adelaide, but I'll bet you anything you bloody-well like that it's not fucking open.'

Teddi was used to me getting mad over trivialities like money. 'Well,' she said patiently, 'We'll just have to wait 'til it's open.'

'We can go to Disneyland while we wait!' said Sylvie.

I swallowed my fury and said nothing. I reached in my jeans for my wallet and looked inside, hoping to make the miracle discovery of a little hoard. There were two tens and a scattering of ones. 'Sorry, sweetie,' I said, 'But until I can get this business with the bank sorted out, we can't go to Disneyland.'

Teddi was working on a practical solution. She fished in her bag and pulled out her address book. Inside the front cover she kept a tattered World Time Indicator she got from Qantas sometime back in the time-fogged past. 'Let's see,' she said, squinting shortsighted at the little figures and characters. 'It's 8 am here, close enough. That makes it 1.30 am in Adelaide. No, it's 2.30 am because of Daylight Saving. The bank opens when?'

'Nine o'clock,' I answered sullenly.

She counted hours on her fingers, one by one. 'So the bank opens at 2.30 pm LA time. We have six and a half hours to wait. What's it like outside?'

'Nice enough. Cool. Sunny.'

'Good. We'll have some breakfast. Sylv can help me with a load of laundry, then she can have a swim while you go find a local bank and see if they can access our account records to find out what's happened. Then, if we're still in a pickle, you can call the bank, and you can call your boss to organise an advance on your pay.'

'There's no way I'm calling JD.'

(There was a time not so long ago that I could have been JD's boss. When Mac finally quit, JD and I were the only candidates to take over. But he was the one who parked his fancy new company Ford in front of the newsroom windows every morning while I eased my second-hand Holden into a gravel lot across the street. JD flew to the States, business class, to study TV news and visit the network office here in LA on company money. I got to the States cattle class, courtesy of my long service leave and a personal loan, because Teddi hadn't seen her family for years and nobody was getting any younger. With JD in his charcoal suit and me in my jeans and lumberjack check shirts, the station executives divined that JD was the better man for the job. There was no way I was going to let him think I was a financial fuck-up as well as being second best – loyal, talented, valued, yes, but *definitely* second best.)

'Ro,' said Teddi soothingly. 'Maybe you won't have to call him.'

I took a gulp of beer and was mildly surprised to discover I'd already emptied the bottle. 'I sure as shit hope not.'

We breakfasted on leftover pizza while I sorted out the last of the food we'd brought along in a foam cooler. There was some cheese and baloney, some bread and crackers, a few pieces of fruit and half a quart of juice – enough to keep Sylvie from starving, for now at least.

By mid-morning, I'd made a useless visit to the same local bank that started all the trouble and was politely but firmly told there was no way they'd even *try* to access an international account, even if it was linked to a global credit card. The girl at the inquiries counter had a big toothy smile and invited me to have a nice day. I nearly leaned over and deprived her of her perfect incisors.

When I got back to the motel it was time to call Adelaide. I got furious all over again, trying to get hold of a phone company operator who was an actual human being, but eventually I was connected and was told what I already knew: there was no money in our account.

'Take me through the transactions,' I demanded.

'Which ones, sir?' said the customer service woman.

'All of them,' I snapped, then immediately apologised. 'Sorry, starting with the most recent and going backwards.'

It was all there – starting with the exact amount Budget had quoted when Ted took me out to Denver airport to pick up the Taurus. There was nothing out of order. I asked how long it would take if I asked for a temporary increase in my credit limit and was told not long, a couple of days at the longest. I didn't have a couple of days. I didn't know what to do next, what to ask, so I just mumbled thanks and hung up. I looked miserably at Teddi. 'I'm going to have to call JD.' She just nodded and started sorting clothes.

JD was terrific. He listened sympathetically and without any hint of judgment as I explained the predicament, interrupting only to ask some pertinent practical questions, and then he took up our cause like it was his own.

'Here's what we'll do. I'll have Accounts raise a thousand dollar advance loan for you and I'll see to it personally that it's banked – and cleared – this afternoon. Plus I'll call the LA office and get them to organise you some immediate cash. How much do you need?'

I was so embarrassed to be asking. 'Two hundred, maybe?'

'Greenbacks, of course. Plus I reckon they could swing you and your family some freebie tickets for Disneyland. They have a deal with the PR people. What's your number there? I'll call you back in five or ten.'

I sat by the phone, feeling stupid and humble. I let it ring twice, not to seem too eager. 'Rod? Okay, they can have the money for you tomorrow morning first thing, but you'll have to go into the office and pick it up.' He gave me an address on Sunset Boulevard. 'The tickets are okay for tomorrow, too. You just go to the hospitality entrance at the main gate and give your name.'

In Adelaide, we have two large albums, crammed with photos, clippings, diary notes, postcards, Amtrak tickets and airline boarding passes, fragments and mementos of that 1995–96 journey.

Right at the end of the second album are the photos of Teddi and Sylvie at Disneyland: Sylvie with a hairy monster's arms around her; Sylvie and Mickey; Teddi standing in front of a horse and cart resting in front of the Fantasyland castle; fake zebras and giraffes grazing beside a pool full of goldfish and crocodiles; people sitting in giant teacups. To me these photos are strange and surreal. I wasn't there.

We'd gone to bed unsatisfied by the last of the travel hamper. In the morning we scraped together every cent we owned. I kept a few dollars for bus fare and left Teddi and Sylvie at the Disneyland gates to make the best of their poverty stricken freebie day in a place where the hotdog napkins have a picture of Mickey telling Minnie, 'Golly, this food sure looks good.' For Teddi and Sylvie *that* was Fantasyland: they starved all day. But, like I said, I wasn't there. I was on a bus.

To get to the Channel 9 network office I had to catch one bus into downtown Los Angeles, and then another one out to Hollywood. As the crow flies, it's a distance of maybe 30–35 miles. If you have a car you can follow the Santa Ana Freeway all the way downtown, and the Hollywood Freeway out to Tinsel Town itself. If the traffic's flowing freely, you could do it in maybe one hour. It took me more than three.

At first I thought the bus was going to be a blessed express, because the driver almost immediately rolled it onto the city-bound freeway. Then he almost immediately rolled it off again, and started following a zigzagging suburban route. Passengers got on and off, mostly blacks and Latinos, placid and domestic-looking people, some kids up the back making noise and tomfoolery like they do everywhere on buses. The ride took so long the drivers changed shifts.

Close to East Los Angeles the bus rolled into a shabby neighborhood where passengers and pedestrians looked desperate. We passed a shelter for the homeless. Dozens of grey-faced men loitered outside. The driver told me to get off for the outbound connection. I stood among dozens of tired, black people, dressed warm against a sudden chill wind that rattled litter through the canyons of these rundown streets where all the store windows were protected by heavy metal grilles.

The second ride was shorter, but it was close to 3 pm when I got off on Sunset Boulevard, only a block from the office tower that housed the network studios. I went inside and entered a carpeted world of glass and chrome and enormous flower arrangements. The elevator had a huge mirror. I smoothed down my hair and tucked in my travel-rumpled shirt. I was glad I'd taken time to shave that morning. I was presenting myself to benefactors, network luminaries too, people you read about in gossip columns.

The network's United States correspondent took me under his wing. Friendly and welcoming, he showed me around the studios and introduced me to the office comptroller, who counted me out the pre-arranged wad of cash and had me sign a piece of paper agreeing to pay it back again. By the time the formalities were done, the reporter was in an edit suite cutting a story, so I just asked to use the phone so I could call the bank in Adelaide and make sure my pay advance had been deposited.

He showed me into a small empty office and left. I dialed Adelaide and asked for the customer service lady I'd spoken to the day before.

She happily confirmed the money was there. I asked for the amount of cash available to me, exactly. I was given a figure nearly twice as high as I'd expected. I asked how much had just been deposited.

'A thousand dollars, sir.'

'I don't understand,' I said. 'The only reason the grand was deposited was to put some money in the account, and now you're telling me there's nearly two thousand.'

'Yes, sir.'

'But when I called yesterday . . .'

'There *is* something else showing . . .'

'What?'

'Well, it seems Budget Rent-a-Car had a pledge amount held aside on your card account. It wasn't showing when you called yesterday.'

'A what?'

'A pledge. A lot of companies do that, as a security on their property until they've got it back undamaged.'

'A pledge. How much?'

'Five hundred US dollars. It was released yesterday, just after you called. Your account details were still up on my screen. They refreshed in front of my eyes. I would have called to let you know, but you didn't leave your number.'

My God. I could have left a number, waited half an hour yesterday, and saved myself all this angst and humiliation. I'd be happily hopping about with Teddi and Sylvie in Never-Never Land. I croaked my thanks and hung up the phone.

I went to thank the comptroller. I was in no hurry to tell my idiot's tale. So I just shook her hand and said I'd better get going if I was going to get back to Anaheim before it got dark. The woman looked at me like I'd gone crazy. 'It's not even four o'clock! How're you *getting* there?'

'By bus,' I said simply.

'No way! Is that how you *got* here?' I nodded. She gaped at me like I was the only person she'd ever met who had actually ridden an LA bus. Maybe I was.

'Well,' she said, 'you'll get there in a fraction of the time if you take a town car. It's only a couple bucks more expensive than a cab, and much more comfortable.'

'How much more?'

'Maybe altogether you'd pay fifty bucks. Plus tip. Call it sixty.'

I'd paid one dollar and eighty cents for the bus ride, but suddenly I was feeling tired and sad. There was no way I was going back the same way I'd arrived. 'Okay,' I said, and I let the nice lady order me a town car. I couldn't get out of those offices fast enough.

Teddi and Sylvie were in our room, watching TV. Broke as they were, they'd had a good time. But Teddi wanted me to do her a favour before Disneyland closed for the day. She wanted to buy a present for Myra, who was still on her two-month student exchange in Sicily. 'An Eeyore.'

'A what?'

'You know, Eeyore, from *Winnie the Pooh*. They sell stuffed toys. Myra loves Eeyore!'

'Oh. Okay.'

I hurried over Harbor Boulevard, and ran across that huge parking lot against a tide of tired and flushed looking families heading for their evening feeding troughs. I got to the gates and showed the unused pass that my Channel 9 benefactors had left for me. I made my way up Main Street USA until I found a likely looking stall. It was getting set to close down, but I quickly found what I wanted. Starving hungry and dying for a beer, I ran back to the Saga Inn.

'That's nice,' said Teddi, with the sort of smile people reserve to indulge the village idiot. 'But that's not Eeyore. It's Piglet.'

Next day we checked out early and caught an airport shuttle to LAX. Ahead of us, across the Pacific, was a resumption of work for Teddi and me, school for Sylvie and Myra. We'd had a fantastic holiday, but somehow I felt I'd ruined it with the failures of the past few days. Back at work, there'd be JD to thank, and the resumption of Channel 9's endless battle to win the TV ratings – so meaningless to anyone outside the industry itself. The thought of that sank me deep in gloom.

On the plane to Tokyo, I got stuck into the sake.

Somewhere over the Aleutian Islands archipelago, the infinite white bed of clouds cleared and I looked down to see a lonely ship anchored in the lee of a mountainous, apparently deserted islet. I wished I were a sailor on board that boat.

Chapter 15

Where eagles fly

Somehow, we kept our noses in front with the ratings that year. I found it hard to care.

JD knew I was getting restless. He'd known it for some time. Before our US trip he had offered me the chance to produce a pilot series of half-hour travel programs, based on South Australian tourism and lifestyle destinations, called *Postcards*. The program was successful, and still is. It kept me busy for the three months prior to America, and I could have dropped back into the job, but the hours were too irregular.

Even though I was bored with the news, I voluntarily returned to producing it. I wanted the regular hours, because I also wanted regular hours at my keyboard at home.

In my spare time, I had been writing a novel called *Eric and Ian get a life*, and a publisher was now encouraging me to finish the draft. My workdays merged into each other. They were hours to get through before I could get up early next morning and hammer away on my manuscript while the household still slumbered.

This went on through 1996 and into 1997. Late that year the publisher agreed to do the book. Contracts had not even been signed but I was convinced I was embarking on a long dreamed-of career as a creative writer. Even before *Eric and Ian* was close to being typeset, I was looking for another book project.

I found it at Arkaroola.

Arkaroola is a tourist oasis and wilderness sanctuary nestled in a rugged niche of the far northern Flinders Ranges of South Australia, a full day's drive north of Adelaide into the arid Outback.

When Peter Mac quit Channel 9, he headed for Arkaroola. Over the years, he helped keep down the population of feral goats that threatened the native vegetation in Arkaroola and in the neighbouring Gammon Ranges National Park, and the place became a home away from home. But the main reason he high-tailed it to Arkaroola was the fact that, late in 1994, he married Margaret Sprigg, daughter of Arkaroola's founding proprietors, Reg and Griselda Sprigg.

'Rocket,' he said to me, as we said our goodbyes, 'Arkaroola's a great place. It's the *real* Outback. One day you've got to come up and visit.'

I promised we would, not really sure when the chance would come.

At St Aloysius College, Myra and Sylvie were studying Italian. The college was involved in a student exchange program, and we were a host family. For two months we had an extra daughter, a big-eyed, dark-haired Calabrian teenager named Rita Manuli. During the time she stayed with us, there was a two-week school vacation. We decided Rita should see some of the *real* Outback. I called Mac and told him we were coming.

Our route took us out of Adelaide on National Highway One, towards Port Augusta past the pink lake at Locheil, through the wheat and barley country of the mid-north towards the big smokestack of the Port Pirie lead smelter. Spencer Gulf was occasionally visible through ugly low scrub to the west, the Flinders Ranges rising impressively to the east.

Just before Port Augusta there is a hamlet unaccountably named Stirling North. There is no visible evidence of a South or Central Stirling. This is where you turn off to head for Quorn and Hawker and the Flinders Ranges. We stopped there to top up the fuel, stretch our legs and have a picnic lunch.

We still had four hundred northbound kilometres to travel. As we commenced our climb from Stirling North into the foothills towards Quorn, we started what for all of us would be a journey of discovery.

The road intertwines with the narrow-gauge tracks of the Pichi Richi Railway, through cuttings and beneath arched iron bridges. A sign indicates the site of Pichi Richi itself, a town surveyed in 1878. Despite the construction of two pubs and two breweries after the railway went through, it was never completed. Other homesteads were finished. Some stand today, nestled solidly in a copse of trees well back from the road. Others are ruined, empty stone shells with black window sockets and chimneys reaching towards the bone dry sky. The creeks are dry too, and boulder strewn, the River Gums screeching with hurtling parrots and roosting white corellas.

These days the railway terminates at a museum across the street from a couple of inviting and active pubs in Quorn. For fifty years after it reached Quorn in 1879, the steel line worked its way north to Marree, then below Lake Eyre South past William Creek along the Oodnadatta Track, on to Finke in the Northern Territory, and finally to Alice Springs. It was completed in 1927. The train was called the Ghan, after the Afghan camel drivers who helped open up the Outback in the days before the train, and the trip became famous as one of the great steam journeys of the world.

The next stage of our journey followed parts of the Old Ghan line.

It's a ruin now, like so many of the original service buildings along the track. There is still one working railway line in the area, which also runs through Parachilna, and follows the road to the modern township of Leigh Creek. The town and the line exist because of huge local deposits of coal. One enormous train travels that track every day, and loads up with fuel for the power station at Port Augusta.

The final part of the trip takes you through arid, undulating plateau country full of rocky sedimentary outcrops. It's grazing country, cattle mostly, though Rita was thrilled to see her first emus and kangaroos in the wild. Beyond the Aboriginal settlement of Nepabunna, you're in the Gammon Ranges National Park, and the countryside gets rugged, the road descending into the Italowie Gorge and onto the debouch to Balcanoona Station, once a major sheep run, now headquarters for the Park rangers.

From Balcanoona into Arkaroola it's another 30 kilometres, and the road dropped frequently into stony floodways. More than once I had to brake hard to save the car from bottoming out. Then it was a case of squinting into the setting sun as the road turned west and wound into the hills surrounding Arkaroola. Anyone who has seen Rolf de Heer's brilliant film *The Tracker* will know how this country looks. There are hills that suddenly rise to mountains, steep sided, ribbed with rocky ridges, glaring a brilliant red-purple in the sunset. We passed a homestead with a farm of old windmills then, a few kilometres on, crossed the dry bed of Wywhyana Creek and found ourselves in 'the village'

I knew virtually nothing about the history of Arkaroola or any of its attractions when we pulled up outside a building that housed a shop, a reception area and a huge wooden door leading to an invitingly dark, relic-hung bar called The Pick and Shovel Lounge.

The girls and us 'oldies' were given adjacent rooms in Greenwood Lodge, one of Arkaroola's earliest motel units, a rectangular affair with wide verandahs and a covered inner courtyard with table settings and a couple of large refrigerators, mysteriously hung with Scottish tea towels. We dumped our bags, left the three girls giggling in their room and went for a walk to get our bearings.

The village felt like an oasis in wild and rugged country, framed on three sides by the horseshoe bend of the bone-dry creekbed. Behind the village, on the fourth side, was a series of low hills, rising to a much taller ridge. Atop the closest was a silver-domed stone observatory that – even from a distance – looked capable of serious astronomy. In front of the village, dominating the scenery, was a magnificent towering triangle of red rock, its ancient sedimentary layers tilted at a steep angle, glowing beautifully in the setting sun. This was the famous Griselda Hill.

From the top of Observatory Hill we could see across the creek, a caravan and camping ground. It was a popular one, too, judging by the number of tents and family groups poking about in the last sun, preparing for dinner.

We were famished ourselves, and thirsty too after the day-long drive. So we rounded up the girls and headed for the Pick and Shovel Lounge.

Being a Friday night, the bar was doing a busy trade. As well as tourists there were half a dozen roustabouts in from neighbouring sheep and cattle stations, bent on having a good time with the few members of Arkaroola's staff who had the evening off. Their eyes lit up when three teenaged city girls sashayed through the door.

There was no sign of Mac yet, so we ordered drinks from an elegantly dressed woman who looked to be maybe in her late sixties. Resplendent in heavy expensive jewelry, she spoke with a genteel Scottish accent. This, we figured, must be Griselda Sprigg, the mother of Mac's wife Marg. When Mac showed up soon afterwards he confirmed it, adding that Griselda still helped run the place despite her official retirement. It gave her continuity and involvement since the sudden death of her beloved Reg, while he and Griselda were holidaying in Scotland, late in 1994.

Mac introduced us to Griselda, and for the first time I shook hands with the woman whose life story I would help to write and publish. Of course, I could not know then that this was fated. The idea for a book came a year later, on our second visit. The first visit was just good fun.

After dinner, Rita gamely digging into a kangaroo steak, we were back in the bar and the carousing was well under way. Somebody had dug up tapes and a space was cleared for a dance floor, and a wild hootenanny started up, led by Marg and one of the station lads. Griselda had no intention of being left out, and was holding her own in the drinking department too. Doug Sprigg showed up after taking visitors for a tour of his pride and joy, the hilltop observatory. It was clear he fancied himself as a ladies' man, and he seemed to take a shine to Myra. The other lads and lasses were conspiring and giggling harmlessly in various corners as we all got progressively hammered.

Which was not, I should warn you, a good way to prepare for Arkaroola's most famous attraction.

Before Reg and Griselda created the Arkaroola Wilderness Sanctuary in 1968, Arkaroola had a long but sketchy history as a sheep run. The pastoral lease was often idle, because years can go by without a decent fall of rain. When the Spriggs purchased the lease from the pioneering Greenwood clan they too became pioneers, in the relatively unheard-of world of eco-tourism. They worked to eradicate feral goats and other pests that threatened any re-growth of vegetation like the Native Pine and competed against local fauna like the endangered yellow-footed rock wallaby. The Arkaroola area is also a geologist's paradise and Reg – a geologist himself – wanted people to learn about and enjoy that aspect of the natural history, too. It was he who named the wonderful specimen of Griselda Hill, in tribute to his wife *and* his beloved geology. As well as grading tracks to the many abandoned mines and beautiful permanent waterholes in the area, they also improved a network of mountainous tracks, originally created by explorers from companies like Exoil, attracted to the area by copper, uranium and the lure of petroleum, and introduced the Ridgetop Tour.

Mac had organised for Doug to take us on a tour. Along with Griselda and a Swiss woman who apparently visited every year, we were loaded into an open-sided four-wheel-drive troop carrier, supplied with blankets and told to hang on tight.

It was a warm day, and at first the idea of needing blankets seemed ludicrous. We bumped along on the track we'd seen the day before and Doug kept up a running commentary. 'When it rains around here it usually rains buckets. A flash flood will smash trees and move boulders. When it rains, you get out of the creek-bed quick.'

There was no danger of that today. The sky was a bright and cloudless blue. We left the creek and started climbing, Doug prattling enthusiastically about the arid landscape vegetation and pointing out aspects of the geological contortions. We stopped at Coulthard's Lookout, where Arkaroola's paying customers get a barbecue and a good bottle of wine as part of the package.

'After the amount of grog you lot drank last night,' said Myra. 'I'd hope that would be the furthest thing from your mind right now.'

It was. The vehicle was straining as its tyres slipped and gripped on the uneven track. Higher we climbed, approaching ridge tops with nothing in front of us but empty blue sky and the occasional soaring eagle. It was windy up there – now we knew why we needed those blankets!

Doug stopped and Griselda climbed out, telling us she'd meet us at this same spot on our way back. As we drove off she was walking slowly into the scrub. Doug explained, 'She often tags along on a tour and gets off here. It's to spend some time alone with Dad. His ashes were scattered here.'

We approached a soaring ridge that abruptly ended in a vertical plunge that seemed like a thousand feet or more. Teddi, who had already started dealing with the vertiginous views by shutting her eyes and refusing to look at them, announced she wasn't going up there!

'It's perfectly safe,' said Doug.

It didn't look it to me. It didn't look like the summit even had the space to turn the troop carrier. We'd have to back down!

'No worries,' said Doug. 'Leave it to me.'

So we did and the reward was one of the most stunning Outback views I've seen. From the northwest to the southeast we could see to the horizon: flood-outs meandering across parched plains towards Lake Frome, the glittering white expanse of the lake itself, dessicated red-brown station lands stretching to infinity. Behind us were the brilliant colours of the northern Flinders Ranges, ancient and mysterious. The mountains ripped out of the plains to east and west as if some giant hand had pushed the plains together and all the hills, ancient rocks and seabeds burst up from below. It was awesome. Now we knew why the Ridgetop Tour was so special.

We collected Griselda on our return. She asked what we thought of Siller's Lookout. We raved. She nodded.

The following year we had another Italian exchange student, Ilaria Brighi, a self-assured blonde kid from the wealthy North. She arrived with a suitcase full of designer *everything*. Unfortunately, our new Commodore had a leaking window seal where Ilaria was sitting on the run to Arkaroola.

According to her voluminous introductory documents, Ilaria was allergic to dust. She spent most of the 130 kilometres of bumping road from Copley to Arkaroola with a handerchief over her nose and mouth, looking like she was about to expire from the trauma.

I am glad to report that we got to Arkaroola before Ilaria died from *asma*. Also to observe that, when confronted by a bar full of lusty cowpokes and off-duty Spanish bartenders, she showed *niente* of Rita Manuli's scholastic Southern conservatism. She was soon on the dance floor with Myra, twirling and gyrating, the lads clearly hoping that – this night – the mountains of the northern Flinders Ranges might once again volcanically erupt!

I was not able to chaperone these shenanigans as fully as perhaps I might. Teddi and I were dining in the adjacent restaurant with Mac and Marg, and Mac was trying out a new idea.

'How's your writing going, with that book *Eric and Ian* whatsit?'

'*Eric and Ian get a life.* Slow. First they said it was too short, now it's too long and they want to cut it back. They've put an editor on it though, and they've committed to publishing.'

That seemed good enough for Mac. 'You know, Griselda's had a fascinating life. She's the first woman to cross the Simpson Desert. Actually she did it three times, with Marg and Doug in tow. She's trying to knock a book into shape, but nothings holding it together. I'm supposed to be helping, but I'm too busy around here, with the tours and everything. I was wondering if you'd like to have a go.'

In the morning, Sylvie woke Teddi and me to tell us Myra and Ilaria had not returned to their room last night.

I knew where the staff quarters were. I went about, hammering on doors, yelling their names and ordering them to get their sorry bums back to where they belonged. Then I marched to Greenwood Lodge and waited in the frosty dawn for them to come grovelling back to face the music.

Myra attempted to put on a brave face, which was hard to achieve with a large carpet burn on her chin. Ilaria was on the verge of tears – terrified that I would phone the folks in Forli and inform them that their formerly well-behaved and God-fearing Catholic daughter had been engaging in debaucheries. I told her not to be so bloody silly. I also told them both to be bloody sure they let us know where the hell they were going, if they planned on another overnight disappearing trick.

They sat in silence, thoroughly chastised, as I filled the car with petrol and said some goodbyes. Griselda was still abed, but Mac and Marg were out for a morning walk with their pair of beautiful Andalusian Shepherds.

'I'll get Griselda to send you all her notes,' Marg promised. 'And she'll be in Adelaide soon enough. I'll get her to look you up.'

Which is how my second book – ultimately published as *Dune is a four-letter word* – got under way.

We traversed the dusty 130 kilometres from Arkaroola to Copley, stopping at the Quandong Bakery for terrific home made pies and pastries. Still sheepish, and no doubt biliously hung over, Myra and Ilaria munched their food cautiously. They would be grateful that we were now on tarred road to Adelaide.

Ilaria's Outback Adventure was, however, far from over. Teddi had booked us an overnight stay in tiny Parachilna, about 70 kilometres south from Copley and the coal-mining hub of Leigh Creek.

You can see the communications tower at Parachilna many kilometres before you see the town itself. Just off the road an Afghan character was sitting beneath a battered umbrella with half-a-dozen dusty red-brown camels, complete with blankets and saddles and a sign offering rides.

'Stop!' said Teddi. 'Girls! Who wants a camel ride?'

Sylvie the whistleblower was all for it. The boozers were another matter. They attempted to decline.

'No way! You'll love it! C'mon now, out you get.'

Before they could disobey, Teddi was out of the car and marching over to the cameleer. She negotiated with the man, who had lowered his umbrella to reveal a thick grey beard and a thick head of hair, atop caftan-like robes and flared cotton pants.

'C'mon girls! It's all set! Rod, give the man twenty bucks.'

'Dad,' pleaded Myra, 'I'm feeling sick!'

That was cutting no ice with me. 'Off you go, all of you. You'll have a *great* time. It'll be twenty bucks very well spent!'

We watched as the girls were lurched aboard their camels, taking photos and giving advice about not getting seasick on the ships of the desert, ha ha! The caravan wandered off across the railway tracks and into the parched saltbush country to the west.

Our lodgings were in a large former schoolroom featuring old maps and posters of the local wildlife, wildflowers, fossils and geology. Along one wall was a dormitory style row of beds – perfect for the girls! Another wall, another row of beds. We commandeered two, and went outside to fire up the barbecue.

We had steak, fried spuds and onions, and a salad of tomatoes and cucumber all set to go for the girls when they got back from their camel ride, looking sunburned and green about the gills.

'Eat!' we ordered. Flocks of galahs and corellas wheeled about, screeching, settling in brilliant clouds of white on gum trees flaring red-gold in the glowering sunset, then erupting again, wings flapping in a sudden desert silence.

Chapter 16

Changing times

When I was a kid I played a lot of hockey – I even represented the ACT one year.In my forties, I exercised by playing Sunday morning soccer with a bunch of similarly ageing journos, and some skilled mature-age university students from countries like Egypt, Jordan and the Sudan.

We played every Sunday except when Easter or Christmas or important Moslem holidays kept half the players home with their families. Rain or shine, there we'd be, rampaging up and down the grassy strip in front of the university gym on McKinnon Parade, North Adelaide.

It was a rag-tag sight. Everyone was supposed to show up with two shirt options, one white, the other any sort of dark colour. In winter we'd be rugged up in muddy tracksuits; in summer, it was often agreed that it was so hot that one side would wear no shirt. We applied sunscreen, but with the sweating we all did, the stuff was soon washed away.

One day, I was reapplying my 15+ at half time, when I noticed a mole on my left bicep was changing colour. It had darkened, and its edges were less regular.

Soon afterwards, as I climbed from the shower to dress for work, Teddi too, noticed the changing mole. 'You better get that looked at.'

I tried to prevaricate, as blokes so often do when it comes to seeing a doctor about *anything*, but she insisted and I made an appointment.

'We'd better take that out,' said Doctor K. 'Just to be on the safe side.'

It was a minor operation. With a felt-tipped pen, he drew a border around the offending mole, gave me a local anaesthetic, and sliced away the flesh along the pen line. Then he neatly stitched me up and saved the flesh for biopsy. Despite the profusion of moles on my body, Doctor K seemed sure that would be the end of the saga. Maybe he didn't want me fretting. It was like a punch in the guts when he called me up and told me the bloody thing had turned out to be a malignant melanoma.

'We're going to have to go deeper and wider,' he said.

This time the pen mark was three centimetres wide and more than twice that long leaving an ugly indentation on my bicep. You can still see the near-dozen stitch marks on my arm. By now I was freaking out. So were Teddi and the kids. The dreaded Unknown lurked. What if the second lot of tissue Doctor K took *also* proved malignant and the invisible melanoma cells had invaded my body?

The biopsy came back clear. I was so relieved that I wanted to forget the whole horrible episode. But Teddi joined forces with my stepfather Peter (the Brisbane GP) and insisted that I consult a specialist. Doctor K happily referred me to an eminent dermatologist and skin cancer expert, Doctor H.

Doctor H has a lot of patients. I saw some as I waited. There were people with holes in their faces, one with no nose to speak of, a lady with a huge white gauze patch over an eye.

Doctor H had more diagnostic tools than your average suburban GP. He examined me with special glasses, roving a glaring light all over my body, classical music soothing in the background as he hummed along optimistically. When he had finished he said he was afraid he was about to put me through another round of surgery. My heart sank once more. He showed me what looked (to me) like a perfectly harmless freckle in the valley between my neck and right shoulder. We made an appointment to have it removed.

This mole also turned out to be malignant, and once again I went through the 'deeper and wider' rigmarole. This time the scar was close to 12 centimetres long. For weeks, my neck felt like it was welded to the tip of my shoulder. At work I carried my head at a tilt and my arm in a sling to prevent a sudden tearing of the stitches.

Mercifully, the second biopsy also proved clear. But now, I was destined to see H annually, and K every three months. It was likely these melanomas would not be my last.

Melanoma is aggressive, and resistant to treatment if it spreads to inner organs. Early intervention was the only way to preserve a person's life once the 'history' was established.

Dutifully, earnestly, hopefully, I commenced the medical routine.

In 1998, Channel 9 Adelaide was sold to the Melbourne-based Southern Cross. They paid more than 90 million bucks, twice the industry expectation. The station was fecund with speculation that it was set for a carve-up.

Southern Cross held a lunchtime staff meeting to say they were axing 59 permanent and 11 casual jobs, leaving 108 from 178. The newsroom lost three reporters, one cameraman, two editors, our library/archive/autocue girl, two casual production assistants, and my production desk was cut from four to two, making a mockery of my official title – Executive Producer.

The meeting was also offered a pathetic redundancy offer. There was a vote to strike if it was not immediately and significantly improved. The rest of the Adelaide media camped like vultures in the street, cameras ready, waiting for picket lines and strident comment. They were set to report on one local news story Channel 9 was *certain* not to air itself. The threat of strike action and bad publicity successfully bullied the new owners into a substantial improvement in the redundancy offer.

Even though I was bored to death by the constant petty wrangle for ratings, I had not seriously regarded myself as a redundancy candidate, voluntary or otherwise. But this was a good offer for someone who'd been an employee for 13 years, and with my novel on the verge of publication I allowed myself to fantasise I could become a successful freelance writer, using the payout as a nest egg. Teddi and I discussed it, and we agreed the time had come to take a risk.

I put my hand up for redundancy. I got the payout the same day my book arrived from the printers.

The trouble with starting out in freelancing is you never quite know when the jobs might start to dry up, so you take on every offer. Before long I was simultaneously writing an advertising booklet, four corporate videos, training visiting Vietnamese TV producers, and working casual production shifts at the ABC. I was working seven days a week. I had no time to help flog the book. My Griselda project was completely ignored. There was an Ashes-series cricket test at the Adelaide Oval. I got to see a single session.

In 1999 Grant Heading, news director at Adelaide's Channel 10, offered me well paid and steady work as state political reporter, in the same newsroom where Teddi worked. After several weeks of enduring the farce of State Parliament, I was 'rewarded' by being sent to cover the official opening by Australia's Prime Minister, of WMC Resources' $1.94 billion expansion of the Roxby Downs-Olympic Dam copper, uranium, gold and silver mine.

WMC spared no expense to have the occasion big-noted. They chartered three ten-seat media planes, one from Adelaide with the South Australian media, the others from Canberra and Sydney, ferrying the 'national' media.

Roxby is 80-plus kilometres north from Woomera and its one-time rocket range and weapons testing facility. Woomera is still a prohibited area. From the air, all the way to Roxby, the landscape is flat and – apart from low hills, meandering washouts and distant, huge salt lakes – quite featureless. Yet Aboriginal people not only lived there before whites moved them away or killed them to make way for their cattle runs, they also traversed this land to trade with other groups.

The media were decked out with dustcoats, hard hats and protective goggles and put aboard a large passenger bus. Our journey to the new smelter was a short one, mandating a tour by the Prime Minister, John Howard.

We passed sand and an expanse of low shrubs and grasses. Then came an enormous electricity station. We passed rows of one-tonne copper ingots. Then we were at the smelter itself, a huge multi-level tangle of pipes and metalwork. The focus of attention were the PM, and John 'Ollie' Olsen, South Australia's Premier. They probably *were* impressed at the sight of streams of molten copper pouring into their casts. Copper mined at least 300 metres below a vast over-burden of sand and rock. It's the biggest underground mine in Australia, and – thanks to the expansion – the fifth-largest uranium prospect in the world.

I wondered how much water WMC was draining from the Great Artesian Basin, to support this colossal operation. I didn't get a chance to ask. The minders chucked us back on the bus and it was off to the Roxby Downs mess hall for lunch and congratulatory speeches.

The mess hall was transformed into a modern-day Hanging Gardens of Babylon. The Roxby high school kids were all decked out in gleaming new sport shirts with 'New Era at Olympic Dam' logos, running back and forth, splashing beer and wine in every available glass. WMC had flown in 500 guests, including half the Federal and State Cabinets and table-loads of Japanese executives. The primary school kids were taking lunch orders, flying about with platters of fresh seafood and succulent lamb.

Not that the Adelaide media had time to put our noses in the trough. Our hosts had us pinned in position, forcing us to record five speeches before we could shoot some overlay and consider a story that went beyond the safe and predictable 'good news for Roxby' yarn. No such luck. The PM had said all he was going to say and so had Ollie. We were bussed back to our plane.

Unlike my commercial competitors who went to air at 6 pm, and the ABC, with the luxury of a 7 pm kick-off, I had to have my stuff ready by 5 pm in case the producer wanted to lead with it. So, still dripping with perspiration, I started scribbling a script into my notebook. It didn't take long to rough it out. Then I picked out some grabs, using our camera and its viewfinder as a playback machine. I slotted the grabs, structured a final script, plus an intro and supers to phone through to another Channel 9 defector Tony Morabito, who subbed everyone's yarns.

We landed at 4 pm. We sped to the studios and an edit booth and the yarn was cut by 4.50 pm. I never saw it. It was just another day in the dream factory.

Maybe I should have said 'sausage factory'. The toe-cutters had already been through this newsroom. Channel 10 was good at getting maximum work mileage out of its staff and its operations could be flowcharted. But life can be unpredictable. One day I went for a run to see how work was progressing on the controversial Hindmarsh Island bridge, and ended with a yarn about the lucky escape of a cropduster pilot who drilled his rig into the side of a hill near Strathalbyn.

For me, the worst time was when parliament was sitting. I'd often find myself hurtling back to North Adelaide with an armful of tapes and notes, scribbling a script, Labor PR people on the mobile hassling me to make sure their point of view was covered, the Liberals doing the same with their last-minute spin. I'd hustle into an editing booth, lay down my voiceover and grabs, until we had a story base. Then I'd leave the cutter to it and hustle with another crew back down to Parliament House, where I'd do one or more live crosses into the news.

I was beginning to wonder if I would not have been better off hanging on as a freelancer.

At least my skin tests were drawing the all clear. We booked a week in Bali.

Kuta was ablaze with neon lights and thumping with nightclub noise, the narrow streets packed with touts and tourists, taxis and hundreds of motor scooters weaving through the karaoke bedlam as we made our way towards the Prawita Hotel.

There was the ill-fated Sari Club – to be blown apart by a terrorist bomb on 12 October 2002. Not that we had any premonitions about that night of hell, but hindsight offers one or two clues about how it may have been possible.

The first came on Nusa Lembongan, a tiny island in the Lombok Strait between Bali and Nusa Panida. This was a place that offered an agonising contrast between the ostetnatious wealth of the tourists and the day to day subsistence of the seaweed farmers and fisher folk, in their thatched huts along a coastal path to a village. The unpainted timbers and lateen-sailed outriggers spread along a beach fouled by thousands of plastic bottles abondoned by the tides.

I loved that village. There was a shop where one man was making yellow-tuna satays on a tiny charcoal griddle; another wanted to take us snorkeling; a third was preening and massaging his bantam rooster for the evening cockfights. An old woman walked a large boar on a leash, enjoying an afternoon out. In a grove at the end of the street, a weather-tanned fisherman sharpened the hooks on his tuna lures, set at the end of long traces dangling from lines strung out on nails driven into the boles of the palm trees.

By contrast, some of the guests at our beachside cottages fit the image of the indolent and the ignorant. One quartet of Italians – slathered with tanning oil, and wearing little more than designer sunglasses – particularly irritated me. They did nothing but swim in the pool or dominate the tables beside it. They ordered drinks in loud imperious voices. They ignored everybody. Had they stepped outside the cottage gates, would they have noticed the glare of the weed fisherman, or wondered how he survived when the paddy terrace was dry and the papaya was yet to fruit?

The Aussies partying at the Sari club on the night of the bombing were no more guilty for their wealth than that quartet of Italians, but among the jealous and materially deprived would have been a few who shared Amrozi's smile.

The second clue came back in Kuta. Enjoying another sunny afternoon of body surfing and beer drinking, we fell into conversation with a Balinese man who spoke fluent English.

'Bali has an independence movement,' he was saying. 'We're a Hindu minority in the largest Moslem nation on Earth. It's our history and the natural wonders of the place that makes Bali so wonderful to the visitors. Why else do they come, so many? Then, Jakarta taxes this island so heavily, you see. Many people resent that. Why should they lose most of what they earn to Jakarta?'

This talk was almost mutinous. The man was perhaps in his mid-forties but (like Amrozi) he looked far younger. He gazed alertly about as he spoke, to be sure he wasn't overheard.

I didn't blame him. This was 1999. Our chat was taking place at the same time as events further east along the Indonesian archipelago in East Timor. At last the Indonesians had allowed an independence vote. The pro-Jakarta militia had done their best to wreck the vote. The bloodshed was huge. The poorly armed international observers could not stop the violence. The militia could not stop the vote, which was overwhelmingly pro-independence. The violence continued. Failure to suppress the Timorese would encourage independence movements elsewhere – as was already happening in Aceh and Irian Jaya. In Bali that year, the military were everywhere.

'This is bad for Indonesia,' declared our mentor on the subject of

Timor's vote. 'Indonesia loses face. Jakarta is rejected by the people. The independence movement in Aceh Province watches closely. Indonesia will not control the militia. They do not want an independent Timor. There will be more trouble.'

There was, and when it happened I got the chance to cover the politics direct from Parliament House in Canberra.

Chapter 17

Pundits of the press

I flew into Canberra on a Sunday night in September 1999 and headed to my hotel. I got that powerful sense of homecoming. The streets were virtually empty. The driver sped along the parkway beside the Molonglo River, past the gates of the Duntroon military college, past the tall American Eagle that guards the Defence Department offices at Russell, across Kings Avenue Bridge and through the maze of bureaucracies that occupies the 'suburb' of Barton.

The hotel was built on the site of the former Wellington Hotel – where as 16-year-olds my mate Bruce and I would illegally purchase hip flasks of vodka, downing the contents before a Saturday night of chess and cigarettes and raisin toast in the church-run young-folks' coffee house next door. The church is still there, and so are the pine trees beneath which we threw up.

This hotel was a far cry from the beery days of the Wellington. I was checked into a suite with a fancy spa and watched live on CNN as Indonesia's President Habibie, under huge international pressure and threatened domestically by the rise of his deputy Megawati Sukarnoputri, announced that an international peace-keeping force would be allowed into East Timor, if the United Nations Security Council agreed to the deployment.

Australia was well known to be the leading lobby in favour of peacekeepers with *teeth*, armed forces that could push the pro-Jakarta militia across the border into West Timor and keep them there. The work agenda at Channel 10's bureau in Canberra's Parliament House had been set.

In days to come, Australia would lobby the UN vote and take a leading role in putting troops into the ravaged towns and villages of the former Portuguese colony. For a brief and exciting time, I'd be reporting on it all, for a national audience.

Australia's Parliamentary Press Gallery plies its pack-hound trade on the second floor of the Senate side of Parliament House. Before heading for my office I would check the press release 'boxes'. Commentator and journo Laurie Oakes, turned right and went down a long corridor to a secluded spot, almost unseen by the competition. The Press from Channels 10 or 7, ABC or SBS, went left into an unreal environment.

The strangest thing was that reporters and cameramen working for rival networks helped each other, swapping tapes, providing dubs and feeds, shooting cutaways while another camera got the head shots. This was unheard of in competitive Adelaide.

People lived and breathed politics to the point they were consumed by it and could not see beyond it. Ministerial media minders were constantly drifting in for a chat, alerting us to an upcoming doorstop or formal news conference. Doors closed. Phone calls were made.

I had a simple assignment: keep an eye on any domestic or overseas developments regarding Timor, import any extra pictures and grabs from Sydney, and repackage the day's Timor material for the network's late news with newsreader, Sandra Sully.

One night, the Deputy Prime Minister, John Anderson, went out to Fairbairn Airport to welcome home a contingent of Federal Police who'd been in Dili to monitor the elections and I got an interview to freshen that night's package.

But mostly it was a case of keeping an eye on the news wires and the boxes. Most nights it was so quiet I was able to knock off a few minutes early and get in a goodnight call to Teddi, and – because my shift didn't start until 1 pm – in the still-frosty mornings I had plenty of time to walk the streets of my childhood.

There were memories waiting on every corner. There was the art deco edifice of the Manuka Pool, where me and my brother Jamie and sister Andy escaped the heat of summer doing bombs off the three-metre diving board. Not far from there was Manuka Oval, where the famous Alex Jesaulenko starred for the Eastlake Football Club before being recruited to Victorian Football League greatness at Carlton. The Manuka shops had been transformed into an oasis of trendy cafes and wine shops. Gone was the white movie palace called the Capitol Theatre, replaced by a boxy multiplex.

Buildings were going up all over Kingston too. The shops were crowded in by multi-level apartments and serviced hotels, and the barber shop where I got my pudding-bowl college cuts was transformed into some sort of pseudo-Irish pub.

One weekend Teddi flew in from Adelaide for more nostalgia, and some exploring too.

I hired a car and went to the airport to pick her up. Her plane was three hours late. Rather than hang around I went for a look at the Australian War Memorial, still mesmerised by the detailed battlefield panoramas and the brutal paraphernalia of war. I remembered the Anzac Day Dawn Services my Dad would take me to, the solemn hymns and the candles flickering in the grainy pre-dawn fog, and the incantations of Lest We Forget for the souls of Diggers dead on the hillsides of Gallipoli or in the mud at Passchendael.

I missed the old aircraft hall with its enormous centrepiece, the Lancaster bomber G for George, and the galaxy of smaller warplanes that sat or hung like satellites around the venerable warhorse. I missed the freedom to climb in the shell-wrecked hull of the Japanese mini-submarine sunk in Sydney Harbour. I welcomed the sombre veneration of valour in VC Corner.

There is a genuine sense of generational sacrifice in the myriad museum displays, and especially in the Hall of Remembrance where blood-red poppies erupt next to the names of the lost. In the shallow pool between the halls children toss coins and make their wishes.

For what?

The Americans 'mop up' in the wake of the *second* war against Iraq, to rid the world of Saddam Hussein and his murderous filial sidekicks, and Prime Minister John Howard, thanks his lucky stars no Aussies have been killed so far. Surely it wasn't for peace?

When Teddi's plane finally touched down I offered her the chance to take a look at the War Memorial for herself. Men are from Mars, women are from Venus and she knocked me back flat.

At the top of Mount Ainslie, we got a panorama of a different kind – a sensational view down Anzac Parade across Lake Burley Griffin to Parliament House on Capital Hill, to the needle-like communications tower on top of Black Mountain, and beyond to the golden-brown pasturelands and hazy-blue hills of the Southern Tablelands.

It was cold up there, ranks of cloud scudding along in a stiff south-west wind. But we stood awhile and took it in, all the changes the city had been through made manifest in this huge and sweeping view.

Next day, in no rush, we found a picturesque route towards the Southern Alps. Beyond Tharwa, gateway to Namadji National Park, the countryside is awesome, and in some ways tragic. There are signs of abandoned homesteads – their stories told perhaps and forgotten in some dusty library – overrun by nature and forests of venerable old-growth gum trees. These magnificent trees also hide the stories of the Honeysuckle Creek and Orroral Valley space tracking stations.

Boboyan Road emerges from Namadji National Park at the NSW border and crosses more high country to Shannons Flat, where one of the local farm families was holding a child's birthday party, with balloons festooning the gateway to a beautiful old homestead. Beyond, we had near-aerial views of the Murrumbidgee River babbling downhill, running clear and strong with snowmelt, through pasture country with well-fed cattle and merino sheep. Not long out of its headwaters in the Brindabellas, the Murrumbidgee was snaking south towards Adaminaby, before doing an unpredictable U-turn and heading back towards Canberra. The road climbed away from Adaminaby towards Lake Eucumbene's northernmost point at Providence Portal. There were tiny boats out on the lake, but this was not a holiday season and the roads were almost empty.

We came on a sign for a place called Chain Fitting Bay. I thought it indicated another resort, invisible in a cove far below. Teddi pointed out that it was actually a place where you could pull off the road and fit snow chains to the car's wheels.

As the road climbed towards Kosciusko National Park, we saw why in darker seasons you might need chains. Coloured sticks along the roadside to measure the depth of snow were marked in metres. It was a warm spring day, and the sky was glaring, but in the roadside verges, and in shady pockets and forest hollows there was still plenty of snow. We stopped and threw snowballs at each other, dwarfed by enormous gums.

Next stop was the Yarrangobilly Caves, a complex of contorted sinkholes and caverns formed along a 14-kilometre belt of limestone by water erosion and underground streams. New caves are still being discovered – the most recent was Mutmut in 1986.

Before the caves became popular with tourists, the Yarrangobilly stalagmites and stalactites were pure white calcite. Now they are green, discoloured by the algae that's grown due to the lights that guide visitors up through the frigid, dankly dripping caverns.

We were the only people inside Glory Hole. At first, in the enormous first chambers, the place was imposing, but as the pathway ascended through clammy narrow corridors to smaller chambers dripping with freezing water, and on into the darkness and the frightening unknown of the under-earth it became claustrophobic, and for Teddi quite terrifying. She has always been a worshipper of the sun, and she couldn't wait to get back to the warmth of its rays.

Far more welcoming was the nearby thermal spring, clear warm waters that rise from 760 metres below the earth's surface – set by nature's thermostat at a constant 27 degrees Celsius – captured in a man-made swimming pool and surrounded by native bush and a park of new-flowering wattles, proof of spring. We had a swim and our lunch, then another swim.

Rather than backtrack, we decided to return to Canberra across the extraordinary tundra-like Bogong Wilderness. Somewhere nearby would have been the property called Talbingo, where the famous author Stella Maria Sarah Miles Franklin was born in 1879. Brindabella is in high country where the child grew up before her family moved on to Goulburn and Sydney, and where the child wrote *My Brilliant Career*, aged 18.

The networks' gun journalists were being fitted with flak jackets and preparing to go ashore with the troops in East Timor. Their yarns would be filed by satellite. The bureau's chief correspondent Paul Bongiorno was back at the helm after chasing the Prime Minister to New Zealand for a Commonwealth Heads of Government meeting. My tour of duty at Parliament House was almost over. I was kept useful with reporting on 'worthy but dull' political issues like a blueprint for federal tax reform.

Teddi was left to her own devices, becoming a tourist in the city she'd lived in for two years, nearly two decades ago. Part of the time, she was actually in the same building as me. She sat in on a debate in the Senate where the young Australian Democrat Natasha Stott-Despoja was making a speech, hardly knowing that before much longer she'd be the youngest woman to lead an Australian political party. And hardly knowing she'd soon be dumped as well.

While I found Parliament a maze-like workplace, Teddi found it a stunning work of art. She raved about it when we caught up for dinner, and also about the Sculpture Garden outside the National Gallery, and the fabulous fog garden that mesmerises diners in the gallery's award-winning restaurant.

It's strange. I've crammed for exams inside the National Library, but never seen it with a tourist's eye. For me, the War Memorial with its ghosts and histories is part of who I am. I've navigated the city's crazily curving streets without ever losing my way.

Too soon, we said goodbye.

Chapter 18

Ground zero

At the end of 1999 I decided I still wasn't getting enough time for my private writing. Life at Channel 10 was too hectic. To report politics properly, you have to live and breathe the bloody subject. I was a jabbering stress case. So was Teddi. Channel 10 had undergone a new round of toe-cutting and declared 11 staff redundant. Among them was Teddi, so she called the ABC newsroom and volunteered her services. She was immediately placed on the casual roster as a part-time News Operations Assistant. She started working at Collinswood HQ before I did.

Once again, the ABC wasn't quite sure what to do with me. I did a stint of radio news reporting, then TV bulletin producing and TV news political reporting.

I was sent to Maralinga, the site of one of Australia's biggest and most controversial atomic weapons tests. I was to see how the legacy of Los Alamos had affected the Aboriginals of the South Australian desert. The assignment was to cover the Federal Government claim that Maralinga is 'safe' again, after a 100-million dollar clean-up sponsored by the Australian and British governments.

I arrived at ABC HQ for the rendezvous with the camera crew on a tropically muggy morning. At 5 am the temperature was already 29 degrees Celsius on the way to 39 in Adelaide and 43 at Ceduna. Remote Maralinga did not rate a forecast, but we reckoned 43 was conservative.

Important people started arriving. I saw Hugh Morgan from WMC Resources dressed as though he was about to go boating. Nick Minchin arrived in a flurry of handshakes, SA's Aboriginal Affairs Minister, Dorothy Kotz, close behind. They were flying in a different plane. They would take off after the media plane and get there before us, flying direct to Maralinga while our old bus tracked to Ceduna and refuelled there.

We took off in darkness, the cockpit lights glowing red and green. Everyone was reading newspapers or dozing as the plane droned across the Yorke Peninsula and Spencer Gulf. I read some stuff on Maralinga; how it had become the base for seven British atomic weapons tests between 1955 and 1963. The biggest blast was a 27-kiloton balloon-launched atmospheric affair above Ground Zero at Test Site Taranaki in 1957, twice the size of the bomb that obliterated Hiroshima. There had also been a dozen smaller experiments in and around Taranaki, so-called safety tests simulating accidents involving radioactive material, and these had created the worst residual contamination, including a total of 22 kilograms of widely dispersed plutonium.

The Maralinga-Tjarutja had been physically rounded up and evicted from the early 1950s, so that the tests were, theoretically at least, taking place in true *terra nullius*.

In all, 3200 square kilometres of the Maralinga lands had been declared off limits and, despite a British clean-up called Operation Brumby in 1967, they remained that way.

Led by the patient Archie Barton, the traditional owners had agitated for their lands to be restored and returned to them since the mid 1970s. The politicians of the day thought this a good idea, until someone correctly observed that the land was probably still poisoned by plutonium.

One lengthy and expensive Royal Commission of Inquiry later, the recommendation for a cleanup, paid for by the British as well as Australia, was won. The Brits stalled, but after several visits to London, one time with a few kilos of plutonium-bearing soil in his dilly bag, Archie and the diplomats eventually persuaded the Poms to cough up 20 million quid and the $108 million cleanup was on.

The plane landed with the wind, bumping onto the airstrip and bloody nearly going off the end. Two other planes were already there, Minchin's and another, which we discovered was a charter job that had brought Archie Barton and the Tjaratja elders from Yalata west of Ceduna. They were to have a formal meeting with Nick and Dot Kotz about giving the freehold title back to the Tjaratja. There was a convoy of Toyota troop carriers driven by burly Army blokes to take us into the village, where we were officially welcomed and shown a video about the cleanup and its technology. Then it was back into the troop carriers for the 40-kilometre run to Taranaki and the 'this-ground-is-safe' ceremony.

Closer to Ground Zero the trees thinned noticeably, and when we reached the knoll overlooking the Taranaki commemorative plinth, there was nothing but undulating earthworks, with huge graders working clean soil over the top of the burial pits and a vehicle beetling up and down with its antennae, probing for radiation readings.

Nick said it was an historical moment. Archie said it was proof that persistence pays. Dot said her bit about the planned hand-over. Nick's minder said the Senator had to leave soon so let's hurry up and have the doorstop. Archie said something to Dot and Dot said, 'Wait, Willy wants to say something, too.'

'Huey,' corrected Archie.

'Oh, sorry,' said Dot. 'Huey.'

Huey Windlass, 72, stole the show. He told how he remembered being herded off the Maralinga lands by the army before the tests and how it was a time of tears for everyone to be so abruptly dispossessed. All the reporters crowded round and took his picture and got him to tell his story, and Nick flew off to Woomera, a forgotten dignitary. For me, then, the story became as much about how the land was being given back, as about the science of how safe the land is. One hundred and twenty square kilometres of the Maralinga country remains classified as safe to travel through and hunt in, but not to camp on permanently. Before they get the land back, the Tjarutja have to develop protocols that will prevent people from souveniring the stray bits of debris they may still encounter beyond the areas that have been actively dug up and revegetated.

The Tjarutja have agreed to tell the people to stay out of that zone, which will be marked with warning signs but not fenced off. For this, they have been compensated $13.5 million. Safe or not, the land is supposed once again to belong to the Maralinga-Tjarutja. Once again, Australia's Aborigines have been allowed the land nobody else wants.

Chapter 19

The apple at last

In the year 2000, Sylvie our youngest turned 18 and completed a veterinary nursing certificate while working part-time with our local vet. Later she preferred to earn better money in a dog-grooming parlour.

Myra had left her first true love at home and flown to Milwaukee where she found work managing La Casita, a Mexican bar and restaurant. Now she was home again and into the first year of a degree in Italian and International Studies at Flinders University.

Wyeth too had flown to Milwaukee. First he worked as a carpenter's apprentice with his Uncle Kurt. Wyeth soon landed a new job, managing the vast and unkempt storeroom at an exclusive homewear retailer called George Watts. Wyeth had also found himself a gal, name of Jill Ortiz, and the couple was planning to marry. They'd set the date for 26 August.

It was time for another visit to the United States, but this time – at last! – Teddi and I would go via the Big Apple, and visit Jonathan Bear.

Ever since I was a kid I have loved travelling by air. To this day I cannot help souveniring uneaten bread rolls and in-flight magazines. I'll happily climb into helicopters and light aircraft too.

Teddi, as you know, considers aircraft cigar-shaped deathtraps. She gets anticipatory jitters days in advance of a flight. Valium is no good, nor is booze. Adrenaline overpowers the drugs every time. She cries and startles like a baby at every terrifying change of engine pitch and every twitch of the wing-tip controls. On the Ansett Airlines 'red eye' flight from Adelaide, the cabin crew took pity on Teddi and took her up to the cockpit to prove that the sophisticated controls meant we were safe. Poor fools.

'There were only *two* guys up there,' she reported when she came back and slumped despairingly in her seat. 'The co-pilot's *American*!'

It was raining when we landed. We got a New York yellow cab from JFK to the Gershwin Hotel on East 27th Street near Park Avenue. The city's skyscrapers climbed into the cloud and disappeared as the cab crossed into Manhattan. At the Gershwin desk they told us we had several hours to wait before our room would be ready. We dumped our bags and went to get food and booze in a two-floor wooden joint a few blocks downtown.

When we finally got to see it, our dorm-style room turned out to be a cramped, plaster-flaking, pipe-rattling, double-bunked rat hole – occupied at the time we lumbered through the door beneath the weight of our bags by a supine young German. He lifted his head and grunted. Then he regained unconsciousness.

'I don't want to stay here.'

This wasn't Teddi talking. It was *me*, muttering darkly. Downstairs, in the lobby with its colourful plasterworks and walls full of art, the hotel had seemed fun and funky. This room was merely filthy.

Teddi was looking equally disgusted, apparently stunned speechless. I told her I'd phone Jonathan Bear, then see about getting a room upgrade. She just nodded and sat among our bags on a sagging bottom bunk, hoping she wouldn't have to open them. She didn't. Friday 18 August turned out to be our lucky day.

Jonathan's brother Steve was in Switzerland. This meant someone had to water the herbs in window boxes in Steve's apartment – a third floor walk-up in a brownstone building just off 5th Avenue in the East Village. Jonathan had suggested to Steve that Teddi and I might use the apartment as a base during our visit. Jonathan came to collect us in a cab and it was all aboard for Steve's apartment.

This was where we found out just what unbelievably good news it really was. Jonathan slotted the key in the lock and our home for the next four nights was revealed: a neat two-room flat with minute kitchen and bathroom and the living room lined with books and CDs. There were big sunlit windows looking out on Steve's lovingly tended cooking herbs and beyond, the 'backyards' of other New Yorkers, zigzagging iron fire escapes, brown bricks, garbage alleys, roof gardens, a lone woman smoking a cigarette by somebody's back door, traffic noise and music drifting up from the street.

'Jonathan, this is fabulous!' Teddi enthused, planting him a big kiss. Then Jonathan made us officially welcome by cracking a bottle of good South Australian red. This was demolished while we planned the evening.

The East Village was Jonathan's home turf. He learned folk singing from Pete Seeger at summer kibbutz. Good at sports, he worshipped the Boston Redsox in major league baseball. Despite this geographical aberration and a consequent hostility towards the New York Yankees, Jonathan knew and loved Manhattan. He was proud of his local knowledge and the benefits.

He led us along 10th Street, among people chatting on their stoops or walking exotic dogs in the rain-cooled air, dodging the iron lattice work that borders sidewalk plantations of pansies and *impatiens* and their centrepieces – tall leafy trees lining the streets full of ubiquitous yellow cabs and double parked delivery vans. Restaurants and coffee houses were already jammed with diners. When we reached thronging 2nd Avenue, Jonathan announced that he knew a district of Indian and Bangladeshi restaurants along 6th Street.

You could see it coming, a strip of storefronts blazing with multi-coloured fairy lights. The sidewalk touts beckoned and boasted their specials. Jonathan ignored them, peering inside instead, through windows and doorways, his clothing reflecting the fairy lights like a Christmas tree. After three or four such examinations, he announced a place called Taj Mahal should do us nicely.

To me it seemed identical to the rest. 'It's crowded,' said Jonathan. 'It has only one spare table. It has to be good!'

It was, mostly. We shared a multi-course meal that cost maybe twenty bucks, me diplomatically avoiding a gurgling dish of melted okra. I skipped that with the excuse that I was saving myself for dessert.

'For that,' declared Jonathan, 'We go to Veniero's.'

Veniero's was a popular pasticceria on 11th Street, and there we walked, for coffee and canola crammed in a tiny booth surrounded by dozens of couples and laughing groups in equally crammed booths, the multilingual din so loud you could swear you just turned up in Babel.

And here's a wonderful thing: we had not seen Jonathan for twenty years, yet he was about to take five days out of his life to be our guide and raconteur, and during this time nothing but our happiness would matter to him. This seemed quite right. Our friendship just *resumed*, as if we'd never been away.

In the days that followed, we ate noodles in Chinatown, corned beef and pastrami sandwiches at the Carnegie Deli, Jamaican curries and blackened fish on the Hudson River side of Greenwich Village, vegan with Jonathan's mother, sensational pizza at a joint in the Village called John's, and more great kosher food, this time at the 2nd Avenue Deli. Despite New York's reputation for huge expense, we never shelled out much more than thirty bucks. Without beer or a glass of wine, the tab would have been even less.

I can assure you we *earned* those meals. Jonathan clearly knew the value of exercise – in particular, the art of walking.

Next morning we made a rendezvous at Steve's place, Teddi and myself trundling blearily as Jonathan led us to a breakfast of hot sweet rolls and coffee at a now famous place called Dean & DeLuca, where collegiate and svelte business types sat immersed in magazines and laptops, sipping now and then at their lattes. Then we commenced our trek.

At Christopher Street we got ourselves day-ride tickets and rode downtown on a subway train so clean of graffiti I could only surmise that Mayor Rudolph Giuliani's 'zero tolerance' regime had moved from the streets of New York to its tunnels and the tiled subway stations along the way.

At a stop called South Ferry, we joined hundreds of locals and eager tourists as they disgorged from the station, blinking briefly in the sunshine, lining up to get aboard the Staten Island Ferry, which – speaking from the point of view of this always-parsimonious traveller – was admirably free to all.

Our barge was called the *John F Kennedy*. It proudly flew a Stars and Stripes so pristine you could see the creases from its recent laundering. Never mistake their pride: Americans take the Stars and Stripes most seriously. The locals parked themselves on uncomfortable wooden benches and resumed their tabloid readings. But the rest of the passengers, Teddi and Jonathan included, were heading directly for the bows, which were filling with rubbernecks, cameras and videos ready for that seaborne shot of the Statue of Liberty. Part of the foredeck was cordoned off to accommodate a commercial photography crew and a pair of young models, one black, one white, showing off a range of fall jackets. Despite the jam we saw Ellis Island and the statue that symbolizes why America believes in itself – and, more recently, why it claims the moral *right* to assert its mighty power.

And we got a good look, too, on the way back, at the Manhattan skyline. In my journal I merely remark that the doomed twin towers of the World Trade Centre and the older, smaller skyscrapers that front Manhattan's southern tip are 'the buildings that symbolise the New York of today – financial capital of the world – an awesome testimony to the power of money.'

Jonathan steered us, cameras snapping, along Broad Street to Wall Street, then north on Nassau to the Civic Centre, which contains august institutions like the New York Supreme Court and City Hall. Television link trucks were set up to report live on Mayor Giuliani's choice for a new police commissioner.

New York's neighbourhoods and zones, evocative names like the Garment and Meat Packing Districts, Hell's Kitchen, the Bowery and Stuyvesant Town, all begin and end very tangibly. The Financial District gave over to the Civic Centre, which in turn gave over – literally across a single street – to the chaos of Chinatown. The place was jammed with sightseers and thousands of the city's ethnic Chinese going busily and noisily about their daily business. The restaurants were crammed with Saturday lunchtime diners. Jonathan was unconcerned. His favourite place would find him a table. It did. We demolished plates of beef with snow peas, Singapore noodles and fresh flat rice noodles stir-fried with chicken and bok choi. Jonathan sipped green tea, but an Australian's duty in life is to sample the beers of the world. Teddi has lived in Australia long enough to have adopted this simple imperative, so we allowed ourselves a bottle each of cold beer, direct from the People's Republic. (No offence, comrades, but the stuff tasted like bats' piss.) We tottered off into the streets once more, Jonathan telling yarns about his life in the Big Apple as we hoofed it across Canal Street into Little Italy. Jonathan was heading towards Central Park and some of the world's most exclusive shopping and residential addresses, along Madison and Park Avenues.

Charles Clay Frick was an industrialist who made his fortune selling Pennsylvania coal to the steel baron JP Morgan in the boom times of the late 19th Century. He built a magnificent home at Number 1 East 70th Street, and set about collecting some of the world's great art treasures – paintings, sculptures, vases and furniture. We viewed works by Monet, Corot, Turner, Constable, Gainsborough, El Greco and Picasso. When Frick died, the house was turned into a museum to permanently house the fabulous Frick Collection. We were in masterpiece overload when we stepped outside and made our way towards Central Park.

This was the commencement of a Really Big Walk. We walked over three miles, crossing the park from the Upper East Side to the Upper West. Jonathan wanted us to see everything. People were out in the thousands, enjoying the now perfect weather of early fall. They had their towels spread out like postage stamps as they sunbathed in the Sheep Meadow. A group of black kids entertained a knot of admirers with their rap dancing skills, and there was a multiracial roller-blades conga line. There were pleasure boaters oaring aimlessly across a lake, and people munching sandwiches and hotdogs perched like pigeons around the circular base of a huge bronzed and gurgling fountain. A man walked a brace of giant black poodles. Others walked dozens of other peoples' mutts, for a minder's fee. People were playing soccer and baseball and fast-pitch softball. Patient old horses clopped along with weathered reinsmen and white carriages. The ritzy apartments and hotels and towers of the Upper West Side smiled with the calm assurance of the utterly wealthy, high above.

We exited the park and made our way south past Trump Tower and the opulent Fifth Avenue shopping places like Tiffany, where

Teddi was outraged that they let guys with dogs inside the store. I saw a ring with a price tag of $1.25 million. I couldn't get out of that place quick enough. I failed to do so without promising Teddi a bauble of her choice, on Designated Shopping Day.

We stopped in at St Patrick's Cathedral. There was a mass going on and I managed to avoid getting hit by lightning. Teddi looked very pious. Jonathan, remained respectfully inscrutable.

Onwards we rambled. We passed the Metropolitan Museum of Art en route to Rockefeller Plaza. Here you can be live audience for one of those *Today*-type TV shows, where insanely cheerful hosts get the audience revved up and ready to face yet another Groundhog Day in the bustling workhouses of the USA. Still in the dream factory, we marched past the neon-lit NBC television studios. Not far beyond were the Radio City Music Hall and Carnegie Hall.

We went north on Broadway to the Lincoln Centre, where a fancy crowd was gathering for *Mostly Mozart* while another, rather more casual mob, was finding its way through trees and gardens to an open-air sound shell where Arlo Guthrie was headlining a free folkies' concert. We listened to the warm-up group, close harmonies from a bunch of Canadian cowboys. It was about then that we realised we'd been on the go for nearly 14 hours and we'd already heard Arlo do 'Coming into Los Angeles' about a thousand times, and we'd all seen *Alice's Restaurant* at least once, and we were bloody tired and could we go home now please?

The train rattled and howled through the tunnels. We stumbled out and drowsily up the steps at Number 12 East 10th Street. Goodnight.

The train rattled and howled through the tunnels. Was this a dream? Was I here before? If yes, who were all these people, with their dark blue caps and satiny blue windbreakers with the big proud 'Y' stitched into the breast and onto the peak? Here we were, crossing the East River into the Bronx. At every stop the fans were getting on. There was a sea of blue and white.

No, it was no dream. Jonathan had procured tickets at a sinful price and prayed that the visiting team, the Anaheim Angels, would wipe the floor with the home team. We were heading for Yankee Stadium. We found our seats high along the left field line and called for cups of beer beneath a clear and sunny sky. Apropos of nothing except basic American pride, the Stars and Stripes flew from dozens of flag-poles topping the white colonnades of the stadium's old-fashioned centre field wall, beyond the bleachers and the bullpens. There was an air of expectation.

The protagonists lined up near home plate. A military colour guard slowly marched and the crowd stood as one to hear *The Star Spangled Banner*. The players clutched their caps to their hearts. So did most of the crowd, fifty thousand-plus. They sang, too. Unlike almost any Australian, except kids who grew up with the mumbled phrases of *Advance Australia Fair*, these people knew the words. They sang with love and gusto.

Jonathan's support for Anaheim that day was rewarded. Teddi also brazenly rooted for Anaheim. I retained a diplomatic silence. When the Yanks blew a 3-0 lead to go down 5-3, our neighbouring fans were far from impressed. I figured on being scapegoated if I got too loud. Unlike soccer fanatics the world over and Australian sporting yobbos in general, Americans know how to behave themselves in a stadium, and the vanquished supporters were almost sanguine as we rejoined them for the short walk to the subway station. The carriage was crammed, but nobody talked about the ballgame.

Next day was Designated Shopping Day, with a side serve of Big Walk and instructions from Jonathan to be presentably dressed.

First we met Jonathan's mother, the freelance travel writer Nancy Bear, and had lunch at a vegetarian place full of students from nearby New York University. Then it was back to the subway for an uptown train to 58th Street. We started with window-shopping in Bloomingdale's. At Victoria's Secret, Jonathan and I cleverly spotted diaphanous giftware for the kids back home. At Tiffany, Teddi scored the promised bauble. Actually I should point out that they were baubles – a silver bracelet with matching earrings. I sat recovering from the price shock in an armchair upstairs. Teddi sat beside me and Jonathan broke all the rules by taking a photo of the pair of us, Teddi displaying her egg-blue Tiffany bag. We declared it cocktail hour and walked further uptown to the Plaza Hotel and the legendary Oak Bar. I ordered a martini for the first and only time in my life; Teddi sipped French champagne; Jonathan drank a Bloody Mary with enough garnish to make an evening salad unnecessary. They tasted so good we had seconds. By the time we got out of the Oak Bar it was time for New York's millions of workers to start going home. The subway was full, and so were we.

Early Tuesday afternoon we were due at Penn Station for the overnight Amtrak ride to Chicago, where we'd get a connection for Milwaukee. It was Jonathan who insisted on lunch at the 2nd Avenue deli. It was Teddi who ordered deli sandwiches with sides of pickles for the train ride. The corned beef and pastrami sandwiches weighed about two pounds each.

Before I say goodbye to Jonathan, though, I want to say something more about our ride on the Staten Island ferry and the view of the Manhattan skyline and its centrepiece, the twin towers.

When the day of terror came, one year and 23 days later, it took us hours to get through the panicked and congested phone lines to New York. Eventually we were able to speak to Jonathan. He was shocked, talking 15 to the dozen.

'My God! I'm looking out the window. We could see the towers from here. Now there's just a hole, and smoke, smoke everywhere.'

Jonathan was okay, thank God. He said nothing about what he'd just done. Just as nobody admits to having foreseen what would happen, Jonathan Bear could never have foreseen the role he would play on that awful day.

A couple of days later we got an email from his mother Nancy:

It's been a few days since the world changed and I apologize for my silence, but I have been stranded in Hong Kong – sequestered in my hotel room these few days, transfixed on CNN, not to miss a moment of the reporting. I thought I had already absorbed the shock by the time my plane landed last night at JFK; that I had already shed my share of tears. I wasn't able to phone home right away to hear Steve and Jonathan's voices, but through the magic of email I was assured of their physical safety. Not until I returned did I hear of Jonathan's heroism in aiding evacuees from the nearby building where he works, guiding them through tunnels, toward the Brooklyn Bridge and safety . . . I learned that Steve ran to donate his blood and buy and contribute supplies like socks, helmets, throat lozenges to those who are digging. But really, there are no heroes – only those who survived and those who did not.

I went out of the apartment today, and nothing had prepared me for the acrid odour which permeates my neighborhood, the huge immovable clouds of smoke which have replaced the twin towers, and more than anything, photos with descriptions of the 'missing' plastering phone booths and store windows. I studied every face, read every word and cried for every one of them. Desperate people trudged along the street, clutching such photocopies of the most important people in their lives – as important as my children are to me. There are still 5000 people unaccounted for.

My mind goes back to that innocent drunken night on the boat from Bergen. And again, to that day on the Staten Island ferry when Jonathan and I were brothers in our youth, when the twin towers still stood, and the world was okay, and so were we.

Chapter 20

Lake Shore limited

Jonathan got us to Pennsylvania Street in time for me to join a long line to collect pre-booked boarding tickets and for all of us to watch the listing for the Chicago train inch higher on the departures board, minus a platform to board from. The Lake Shore Limited was about to live up to its name.

'It'll be at least an hour, sir,' my customer service helper smiled apologetically. 'The train's still in Queens. Some kinda problem with the dining car.'

So the three of us went to the bar for beers and waited. And waited. I felt saddened, knowing how long it had been since our first meeting and this one. When would the next one come? Would it ever? Then of course I knew it didn't matter, yes or no. Mates are mates.

Two and a half hours later we hugged our farewells and climbed aboard. We had a comfortable pair of huge reclining chairs fronting a roomy bulkhead at the front of the carriage. We had heaps of hand baggage, including an entire supermarket-size brown bag with the stuff we bought from the 2nd Avenue Deli.

Away at last, we watched a pretty sunset through green-black forest silhouettes as the train hauled north along the glinting Hudson River valley. Soon after dark there came an announcement on the train's public address system: It was the first call for dinner.

It was also the last call for dinner: vital dining car machinery had broken down. A disembodied voice on the PA system promised that an extra lounge car would be added when the train arrived in Albany, New York, still two hours away. Meantime the existing lounge could offer pre-packaged food that did not involve cooking. Passengers started scurrying along corridors, concerned they'd miss out.

Aware that we had New York's finest deli sandwiches stashed, I followed them on the pretext of coffee, to see how they were coping.

It was a long line. The lone attendant, an elderly black man, pepper-and-salt grizzled with beard, bow tie and cummerbund, was running out of offerings: 'Pizza! Ain't got no *pizza*! Whatchew see is whatchew *get*, honey!'

I got my turn. The man glared at me, mutely daring me to ask for something he didn't have. I asked for coffee, and hot water for Teddi's tea.

'Too *easy*, man!' The diatribe resumed. He flicked the wine glass containing his tips – a wad of dollar bills. 'Man! I get to Chicago? Ain't gonna have me no *one* cocktail. Gonna be *ten*!'

It was cruel to open our sandwiches, but we did it anyway. The cabin filled with the striking odours of cured sliced meats mingled with fresh-baked rye, sliced pickles, sauerkraut and mustard. There was too much food for one meal. It was too good to give away! We saved the rest for breakfast.

Through the night we rode the rails. By dawn's early light the lounge car was down to coffee and candy bars. Cleveland was cast in the gloom of heavy cloud. It rained all the way through Toledo. Where the hell was Illinois?

It took 25 hours from Pennsylvania Street, New York, to Union Street, Chicago. The train was a mere four hours late. We scrambled our bags aboard the last train to Milwaukee.

Our friend Dan Ullrich (my former *Cityside* boss) had sensibly anticipated the Amtrak antics and checked before coming to meet the train. Prematurely grey but looking relaxed, there he was waiting at the gate. And Dan, bless him, had a big surprise awaiting us. He had booked us into a nearby apartment hotel, the Plaza, as a gift to us, and Wyeth and Jill, the soon-to-be-newlyweds.

The wedding plan was for a brief ceremony beneath the oldest tree in Cathedral Park, after which there would be a rowdy reception at Taylor's.

The day of the wedding, though, it looked like the ceremony might also take place inside Taylor's bar. Mid-morning there was a heavy thunderstorm. But as we dolled ourselves up the sun appeared, and the skies were blue as we walked down to the park. Jill wore a beautiful gown and her hands and feet were intricately hennaed in the fashion of Indian brides. Teddi wore black crushed velvet with glints of red and she wobbled about in a rare pair of high heels. Sister Christine fussed with all the flowers, including boutonnieres for me and Wyeth and José, all of us tarted up in our suits and silk ties.

Gordy Simons danced about taking photos at the ceremony. I got it right with the rings and there were heartfelt 'I do's' and tears of happiness and the little kids threw rice and blew bubbles. Wyeth and Jill heaved happy sighs of relief that all had gone so well.

I wrote a sentence not unlike the one above in my journal on Sunday morning, 27 August 2000. Now as I review it, three years later, Wyeth and Jill are visiting Teddi and me and his sisters in Adelaide. He and his pregnant (yes pregnant!) bride have taken time out from their busy Milwaukee lives to spend a couple of weeks here. They celebrated their anniversary in a fancy downtown hotel that used to be the financial and political hub of the free British colony of South Australia. It's wonderful to have all my children in the same town again, if only briefly. Who knows when we'll see them again? There's a new pain in my lower back. It's not gone away.

After our return from the States, my boss at the ABC decided the newsroom needed leadership and designated me Chief of Staff.

Anybody who knows anything about newsrooms knows that the Chief of Staff's job is thankless. The COS is like the chief engineer on a ship – they keep the engines turning. He generates story ideas and assigns reporters and camera crews to their tasks. He monitors emergency-services radio scanners and incoming news releases for items containing possibilities, fields phone calls from the genuine and the salesmen and the political minders trying to flog an angle for their minister, ditches an item mercilessly if something better comes along, and tries incessantly to cram as many local stories into the producer's bulletin as possible. It is also the COS who absorbs the blame if a story gets missed.

The COS at the ABC has a long day: starting about 7.30 am and not going home until the 7 pm TV news was safely on air. If a story was breaking, I stayed. It was an intense and stressful day with never enough crews and journos to cover every possible yarn.

For the next three months I was virtually chained to the 'intake' desk, facilitating not only the construction of the local news items but also catering to the rest of the network's newsrooms – especially Parliament House in Canberra, where Jim Middleton and Russell Barton were chasing interviews with South Australians like Alexander Downer or the Defence Minister Robert Hill.

But as the time in the chair wore on, my attitude became a little more sanguine: I had been on the lookout for a job in Alice Springs, ever since we spent that wonderful time there in the early 80s, and now I reckoned I'd found one.

I would be in charge of my own newsroom. Not only that, Teddi's anthropology and research/archival skills had been recognised, and the chances were good she'd be working with me at Australia's only Aboriginal-owned and managed television station, Imparja.

Oh, what innocents we were. We lasted precisely four months.

Chapter 21

Dispatches from the frontier

There was anxiety about us two oldies leaving Guilford Ave. But the girls were young women now, working and making sufficient money to pay us a bit of rent. This was necessary so we could afford to keep up the Adelaide mortgage payment, and also rent a unit in Alice Springs.

We left the menagerie for the 'girls' to look after. If memory serves me right, we had four dogs and five, maybe six cats – only two of which would be joining us in the Alice. Sylvie and Myra ran the place well while we were away. They only had to kick out one intrusive ex-boyfriend of Sylvie's, and they only had to bury one dog.

I'm getting ahead of myself. We read new books on Aboriginal politics, the kind Teddi might have written if she'd stayed in academia. They did little to prepare me for the cultural confrontation ahead. We packed ourselves off to this isolated and mysterious place in the heart of Australia's Red Centre with an innocent optimism that we could share our skills for the benefit of the young indigenous employees actively hired and trained by Imparja.

I remember little of the flight north to the Red Centre. I was on painkillers: my skin cancer specialist had just excised a large basal cell carcinoma from my back (not as fearsome as melanoma but dangerous if left untreated), leaving *another* ten-centimetre scar. Plus I was hung over the morning after Myra's 21st birthday party at the Semaphore Palais. Teddi was very quiet, too. Nothing to do with fear of flying this time: she was devastated to be saying goodbye to the kids. She would miss them to the day we got home.

We spent a 42-degree Celsius Sunday, poolside at the Desert Rose Inn. I was itching to get out again and tour the distinctive red ridges, so redolent of the Caterpillar Dreaming of Aboriginal lore. But I would have to wait until tomorrow to get behind the wheel of the Subaru Forester I'd been promised as part of my package, and in my bleary state it was too hot to walk. We swam and lazed and waited for Monday.

When it came I was ready for action, smart-casual, briefcase in hand, striding optimistically along Parsons Street towards the sailcloth shelter-cum-municipal rotunda in the Todd Street Mall, where small clots of grey-clothed Aboriginal women kept outwardly vague watch on their skylarking kids. The men sat aside, smoking – many in dust and sweat-grimed cowboy hats, others with pure white hair. There seemed to be an air of waiting.

Imparja's offices face directly across South Terrace to the Todd River, that dry sandy expanse, shaded here and there by enormous river gums, where groups of people spend the day, keeping clear of the town zone, a few of them swathed in bandages, many of them drinking from 5-litre casks of Fruity Gordo purchased from the pub just a few doors from the causeway.

My office had a picture-window view of the Todd River, but I do not recall a moment in which I actually stopped and looked out there for a long and lazy moment, to savour the wonderful scene. More than once I stared out at the semi-hidden drinkers and wondered how come all of the money that's been spent to 'empower' Aboriginal Australia still allows the reality of such hopeless destitution.

When I found my way into the news department, Norm Grogan was there to meet me. He was Imparja's Darwin-based reporter, who had been dragooned south to read the news while presenter/journalist Catherine Liddle was having her baby Angus. Norm had stayed on to meet me before he, and the senior cameraman Alan Dowler, drove back to Darwin, resuming duty in the Top End just as everybody else was about to go on holidays.

'Welcome,' he said, 'to the transit lounge.'

The Corporate Vision was somewhat alarming to me. It said something about the station's senior management, who were mostly recruited whitefellas like me. The document made much of the commercial and goodwill opportunities offered by Imparja's kids' show character, Yamba the Honey Ant. But the contribution of the news department was not canvassed at all – it wasn't even *mentioned*!

By the standards of Australia's metropolitan newsrooms, mine was miniscule, but it still drew a million-dollar budget, and paid its way through video sales and co-production work. It took only a few weeks to work out why it was overlooked. My two immediate bosses had divergent views about what direction the news should be taking. One was an expansionist. The other – from a sales background – saw news as financially draining on the station. One wanted shows to support Imparja's charter of bringing news and current affairs items relevent to its indigenous constituency. The other knew the audience contained as many station people and townsfolk as Aborigines, and they wanted to know the major news of the day, what happened in Rugby League

(Queensland and western New South Wales) or Aussie Rules (everywhere else), and how hot it was going to be. The expansionist had unrealistic dreams and ambitions, for which I was supposed to be the catalyst. The other would have been happy to have our news as a Ten Network turn-around from Sydney, for which we paid a fee anyway. It's difficult to write a document about a corporate direction when there isn't one.

I had a third boss, too – the Human Resources executive, a dignified and very senior woman in the local Aboriginal community. I soon learned that I made no hiring and firing or discipline decisions regarding my staff, because she did. I would be 'consulted.'

I suppose I should have been grateful for that. I had other worries. I had two Alice Springs-based cameramen, one indigenous, one a whitefella. They disliked each other enormously, in part because the Aboriginal man was far more useful to me: he could shoot good pictures *and* he could edit field-shot videotape into a half-decent story. His colleague could not, despite constant offers of assistance from my lieutenant, the gregarious and multiskilled David Hayes-Marshall.

That wasn't all. We used incompatible types of camera and editing gear, necessitating a lengthy dubbing process before we could cut local yarns. With Norm back in Darwin, I only had Catherine Liddle and one other journo, a willing but inexperienced Sri Lankan. A third reporter's post was vacant. I had a replacement in mind but my HR boss stalled, saying the candidate might cause bad blood. In the local job market there seemed no one else.

Absenteeism was rife and constant. In the indigenous world, family business *means* family business: if you're called you go. The same goes for sorry business. Some employees also fell victim to the welfare-dependency of their peers: man, you're working for your money and we're getting paid this sit-down money. Sometimes we abandoned any pretence at local story coverage and filled the bulletin with Network Ten stories: Catherine Liddle topping and tailing a list of 100% imported yarns.

One night Catherine got crook and there was nobody to replace her on air. I volunteered and was quietly informed that it was policy that the presenter be indigenous. We turned to the ever-resourceful Yamba, Honey Ant extraordinaire, minus costume.

But in my first few weeks I had none of these worries, only suspicions. We started kicking a few goals with the Ten Network, and morale was good because we were doing most of our shows error-free. I was full of optimism that things would pan out well.

There's a Central Australian wisdom that if you see the Todd River flow three times, you have become a 'local'. The first time Teddi and I saw it happen was quite an occasion. The region gets a lot of its scarce annual rain during the Southern Hemisphere's monsoon season, the Top End Wet, when broken-down cyclones turn into deep rain depressions and drift across the parched lands, bringing flooding downpours that can quickly fill the desert catchments and cause spectacular widespread flooding.

I never expected to get wet so soon. In the Alice it drizzled for two days non-stop then rained intermittently for several more. I got a camera crew to film the Todd River flowing. It was mainly the town's large storm drains emptying into the Todd that caused the flow, but it was great local footage with interest over the borders. The network snapped it up.

After work, two things happened; I got a call of thanks from the network's news editor – apparently a rare feather in our cap. Then, I was taking the Subaru home when a bedraggled quintet of Aborigines came padding on their spindly legs from the riverbed and crossed the street towards the Imparja offices, to shelter from wind and rain. Among them were two old ladies, both drenched and shivering. One of them jabbered at me in Arrernte. Eventually I realised she was imploring me to get her a blanket.

Everyone at Imparja had left and there was nothing – not even a towel – in the car. So I went home and Teddi fished out a blanket of ours. We went back and gave it to the old ladies who immediately put it to grateful use.

Just before Christmas, Gavin Gleeson from police media liaison phoned. 'Some bloke's pinched a plane from the airport and drilled it into the scrub just on the other side of the Santa Theresa Road. Thought you might like to know.'

'The pilot?'

'Cactus. Had no clue. Knew enough to fire it up, snuck in and hotwired it. Got to the runway, got take-off speed, got into the air, then heeled over and wham. The plane exploded.'

I called Dwayne Tickner, my indigenous cameraman, who dropped everything and rushed out to the site to meet us. Dwayne charged about getting various angles of the charred and unrecogniseable wreckage. Gavin Gleeson was there, and he lined up an inspector to give us an interview, and he organised some shots of the local Emergency Service volunteers scouring the bush in line, looking for clues and bits of plane. Dwayne and I soon had everything we needed to cobble together a cut story for Network Ten, and to send pictures to every other Australian TV network. We met the deadline and once again we had calls of thanks.

A few days later I was talking to a local police sergeant. He was telling me how searchers found the burned out wreckage several hours *after* the crash.

'A bunch of Santa Theresa blokes (from an Aboriginal mission 86 kilometres away on the fringe of the Simpson Desert) was sitting beside the road. We asked them if they'd seen anything strange.

"Like what?" they asked.

"Like a plane crash," we said.

"Over there," they pointed, as if it happened every day. They'd been there since before dawn. Saw the whole thing. Never bothered to raise the alarm.'

Not that there would have been much point. The pilot had no hope, and apparently wanted none. He left a note, figuring he had a date with the Almighty.

His name was Bobby G. The crash site is now known as the G Spot.

There was a campfire on the sand by the waterhole, lighting the faces of the dozen Arrernte people gathered there. The women were dressed in shapeless dark brown shifts. They stood in a tight little row, dancing in tiny, shuffling steps, keening softly. The men were bare-chested and cross-legged. They sat with carved music sticks, tapping and chanting a welcome to the messengers. A white-haired elder beckoned the messengers towards the fire.

The Arrernte family stepped up and was presented with a specially carved boomerang and a message stick to be passed on to the Governor-General in Sydney. It contained an invitation for all Australians to come to Alice Springs in September 2001 to take part in the Yeperenye Festival, one of the largest celebrations of Australian indigenous culture ever undertaken, and part of the push for reconciliation and 'treaty' in the year of the centenary of Australian Federation.

The messenger family departed, direct for the airport aboard an air-conditioned government Toyota. The shapeless shift women continued their shuffling dance.

The men sang the messengers on their way.

Teddi had organised a comfortable, no-frills two-bedroom flat at Number 10 Hayes Street. Nearby we could watch the camel teams swing slowly past, kicking up a fine dusty wake at sunset, plodding homeward towards the Rural Area after their leisurely carriage of the day's tourists. Even with our books and CDs arranged on shelves we brought from Adelaide and with our own favourite artworks on the walls, it was difficult not to retain the sense that we were still in a motel room, and in some sense our lives were still in vacation mode.

Modest as it was, there was a postcard element about the units occupied by our neighbours. There was always a pair of saddles airing on the upstairs balustrade and a long row of blue jeans hung out to dry. When the cowboys were home for a few days we could hear their hilarity through their open door, decorated by a poster for Bundaberg Rum. There were usually empty rum bottles and VB green cans on the porch.

The cowboys reckoned they could get Teddi a horse. I rejected that fearing it might stomp some of our other neighbours. Next door lived a young indigenous mother and her toddler with a curly mass of hair so black it was blue, like a crow, like his mum. She had an armchair she sat outside in, talking on her mobile phone, laughing and chattering while the boy ran free with one of his cousins, a silent big-eyed girl with hair of spinifex-blonde.

Those kids loved Teddi. She gave them chunks of cheese and chocolates and they obeyed her when she told them not to hassle our pet bearded dragon while he was sunning outside. They circumnavigated the footpaths and the aloe and the oleander outside our front windows, round and round they'd go. They rattled sticks on the screen door and looked silently inside our world.

One day I took time off work and went out to the airport with Teddi to collect two of our Adelaide menagerie, the cats Ted and Baby. They weren't the kids, but they'd have to do.

The moggies were being ferried in as the excess 'personal' baggage of Peter MacDonald. Yes, my former boss at Channel 9 had relocated to Ross River Homestead, operated at that time by his mate Innamincka Mick Smith and Mick's wife Lee. Mac's marriage and connection with Arkaroola was over, alas just at the time that my book project with Griselda Sprigg was about to be published. But Mac now had a commercial pilot's license and he'd been freelancing scenic flights in his single-engine Cessna.

We relieved Mac of his burden and took off for Hayes Street. The cats were freaked and immediately disappeared inside the nearest cupboards. A few nights later, they allowed themselves to be coaxed out of hiding for a bit of suspicious exploration.

They'd soon settle, we promised ourselves, and so would we.

Imparja's Visions document might not have mentioned the newsroom, but it certainly recognised that a well-established and operated videotape archive was not only an important vehicle for recorded history, but also a source of money. Teddi was given the official title of Materials Collector. She moved into a big room, next to the newsroom's only edit suite. At first she had no phone, no computer, no air-conditioning, just a spare desk from my office and boxes full of jumbled videotapes, dead monitors, forgotten files, souvenirs from the glory days of Yamba the Honey Ant, and some swags for when the news crews went bush. There she commenced to build a library and archival tracking system for the material that had to be conserved.

Imparja's 'parent' organisation is the Central Australian Aboriginal Media Association. CAAMA had decided to do something about its own archiving and video systems, and it had a lot of shelves, plus some new archiving software. Was Teddi interested? You bet she was! Much to the astonishment of the station hierarchy, nobody among them having taken any interest in or responsibility for the direction of Teddi's initiatives, she had suddenly achieved the machinery of a decent tape library.

Her next initiative was to begin a system of preserving news material, shot daily. Introducing the system proved difficult. First Teddi had to persuade the Operations Manager to give her new tapes that she would assign for the daily use of the cameramen. Before she let those daily tapes go back on the road, she looked at the material that had been shot on the tape to decide whether it should be preserved. If so she gave the tape an archival number and a fresh tape would take its place.

Simple? Not for our boys. One was downright uncooperative – the other pretended to care. She persevered, going to great pains to explain this new bit of newsgathering to our small population at Imparja. She wrote memos, even hung up coloured bits of paper explaining to staff that in this box you kept shot material, in this box are your new tapes, and 'PLEASE DON'T SHOOT OVER PREVIOUS TAPES!'

I won't even detail the rigmarole that ensued when Teddi started asking tape operators to dub all local news stories onto an archive tape. This was unheard of!

She started to view the mess of tapes in the 'library' – boxes from various departments that had literally been dumped in her room. There was no context for her to evaluate them properly. She discovered this job would take months. She commenced.

So much valuable material. So little concern for it. She felt heartbroken.

The brilliant thing about having a company car was the weekend. Encouraged to use the Subaru to get out and explore, we did.

One of our favorite escapes was going west on Namatjira Drive through the western MacDonnell Ranges to Glen Helen Homestead on the banks of the Finke River. Here there's a permanent, deep, waterhole and a sheer red-rock gorge and clear, cool mornings, full of birdsong and, for a few moments right on sunrise the howl of a dingo or a dog gone wild in the rugged rocky hills.

We'd swim there, in the waterhole, Teddi and me and nobody else. I'd climb the crazily tilted ancient red rocks and gaze about amazed. I could see clear across to Mount Sonder, the Territory's tallest, glowering away to the northeast. And to my right I could see the valley of the Finke, flashes of still water pools in the sunlight, further legacy of recent rain.

One time we ended up going there, even when we didn't want to. It rained all Friday night. It rained a flood, with booming thunder and spectacular jagged lightning.

It was still drizzling in the morning, when we got a phone call from Mick Smith at Ross River Homestead: 'I wouldn't be coming out here, if I were you. We've had five inches.'

'Jeez. Is there no hope?'

'No way. Trephina Creek's running and there's three feet of sand at Bitter Springs. Mac's stuck in his caravan on the other side of the homestead creek. The water's gone, too.'

Five inches of rain, and the water's gone? Mick knew it sounded strange. 'The pipes are stuffed. They've all been washed downstream to buggery. There's nothing fresh for the dunnies or showers. Sorry, but I wouldn't be coming out.'

We decided to return to Glen Helen.

The return visit was a wonderful opportunity to savour for a second time that sumptuous waterhole but also a chance to read *The Glen Helen Story* by Bryan Bowman, who ran the pastoral lease from 1938 until 1984 and was one of the first to see the place had tourist potential. The homestead oasis there today is actually the third of four homesteads built within the original boundaries of the Glen Helen pastoral lease.

The first, now stony rubble, was built during the 1880s, when cattle were pioneered into country that was until then the exclusive domain of traditional Aborigines. The locals resented the intrusion. In sporadic raids they speared the cattle and, now and then, the invading pastorialists too. Glen Helen's cook, a fellow named Beattie, was speared twice during a raid on sugar and flower. He survived because his organs were protected by the man's 'brisketbone', next because he got his hand in the way and that was gored instead. A mounted copper, from Illamurta Springs south of Hermannsburg Mission, was sent to dispense the necessary justice. This would usually involve a long walk in neck chains to a far-flung courthouse, maybe Port Augusta or Oodnadatta.

Not long after Constable Cowle made his visit to Glen Helen, it was abandoned. The stock roamed unchecked until some time around 1900 when markets improved and a second homestead went up in the shadows of Mount Sonder. It lasted a season or two and was abandoned too. An Englishman named Fred Raggatt built the third homestead on the banks of the Finke, where a sheer red wall of rock plummets to the riverbank. He tried sheep as well as cattle then handed over to Bowman, cattleman turned eco-tourism pioneer turned author. These days his legacy combines comfortable cabins, the homestead restaurant and bar, a plethora of wildlife and brilliant scenery.

On Sunday as we checked out we discovered a deadly King Brown snake in the bar, somewhere under a fridge. There was a ranger coming up from Ormiston Gorge to try and hook it out. Meanwhile, the Glen Helen manageress was keeping well away from the bar until the creature was captured.

Close to the Alice, the usually brilliant colours of the ranges were subdued by heavy rain clouds, which emptied themselves all over town just as we came home.

The Hayes Street cowboys danced about in the deluge, and a boy from across the courtyard was cycling his girl around like Paul Newman and Katherine Ross in *Butch Cassidy and the Sundance Kid*.

In the morning, the ABC radio broadcast police warnings of flooding along the Todd River's low-level causeways. Once again, I flogged Imparja's pictures and yarn to the networks.

Thunderstorms continued all day and into the night. We had 103 millimetres in a single night, a battering downpour that sent January rainfall for Alice Springs into the record books. The rivers and flood-outs we'd crossed incident-free a day or two before were now impassable. By week's end the rain had moved on and the Todd was down to a trickle, decorated once again by the shining silver balloons of empty wine cask bladders caught in trees and clumps of grass during their skelter downstream.

The Todd River had flowed twice in a single season. One to go and we'd be locals.

Chapter 22

Disillusion

For a month or more, I had unavoidably become familiar with the Alice Springs Balloon Launching Centre. It was an institution that demonstrated beyond doubt that – even if NASA, the famous United States National Aeronautics and Space Administration, is involved – if it's happening in the Northern Territory and something can go wrong, it will.

NASA had a big balloon project. The balloon was supposed to be able to carry satellite-scale payloads to the limits of space for a fraction of the cost of rocket launches. Fully inflated, the balloon was boasted to be 'as big as the MCG' – the huge cricket and footy stadium in Melbourne.

Alice Springs is not exactly overcrowded with media outlets, but for weeks and bloody weeks, those of us in control of budgets had been paying our reporters and camera operators zillions in the forlorn expectation that NASA would get the bloody balloon into the air. The failed attempts invariably occurred before dawn on Sundays, thus ensuring the best overtime rates. Imparja's overtime bill alone would have paid for a rocket launch.

But, let the record show that on Sunday 25 February 2001, the balloon, carrying scientific instruments designed to measure something really obscure like cosmic dust motes, was launched at last. It ascended majestically, so slowly we could see it from Hayes Street. It floated west in a sunny blue sky, accompanied by a cheerful 'good riddance' from me.

And, let the record further show that, late that same afternoon, the balloon developed a helium leak and in 'a NASA-controlled descent' was returned to *terra firma* about 200 kilometres away.

I was not rid of the balloon. The NT was my patch. The news got worse. NASA was sending a team to retrieve the payload. *And* they had a spare balloon.

There'd be another launch.

Sometime.

Ka-ching!

Once again we were hoping for a weekend at Ross River, but the ABC radio news had me worried. Residents of Borroloola, a little town on the Territory side of the Gulf of Carpentaria, were 'battening down' for possible destructive winds from the newly declared Cyclone Wylva. Would our plans be scuttled once again?

One of the most infuriating and menial jobs in my strange job description was to keep watch on cyclone activity and warnings for the Top End and most of Queensland. If a warning was made, I had to get in touch with Presentation Control at the station, and dictate a 'crawl' to be run along the bottom of peoples' TV sets. I had protested that the PC operators could write their own crawls – taken straight off the bureau's website – if their computer was given internet access. 'Oh no!' The Operations Manager had retorted. 'They'd be on porn sites all night!'

For this reason, I consulted the Bureau of Meteorology's website warnings page, selected as a favourite on our home computer, and found that in cyclonic terms Wylva had turned into a bit of a wimp.

The Ross River trip was on.

Eighty-seven kilometres east of the Alice, the homestead and the lease were named after the Scottish explorer John Ross, who was helping Charles Todd decide the best route for the Overland Telegraph. The first European settlement there was in 1876.

Ross River ceased being a working station decades ago, most of its land parceled into neighbouring Love Creek. But there were picturesque acres surrounding the old homestead, and leathery stockmen to take the tourists on horse rides or camel treks varying from half an hour to several days. Teddi took a horse ride and I climbed the hill behind the homestead to get a photo of Teddi and her guide clopping across the still-flowing ribbon of Homestead Creek.

The view up there was incredible. We looked across the gap in the range to red cliffs, the white sandy riverbed, the river gums white and green and alive with birds, the long sweep of the valley disappearing towards the western horizon, and along the northern fringes of the valley, more creek beds washing down from the purple MacDonnells that loom behind like the giant caterpillars of the dreamtime they are.

We ate that night on huge rough-hewn picnic tables outside the homestead, meaty woodsmoke smells wafting past in the sudden chill of a cloudless Outback night, the stars above by the billions. But Mick was not his usual bluff charming self.

'You should get going early tomorrow. Forecast's gone to shit again.' He explained they had a big tour bus coming in and they had their fingers crossed it would arrive before the deluge.

I wish we had stayed. At least it would have delayed the news we received from the tearful girls at home in Adelaide. Our gregarious and relentlessly cheerful dog Biggles had fallen sick and died. They buried him near a big lavender bush in the back yard.

Teddi and I both felt terrible that we could not be there to ease their sadness. For the first time since we had arrived in the Alice, I wanted to go home.

From my journal: Saturday 20 January 2001

It's been hot for days – 45 Thursday, 44 Friday, 42 today, century heat all week before that. It's been a week of some substance, and evaporated opportunity. New weather graphics, the start of the digital news exchange. . . . Dwayne's had a week off, dealing with personal demons. Merv C has to decide between Imparja's nebulous promises and a 6-month contract with SBS in Sydney. Katrina R's off to study in Newcastle. Catherine L is hinting she's restless to move on. Nobody at Imparja appears to recognise the risk of implosion. Midweek I started writing a memo to the CEO, but Chris W went off on three weeks leave and asked me to wait until he gets back.

Sunday 11 February 2001

I am in a flithy mood. Fucking filthy. People at Imparja take no responsibility for bloody anything. There is a cyclone warning current, between Numbulwar and the Queensland coast. But according to Imparja there isn't. According to Imparja it's been fucking cancelled. Actually, you imbeciles, if you'd just look at your fucking fax machine, you'd find out that the warning has moved to another part of the coast and the warning has been updated with a new number. Number 16. It follows and updates Number 15. Simple enough? Not for Imparja, no way. Cyclones are fucking dangerous. But fuck it. The whole NT can get blown away for all I care.

After Ross River we decided to stop being soft and go camping. Our destination was the Ellery Creek Big Hole, a spectacular gap in the Lasseter Range, which boasts a frigid permanent waterhole so deep that one cramped-up drowned tourist has never been found.

We tempted no such fate, eating, as all good citizens should, well before we swam. We explored the rocky reaches upstream as the picnickers packed for home in the late afternoon. We set up camp to enjoy a sunset barbecue and rolled out the swags as the stars began to blaze.

Then four carloads of hoons turned up from town, P-platers with slabs of beer and one Eminem CD, which they proceeded to play full-bore and non-stop. Next to show up was a hotted-up Commodore. Its occupants were fans of heavy metal – also played full-bore. Beneath the stars, we tried to tolerate the stereo effect. Until another car-load turned up and built a bonfire about ten metres away and, about 10.30 pm, the party got into full swing, torchlight straying our way regularly to see if they'd managed to get us *really* pissed off. They had. Teddi was seething. We packed up and departed. Alas, during this process, Teddi fell and twisted the ligaments in her knee.

We thought nothing was broken, but after days of agony and no improvement from ice or heat, Teddi agreed we'd better visit the Alice Springs Hospital. The hospital's Casualty section was exactly that. A drunk sleeping it off in a corner cot, a man on emergency dialysis, another with a deep gash on his forehead, and a doctor patiently explaining to a woman who'd complained about the delay: 'You're not an emergency. Last night a guy nearly died from a stab wound right here on your bed. *That* was an emergency.'

A week after the fall Teddi was still virtually immobile. During that week, when I should have been home taking care of my invalid, I lost eight shifts to sickies and another eight to people on leave, which forced me to be at work, coping, coping, only just coping, and wondering whether the company might not be better off saving itself a million bucks a year and turning the news into a relay service.

Bleakly I realised that I had so few resources at my disposal that I was doomed to band-aid work, avoiding corporate embarrassment by getting a part-time presenter to re-hash crap from Network Ten.

I was not prepared to fight. I was coming up to my three-month probationary assessment and I was miserable. One Thursday I got a call from my former boss at the ABC in Adelaide, offering me a job producing the 7 pm TV news for serious pay. I was ready to walk out on this crazy confrontational Third-World oddity of a town.

That same night, the heavens opened once again, and for the third time in as many months, I woke to the sight of the Todd River flowing . . .

There's a local saying about the Alice Spring's hospital and the town's health system generally: 'When in pain, catch a plane.' We heard it a lot during the time of Teddi's knee trouble.

No bones were broken, we knew, but ten days after her fall the pain remained intense. One morning while I was at work, Teddi called an ambulance and checked in to the Casualty Department.

It took almost all day, but eventually she was seen by an orthopaedic surgeon who ordered an arthroscopy under general anaesthetic, during which he and the team 'trimmed a small meniscal lesion' and discovered not only some defective cartilage but also a torn anterior cruciate ligament which might one day demand a full knee reconstruction.

Teddi 'enjoyed' an overnight stay with self-administered morphine, confronting a yet-to-be-determined process of rehabilitation.

Once Teddi was settled in her room, off with the opiate pixies, I had a rendezvous with my immediate boss, who'd been badgering all day for a chance to talk me out of quitting. He was waving a fistful of promised new dollars and waxing enthusiastically about the projects Imparja *needed* if the company was ever to fulfill its charter obligations to produce genuine indigenous news. I sympathised with the man's plight. He'd hired me and right in his face, I was walking out.

I said I'd talk it over with Teddi, but the fact was that we had *already* talked it over – and we'd decided to go home.

The newsroom staff gave me a beautiful didgeridoo and a framed photo of lightning flashing over the Gap. Upstairs in the carpeted offices, there was much muttering and attachment of blame, but nobody really cared that I was leaving. My office was the 'transit lounge', after all. It was an inconvenience only, another ad to be placed in the *Weekend Australian*. I was another one who thought he could make a difference and ended up making none.

One of our last days in Alice Springs, a Sunday, happened to coincide with our 23rd wedding anniversary. Teddi had planned a surprise. She had secretly sought out and engaged a celebrant so we could renew our vows.

By the time she told me this, we were ensconced in a room at the Desert Rose Inn, exiting this time, and at the ABC's expense instead of Imparja's. The room was in chaos: hastily crammed suitcases, their contents strewn about among crutches and walking sticks, and it reeked of liniment.

It was hardly the place for a wedding. But Teddi had thought of that, and selected the motel's poolside garden for our ceremony. It also featured Meredith Campbell the celebrant, and Meredith's husband Michael, who doubled as witness and photographer.

By Sunday afternoon, the skies, which had been leaden all week, cleared to a warm, sunny day. Teddi, who had sneakily suggested she might like a new outfit (a good idea since I'd sent almost her entire wardrobe south with the removalists), was looking terrific. She was warily optimistic after the final days at Hayes Street, staring out the window, *Rear Window*-style, as one of our neighbours went crazy and the cops came to evict him, then two of the cowboys had an awful fist-fight. In those final days, all innocence had been lost.

Meredith looked like a cross between a sixties flower-power girl and a gypsy soothsayer. She and Teddi had devised a simple ceremony featuring the poetry of Robert Louis Stevenson, e e cummings and

Jonathan Bear. It also featured those famous 'I do' words, which that retired judge never had us utter on that snowy Saturday in Milwaukee, 23 years ago. I was permitted to kiss my beautiful bride, and Meredith rewarded us with freshly baked cheesy pumpkin scones.

It was a lovely ceremony and offered a sense of starting again, which is what we now had to do.

Back in Adelaide, Teddi commenced physiotherapy and gym work with a trainer who soon helped restore Teddi's faith in her knee. I commenced producing the ABC's 7 pm TV news.

Our return coincided with an issue that was dominating politics in the Adelaide City Council. The council had just done what many in the Alice would applaud. It declared a 'dry zone' in central Adelaide's parks and streets. Public boozing was to be outlawed in places like Victoria Square, so the tourists at the Hilton Hotel could look out from their balconies and no longer witness the dispossessed splayed senseless on the adjacent lawns. Now, the outcasts are exactly that. They have to take their casks and flagons and get themselves forgotten, out of sight and out of mind, somewhere in the parklands; somewhere beneath the omnipotent, optimistic sweep of Colonel Light's civilizing Vision.

Chapter 23

The days of terror

Just about everybody has their own, personally significant, recollection of what they were doing and where they were on 11 September 2001.

It was just after midnight on Australia's 12 September. Like Nancy Bear, watching helpless in a Hong Kong hotel room, we were riveted to the television newscasts for hours, Teddi and I taking turns trying to get through to Jonathan and make sure he was okay. The dreadful sight of the same plane careening into the same office tower from a half-dozen different angles was too Hollywood to be true, surely! But there too was the Pentagon burning. Desperate tiny figures hurled themselves from the burning towers. This was real and it was appalling, terrible to witness. Teddi was in tears until dawn. I was ready to get in to work way before usual, feeling useless but ready to help.

But there was no Adelaide-produced news bulletin that night, it was anchored from Sydney, sandwiched around wall-to-wall coverage from CNN and the BBC. Apart from producing a short piece on confirmation that an Adelaide expat was one of the first Australians confirmed dead in the World Trade Centre carnage, I did nothing all day. Like many of my ABC colleagues – their programs also pre-empted – I sat stunned and disbelieving, staring at a bank of TV monitors as they carried those awful signals of a world forever changed.

Teddi is no great American patriot, but when the post-mortems began on why Osama Bin Laden and Al Qaida and seemingly half the Islamic world hate America so much and ABC's radio listeners chimed in that America only had itself to blame, Teddi got upset. What could justify such a slaughter? Sure, America wasn't exactly squeaky-clean, but *nobody* deserved what happened in New York. But she kept her trap shut and suffered silently as the anti-American tirades continued.

She was homesick. She'd not worked since the Alice and the night of the knee. The government funded job agencies – having discovered she was married and I had an income – gave Teddi a file number and nothing else. The girls really *were* all grown up, in new and promising relationships. Suddenly Adelaide was feeling tired and parochial. In Taos, we had promised ourselves we'd return to the American south-west. Now we started wondering whether a quiet little nook of the USA might have some answers.

We decided to make a scouting mission. In April 2002, we'd make a near month-long drive from Los Angeles to Denver, and back again via a different route. We'd explore little-known places along the way, with a week in Denver itself to celebrate father Tedd's 80th birthday.

First we would need to renew our passports. Indeed, given the events of 11 September we decided it would be good if Sylvie and Myra were up to date as well. Being Aussies, Sylvie and I had no trouble. Born in the USA, Teddi and Myra remain US citizens and travel on Uncle Sam's passports.

It *seemed* simple enough. Two passports, soon to expire – send 'em off and get 'em renewed. We called the United States' Melbourne consulate and asked for the relevant forms to be posted out.

I have no great beef with bureaucracy. Everyone needs a job. It was easy enough to determine that we needed the pink form not the brown. But I would really like to know why the United States is the only country in the world that demands passport photographs be taken in a format that defies every photographic device except one that produces a brace of two-inch-square stressed-looking faces, at a cost of $12.50 per image (two required, per application, pink form and/or brown).

Getting the photos taken was by no means the end of the expenditure: based on the current pathetic exchange rate, it also cost 152 Aussie dollars for the passport renewals, plus $2.50 for sending the documents off to Melbourne, registered post. The Yanks took the bucks and processed the documents.

Then, they later insisted, they sent out the replacement passports and Australia Post lost them both. It took us a few weeks to realize something was wrong. Eventually, we called the Melbourne-based consulate to check. The consulate gave us the Express Post number the Yanks used when they sent the passports to Adelaide.

Australia Post confirmed the parcel reached the Regency Park Mail Handling Centre in Adelaide and was 'processed' at 6.54 am on the morning of the alleged delivery. After that several Australia Post customer service officials told us they 'assumed' the passports were delivered.

That might have been good enough for Australia Post, but it wouldn't get Teddi to America for sundry events like Tedd's 80th. We called the consulate again, this time for another batch of passports.

Now we learned that, when once the pink form would do the trick, now the brown form was required, *and* a Declaration Regarding Lost or Stolen Passports, *and* a Police Report ('Even if you have misplaced the passport in a house move or thrown it out with the trash, you must still lodge a police report') *and* new passport photos, *and* $228.00 for the *new* new passports.

You may assume that I was now feeling that at least *some* bureaucrats don't deserve jobs. Australia Post remained in official denial regarding their responsibility for the rapid and unnecessary thinning of my hair and wallet. I wrote a letter to the Commonwealth Ombudsman, demanding satisfaction. Sorry sir, no jurisdiction. Fill out an official Australia Post customer complaint form (8834928 (4/99)) and keep your fingers crossed.

I got one of the forms from the Post Office near the ABC, the same day I wanted to post the passport re-applications. It was then that I found out Australia Post does not accept credit cards to pay for Money Orders and I had to drive to the nearest ATM to get the cash. Money Orders are required because the United States government does not accept personal cheques from supplicants who live in Banana Republics like Australia.

Eventually, both the complaint and the passports re-applications were dispatched.

One day not long after, a large envelope arrived with the mail, embossed with important blue lettering: UNITED STATES CONSULAR BUSINESS. At last! The passports had arrived!

Not so fast, Joe. Our re-application documentation had been returned, with a form announcing that it was 'inappropriately witnessed' and informing us that – despite the fact we had earlier lodged to the same consulate full documentation allowing them to issue the brand new valid passports that Australia Post had then proceeded to *lose* – 'current photographic identification is required.'

There was a printed explanation to go with our rejection note. It read:

Identification: *You are required to submit one form of valid photographic identification, such as a driver's licence or Australian passport. A photocopy of your ID, certified by the official who witnessed your application form is acceptable, EXCEPT if you are a first-time applicant, or you are requesting replacement of a lost/stolen/mutilated replacement passport.*

Quite apart from the question of why the hell we'd be applying for an American passport if we already had Australian ones, there now arose the issue of what constituted valid photographic identification. We'd just have to send them Myra's Proof-of-Age card and hope she didn't get thrown out of Heaven Nightclub while the card was 'in the mail.'

As for Teddi, she doesn't drive and had no other photo ID, apart from her passport which was bloody well lost in the mail, old and new together! This was getting ridiculous. In mild desperation I called the US Consulate General and spoke to a guy named Paul.

'Paul,' I said, 'should I take time off work and come over to Melbourne with Teddi and Myra and all their birth certificates and everything else I can find just so you can look up the documentation you already have on file and say to yourselves, "Oh, yeah, they're okay." '

'I have a suggestion,' said Paul.

'What?'

'You could fill out an Affidavit of Identifying Witness.'

'What's that?'

'You certify you've known the applicant for so many years and the applicant is who the applicant says the applicant is.'

'And it gets to be witnessed by who, *appropriately*?'

'A clerk of the courts, a judge, or a Notary Public.'

'What about a Justice of the Peace?'

'No. Nor a policeman or a postal official.'

'Right. Well, can you send me out an Affidavit, plus a couple more brown forms. Or do we need purple ones now?'

'Haha, sir. Certainly, sir.'

The Adelaide *Yellow Pages* lists 27 Notaries Public. We found one and I sent it all off, certified mail. In a few weeks the replacement passports arrived.

But the original replacements were still unaccounted for. Australia Post continued to deny any responsibility – and refused to repay any of our now considerable costs.

In January 2003, more than 14 months later, among a few other sundry items, a small packet turned up in the mail. Inside, without any explanation, were two brand new United States passports, showing the first set of photos we'd paid so dearly for.

This time it was us who got to send stuff back.

While all this was going on, Australians were preparing to head for the nation's ballot boxes and vote for a new Federal government.

September 11 had given Prime Minister John Howard a wonderful political opportunity: he declared that Australia would stand shoulder to shoulder with its great democratic ally in the war against international terrorism.

Fair enough, but while he was uttering brave words like these, John Howard was also allowing would-be refugees from regimes like Afghanistan and Iraq, against which Australia would soon go to war, to be held in immigration detention centres in remote parts of the country – Port Hedland and Woomera to name but two. These people were 'queue jumpers' who must not be allowed to profit from their impertinence. They would be held until their refugee status was confirmed; they would be deported if it were not. Meantime Australian warships would patrol near Indonesian waters, turning back any shiploads of queue jumpers they might find.

The most famous case was that of the *Tampa*, a cargo ship captained by an experienced Norwegian, who ordered the rescue at sea of hundreds of would-be refugees. Their boat was sinking. The rescue was made and the *Tampa* steamed for the Australian territory of Christmas Island. The Navy blockaded the ship. The Norwegian steamed on, and defied the Australian orders. It stood off the island for days, the 'passengers' baking in the tropical sun. Eventually, after days of Australia's consistant refusal to allow the people inside Australia, a compromise was found – sending the ship on to Papua New Guinea, which along with Nauru would house the hundreds of *Tampa* refugees, and others who might happen along in future interceptions.

Another frightening case involved a boat crowded with hundreds of refugees. It sank with the loss of almost all on board. In another, a refugee boat sank and there were people in the water. All the media carried images of people in the drink – Australian navy pictures handed out by the government's minders. The Howard government lied that the queue-jumpers were throwing their children overboard.

I was sympathising with Teddi. The whole country was nuts if it couldn't see the Howard government's hypocrisy, yet my evening political stories from Canberra clearly showed there was public support for the detention policy – and turning back the boats.

The issue loomed as a major one in the election. Except that Labor Leader Kym Beazley knew full-well the PM was on a winner and he cravenly did far too little to argue for a more humane approach. He desperately tried to divert voter attention to domestic issues.

Whether Beazley failed or not, Australians would have to wait until the end of another major public event, an event in which they were probably far more interested: the Melbourne Cup.

Teddi had been there before, with Myra, who was so horse-mad she willingly spent her holiday pre-dawns in the racing stables of Semaphore Park and Morphettville, mucking-out, hoping for a ride, progressing to race-day strapping. The pair of them had become useful tipsters for the occasional foray along Prospect Road to the Blair Athol TAB. Who could forget the killing we made when the Cheltenham battler Len Smith trained Myra's beloved Skybeau to third in the 1996 Melbourne

Cup, then backed up a few days later with My Brightia at 65-1 winning the Oaks! Now it was my turn to try my finery on Flemington.

We got on the road from Adelaide a few ticks after 6 am, on a day that promised sweating showers. We dodged heavy trucks in the drizzle as the ABC radio news informed us with blithe objectivity that according to South Australia's Royal Automobile Association, the state's country roads are the nation's most lethal.

The Windsor Hotel is at 103 Spring Street, across from Victoria's Parliament building, a pair of ornate facades puffed up and regarding each other ceremonially across the street of trundling trams and pedestrians rushing for their trains.

Liveried doormen and valets and a concierge took charge of the car, our luggage and our selves, guiding us to reception across a lushly carpeted lobby filled by Australian landscape paintings and glass cases displaying antique jockey silks, past elaborate floral fantasies and armchairs that would swallow a child, past the entrance to the smoke-hazed Cricketers Bar to an elevator (for which we were given our own security key) and up to Room 127.

The TV weatherman on Channel 10 predicted that Melbourne Cup day would be wet. It might have been wet – at times it *poured* – but Flemington still managed to attract 92,477 paying customers that day. Like Teddi and myself, thousands upon thousands of them had gambled on good weather. There were jams of people guzzling the sponsor's beer and half-bottles of Seppelt's Great Western bubbly in the public concourses and the betting rings. Teddi sensibly suggested we get our Melbourne Cup bets on early, so we found ourselves fronting a bagman and scribe employed by the well-known Melbourne bookmaker Michael Eskander, three hours before the race and with no hope whatever of setting eyes on the twenty-plus runners.

Teddi took the imported Marienbard. I prefered the drifting but once fancied Freemason. Myra wanted ten dollars each-way on Rum, and Marty from Poochera, Teddi's beloved friend for years, fancied Rain Gauge. Teddi had an inspirational final hunch. She took a win-and-place wager on Ethereal, in honour of our man in Manhattan, Jonathan Bear. Never mind that Ethereal would be only the third mare in Cup history to collect the trophy. Never mind that no female trainer had *ever* guided a Cup winner to the post.

Next we tried to upgrade our general admission tickets to get some undercover seating, but everyone had had the same idea and covered seats sold out with me just three places from the ticket window. We had no choice but to brave the rain-swept lawns down by the running rails as close as we could get to the winning post.

There we met – among other colourful, variously inebriated and plastic-wrapped characters – an entirely sober and highly dapper Aboriginal bloke named Gordon Coulthard.

Gordon said he was an Adnyamathana Elder from the Flinders Ranges. I had recently read about him in the Adelaide *Advertiser*. He was the same man who gave the official nod to the Beverley Uranium Mine near Lake Frome, a place that took the wash from the uranium-rich hills of Arkaroola.

I asked Gordon why he made the decision and he told us he did it for the jobs. More importantly, in the context of the day, Gordon gave us his tip for the Cup.

Like his relative Gil from Balcanoona Station near Arkaroola, Gordon said he was an experienced horseman. He said he took riders out on the mountainous trails around Wilpena Pound. Gordon was also tipping Ethereal, 'no worries.'

I pause here to consider, with the wisdom of hindsight, that this was my cosmic cue, ethereally speaking, to head for the nearest bookie and put the entire contents of my wallet on the horse in question. After all, in a crowd of 92,477 people, how many Aboriginal horsemen from Wilpena do you run into, who also like horse number 13, drawn to run from barrier 13? It should have been obvious!

Posterity records that I stayed put, in soggy shoes and trousers now in dire need of a visit to the dry-cleaner, angling the Windsor's brolly into the stinging southwesterly wind attempting to shelter myself and the frantically shivering Teddi and a gaggle of asylum seekers slightly the worse for champagne. It was freezing.

Just before the start of the Cup, the rain stopped and I was able to drop the umbrella. It leaked run-off all over my pants, which just about sums up my fortunes when the race was run and Freemason ran second last, just behind Myra's Rum. Teddi's nag ran sixth ahead of Marty's Rain Gauge.

But as they say in the classics, all eyes were on Ethereal, who flashed home to overhaul the imported fancy Give The Slip, the Flemington sod flying in tribute.

Just after the triumphant mare skittered white-eyed past on the way to the dismounting yard, some idiot threw a streamer that spooked the horse. She reared and tossed the jockey, Scott Seamer, stomping on his foot when he landed, thus ensuring he had the rest of the day off to celebrate his unexpected (by me) win.

There was obviously some good money for Ethereal because we queued for ages in his collect line. While we waited we saw Eskander's bagman engrossed in a verbal altercation with an irritable-looking gent with longish grey hair, immaculately dressed in a duck-egg-blue morning suit. It was none other than Andrew Peacock, once dubbed the 'Colt from Kooyong'. Peacock still strutted the global stage as Australia's Ambassador to the United States, and he sure as shit collected his fist full of dollars that day. What a wad!

I wouldn't have minded a look at Gordon Coulthard's payout, either.

After the Cup was run and won, we took three nights to travel back to Adelaide. Our only timetable was getting home on Saturday, in time to collect Sylvie so she and I could cast our votes in the Federal election – she for the first time.

We were in Geelong by mid-morning. I remembered the city from student days as a pretty run down sort of place, the old inner city houses and warehouses and businesses neglected, many to the point of dereliction. The pubs were dour and cold. There was a film of cement dust on every external surface. Kardinia Park, home of the Cats footy team, was a parochial den of terrors for visiting sides, and their fans.

The city we drove into had been transformed. The town pier was a crowded complex of fun arcades and restaurants. Old warehouses along the Corio Bay waterfront had become new businesses. One was now the National Wool Museum, and the Wool Exchange Hotel looked like it had had a big amount of pokies profit spent on it. The downtown area was thriving. And it was clear that plenty of money too had been spent on renovating the many old homes in the central city area.

Geelong is the gateway to the Great Ocean Road. We travelled via Torquay and Bells Beach, astonished at the new housing developments Torquay had attracted. Torquay had been 'discovered.'

There was no great sense of that in Anglesea. Parts of it had had to be rebuilt after the Ash Wednesday bushfires a year or so after our last visit in the early 1980s. People then had fled for safety to the beach. I could not find Uncle Don and Aunt Bev's place on the slope above the beach. The street we thought we remembered featured new architectural masterpieces. Maybe Anglesea had been discovered too, but by necessity after the fires. Anglesea's 'seachange' was wrought by nature.

The weather was almost as crappy as Melbourne Cup day, but the views we saw along the Great Ocean Road would have been stupendous in any weather. Not far out of Airey's Inlet there's an archway that commemorates the returned World War I Diggers who battered this extraordinary roadway out of the steep coastal slopes of the Otway Ranges. From Lorne to Peterborough on the western side of Cape

Otway, they toiled for 14 years, from the end of the Great War to the depths of the Great Depression. The original road was a dirt track barely wide enough for a single vehicle, with wooden fencing hand-hewn from the Otway forest the only protection from a tumble onto the rocks and into the sea.

Teddi thought the current road was just as bad. It remained a narrow one, and people with fast cars and the attitude of the immortal cornered faster than sedate suburbanites from Adelaide would prefer. They hurtled around oncoming corners and crept towards our lane; or they tailgated all the way to the scenic lookouts. I pissed Teddi off a dozen times by turning in to let the impatient bastards go past, but at least I got some good photos.

We were looking, on a beautiful road that tracked uphill from Apollo Bay, for Arcady Homestead. Once an eyrie for farmers who more than a century ago first felled the timber, then ran perilously sloping paddocks of sheep and dairy cattle, Arcady was now given over to bed and breakfast accommodation.

And a good thing too. We were the only guests and had the white weatherboard homestead to ourselves, playing chess in front of a roaring fire, sipping the wine our hosts had gifted us, sleeping like proverbial logs in a room full of well-matched antiques.

In the morning I walked down through Arcady's gardens to the Barham River Road and followed it upstream for a while. The scene was alive with natural noise. The water rushed and babbled and now and then cracked a river rock against another. As I climbed I could still hear the regular call of Arcady's rooster. It joined a cacophony of magpies and crows, kookaburras and bowerbirds and parrots flapping and feeding and hunting high in the forest of mighty trees, for some reason saved from the axe.

Beyond Apollo Bay the road climbs into the Otway Ranges National Park, where bushwalkers can meet the forests and the ferns, and camp among them. We followed a side road that plunges due south to the Cape Otway Lighthouse. I guess the complex of restored buildings got privatized, because there was an entrance fee, and no such thing as a self-guided walk. Being the world's greatest cheapskate, I suggested we leave and head for the Twelve Apostles, the remarkable group of rocky eruptions that look like they've been speared into the sea. There we found the same thing had happened to sightseers at the local visitor's centre.

It didn't matter to us. Both places were so busy with tourists – the Apostles visitors centre had half a dozen big buses pulled up outside – that we were happier just pulling off the road to check out the Ocean

Road's less popular attractions. There's certainly no lack of them, and they're just as spectacular: the area west of Cape Otway is not called the Shipwreck Coast for nothing.

One such place is the Loch Ard Gorge. The gorge is named for the clipper ship *Loch Ard*, which ran aground on a nearby island en route from England in 1878, with 54 passengers and crew aboard. Only two people survived the grounding and the ship's destruction by wave and rock; both were washed into the wildly pretty gorge with its vertical cliffs and clear turquoise waters and its tiny haven of pure sandy beach. One of them was Eva Carmichael. She was travelling from England with her parents, three sisters and two brothers. The bodies of her mother and elder sister were washed ashore. They are buried in the forlorn little cemetery at the top of the gorge. You can look out from that sad place and feel how pathetic a human body really is, pitted against the immoral blast of nature. Similar wreck sites are spread all along this western coastline. From Moonlight Head to Port Fairy, the maps name dozens of ships that came to grief.

Port Fairy was our next destination, and it was completely different to the improvised pseudo-camping experience we'd had there in the early 1980s. Teddi had found us an attic room in a restored bed and breakfast called Merrijig Inn. Built in 1841 it claims to be Victoria's oldest inn, even if it did service in the 1850s as a police barracks, and was also used as a courthouse. I was ready to concede that this well appointed B and B beat the hell out of camping.

Robe, across the border in South Australia, is also historic and picturesque but we felt it was groaning with more tourists and retirees.

We could have done another night in a B and B there, but suddenly the places we drove up to seemed so bloody naff that all we wanted to do was find a simple motel room with a telly and a fridge to keep a six-pack cold.

We found such a place in Kingston, in southeast South Australia. There was a pool in the courtyard, but the weather was still crappy so we just vegetated in front of the TV news. The news was all about the federal election, and late breaking evidence that the Australian government *had* lied about the circumstances in which boat people 'asylum seekers' allegedly threw their children overboard when their illegal boat voyage was intercepted at sea by HMAS *Adelaide*. The Labor Party huffed about this late outrage, but did nothing to decry the fundamental policy issues. Labor had lost its socialist heart, the unwritten credo that a responsible government would give battlers a fair go. The party would need a miracle to win.

I was in no mood to give them one. We snapped off the news and went for dinner. In the morning we bypassed the Coorong and drove straight into Adelaide. Sylvie and I cast our votes by lunchtime. How she voted is her business, but I will confess that for the first time in my political existence I did not vote a straight Labor ticket. I voted first for the Green Party, because Bob Brown's mob at least took a morally backable stance on the asylum issue.

Plenty of voters did the same. Labor collected its lowest primary vote since 1931.

Labor got what it deserved, and so did we, the voters. As I write, Labor remains in the political wilderness and John Howard is some kind of hero after sending Australian forces to war in Iraq and not losing a single soul. Yet.

Chapter 24

Touring practice

I thought Teddi must be practising for our American journey, still some months away. More likely she was just trying to get me – working 11-plus hour days and a classic stress case – out of town.

We travelled 1268 kilometres over two days to visit our mate Marty in Poochera. In February 2002 we went to Angaston in the Barossa Valley to see how the town makes its annual contribution to South Australia's country show circuit. It contributes horses and girls who make them jump; and a second-hand bookstall where for two dollars I got the book that has told me everything I need – or *want* – to know about the history of Port Pirie.

A long week at work then intervened, our rural meanderings interrupted first by the arrival in Adelaide of the former US President Bill Clinton, then Queen Elizabeth and Phil the Greek, with the associated producer's nightmare of facilitating satellite feeds for visiting hacks from the BBC and other Pommy newshounds. I was sidetracked by all of this, but Teddi had been on the look out for a getaway. One Saturday morning she rustled the morning paper in my half-asleep face and declared: 'There's a shrimp festival at Wallaroo.'

In Australia we call them prawns, and I was sceptical. I was supposed to be a newshound, yet I had heard nothing of it. But on page 35 of the Adelaide *Advertiser*, 2 March, there was the proof:

> Prawnfest 2002: Prawn cooking demonstrations and recipes, food, wine, live entertainment, fireworks over the harbour from 9.30 pm. Fresh prawns from trawlers docked at the marina, being sold at special Prawnfest prices. At Wallaroo Marina, from 11 am.

I am a sucker for a fresh prawn and a bargain. This was all the encouragement I needed. We did the weekly shop in record time, grabbed an Esky for ice and prawns, and hit the road.

Being an optimist, I had a mental image of the Prawnfest: it would be spread out in colourful tents along a sunny, well-grassed foreshore shaded by Norfolk Pines, the prawn trawlers bobbing alongside an historic jetty festooned with fisher folk catching bag limits of garfish, whiting, Tommy Ruffs and ink-squirting squid. The reality was somewhat less inspiring.

Signs directed us into what seemed like a new suburban subdivision.

It *was* a new suburban subdivision called Copper Cove Marina and it featured no less than 310 waterfront allotments and 160 'streetscape' allotments, almost none of which had yet been built on. The marina was so new its waters looked like they trickled in on yesterday's tide and were dyed blue by giants tossing in fists full of food colouring. There was not a tree or a blade of grass. The enormous mud-brown earthworks were barren as a battlefield.

Forced by 'road closed' barricades to park somewhere back near Adelaide, we joined hundreds of our fellow prawn enthusiasts walking down a new, freshly curbed road outrageously called Heritage Drive towards the foreshore-to-be, where people with leather money bags took our three-dollar admission fees before we could actually see what we were paying for.

I had seen such dismal scenes before: the burned and looted caravan of massacred Turks in *Lawrence of Arabia* sprang immediately to mind. The Prawnfest site had been established on top of a bald, sand-covered hillock, the sand billowing like a smoke-cloud, blown straight into our eyes by a stiff southwesterly wind. On the fringes were the stalls where unhappy-looking entrepreneurs offered embroidered pillowcases and Dagwood Dogs just like the ones at Angaston. In the middle was a group of marquees, into which people were crowded for shelter, picking bits of grit out of their ten-dollar paper plates of seafood. One of the marquees had no covering. It was just framework, but people were huddled there too. Their misery was palpable.

As for the prawn trawlers, there was one, tied up at one of Copper Cove's '24 commercial fishing berths' with a sign announcing that prawns would be on sale for 16 dollars per kilo from 3 pm.

The sandstorm intensified. We decided to come back for the prawns and got out quick. We found an outdoor café that faces the town jetty and watched the big grain trucks rolling out to load a freighter. Then we drove south to the pretty little vacation spots of Moonta Bay and Port Hughes. We gobbled ice creams, filled the Esky with ice and started back to Wallaroo.

I managed to get lost in the back blocks of Moonta, and by the time we returned to the Prawnfest it was nearing 4 pm. Considering the prawn sales were supposed to go on until 9.30 pm, we figured this was still plenty of time. No such luck. When I got through the sand cloud to the marina shore, I saw a forlorn gaggle of defeated people standing around the lone trawler. No words were needed.

'Sorry, mate,' said a deckhand when I asked, in the stupid hope that I had misinterpreted the body language. 'There's a truck coming with more at six. We sold out in half an hour!'

By this time I had realized that the Prawnfest was just a ploy by local businesses to get visitors to spend money somewhere else in town while they waited for non-existent trawlers to arrive with non-existent supplies of seafood. I wasn't getting sucked in twice! We left for Adelaide.

Tungali Cottage is a comfortable four-room farmhouse at the foot of Mount Crawford, about an hour's drive northeast of Adelaide and a stone's throw south of the Barossa Range. This range divides South Australia's most famous wine-grape district in the Barossa Valley from the beautiful Eden Valley, nearly as well known for its excellent Rieslings. We'd started going there on our 20th wedding anniversary in 1998, and instantly been charmed by Elizabeth Gordon's welcome trays, with home-made soups and an abundance of local fruits, cheeses, breads, nuts and wine. There was an open fire, plenty of extra wood, and – unless you hoped to catch some footy on the just-this-side-of-colour TV – nothing to do but relax and forget the woes of the world.

The visit before my cancer diagnosis, we were loitering in the sun-drenched kitchen. The sun was up and climbing, magpies and parrots squabbled in the red gums outside the cottage window, beyond which the paddocks were rolling green like a fairway. The Mount Crawford old growth forest glimmered orange and olive as the sun climbed higher and we polished off an enormous breakfast. Teddi sliced and buttered Elizabeth's banana bread for our pincic lunch, while I browsed a pamphlet that suggested a route for the day's explorations: a self-guided drive along the so-called Mount Crawford Heritage Trail.

The trail took us on a zigzagging circuit of about 50 kilometres into the Barossa Range, past historic homesteads like Corryton Park and Pewsey Vale to the Barossa's first German settlement called Hoffnungsthal. On the southern part of the loop, travelling through a state-owned pine forest to the Mount Crawford pioneer cemetery, a long held question about Tungali at last got its answer.

Tungali's own pamphlets tell visitors that their hosts are Doug and Elizabeth Gordon. This was our fourth visit, but we had never encountered Doug. We joked he'd gone loopy and Elizabeth locked him up for the safety of the guests.

At the cemetery, its chapel burned out by a bushfire in the 1880s, we encountered two Gordon graves. One rested the Gordon family patriarch and his bride, the headstones' lettering weathered and overgrown with lichen and moss.

Further down the hill we found Doug's resting place, beautifully made and cherished since his death in 1996. On his plaque, Elizabeth records that Doug was not only her husband, but also her best friend.

Elizabeth is a proud and private person. I would never have asked the whereabouts of Doug. Our silly joke seemed awful now. We returned to Tungali feeling more than a little chastened.

As I dozed off to sleep that night, before the cosy hearth that had seen a thousand fires built by Gordons and the pioneers before them, I mused for a moment on my own predicament.

I wondered, when the time came to lay me down, whether Teddi – like Elizabeth – would recall me not only as her husband, but as a best friend, who was lucky enough to travel with her for the while that became a lifetime.

Chapter 25

Way out west

There was something hopelessly quixotic about the way we approached our trip through scattered parts of the western USA about six months after 11 September. Our only ground rule was to keep off the roaring Interstate freeways as much as possible, and to lob into as many hokey little hamlets and flag-waving tidy towns as possible, to give ourselves an idea of what we would be in for if we actually *moved* there.

This was a rule often to be broken, because freeways are great for reeling in some serious miles if you need to, and we did have to get from LA to Denver and back again in the road trip we'd planned, a distance that ended up totalling 3765 miles (6024 kilometres). But the chief and only definite plan *was* to hit the back roads as often as possible. After that, things would take care of themselves.

The Hertz guy wouldn't have cared if the cops had out an all states alert for a deranged Australian. So long as I had a credit card he was happy to hand me the key to a dark-blue Ford Taurus and a scribbled mud map to Interstate 105, after which we were on our own.

Within minutes we were sucked off a ramp into the eye of an eastbound hurricane. From slick new Mustang convertibles to rust-eaten clunking gas-guzzlers held together by rainbow stickers from 1971, every vehicle on the road was flagrantly flouting the speed limit. Drivers had their spare arms flung casually over passenger seats, fingers tapping in time to blaring sound systems or animatedly connecting for earnest conversations on their cell phones, everybody lane hopping like they were inspired by slalom racers from the Winter Olympic Games, just ended in Salt Lake City.

Teddi fiddled with the air conditioning to try and stop me sweating, calling out in near panic when I strayed in the wrong lane. The ruts in the concrete road surface made the tyres flap madly, like I had a flat. I thought for sure I'd have to stop, but Teddi refused to let me. Then the road surface changed and the tyres sang.

Our destination, the Cozy Chipmunk Inn at Lake Arrowhead, was a serendipitous four-storey pale-blue wooden structure, flying the obligatory Stars and Stripes, festooned with fairy lights and set among forest pines. It had steep wooden stairways and an old letterbox nailed near a top-floor landing with a hand-painted sign saying AIR MAIL, and a toy chipmunk hanging out of it, presumably waiting for the mail plane.

Apart from us, the only guest seemed to be a wheezy old lady who managed to be at street level and on all the landings simultaneously, engaging me in conversation as I lugged our heavy luggage up the stairs. 'Where you from, son?'

I was fresh off the plane: 'Stray-ya', said I.

'Beg pardon?'

I gathered my wits. 'Oh sorry. Oss-trell-ya.'

The penny now dropped and she nodded, businesslike. 'What kinda wildlife you got there, for huntin'?'

I told her that in Australia we killed and/or ate both of our national emblems, kangaroos and emus, with equal delight 'and often with quandong relish'. She considered this small joke as I went back to the car for more bags.

At 3 am, when I woke up and had a sinus attack from the altitude or pollens or something ghastly, Teddi started watching 'Let's talk Sex.' There was a guy with a sleazy black moustache and a horrible Hawaiian print shirt, talking to a blonde who badly needed Andy McDowell's L'oreal anti-ageing products.

They were flogging some miracle pill called Extenz.

'It makes your penis 25 per cent bigger after just a few weeks,' said Mr Hawaii.

'*And* it works in 98 per cent of cases,' said the crone-to-be, looking at Mr Hawaii with baleful lack of conviction, like he must be one of the pathetic two per cent for whom even the famous Swedish Dikkblastter has been a dismal failure.

Suitably emasculated, Mr Hawaii threw to an ad break. It was just for me. 'You know,' said an actor in a white coat who looked like an archetypal caring doctor, 'Americans contend with billions of allergens every day.'

I sneezed and blew my nose for the 19th time on some of the Cozy Chipmunk's complimentary Kleenex and paid attention. There was a voice-over, sympathising with a montage of cute-but-nasally-challenged Americans trying but failing to go about their daily business of clinching huge Wall Street deals *and* winning the Nobel Peace Prize. 'You need SneezBan! Now with extra NoChoke.' The young folk with perfect teeth looked suddenly and fabulously revitalized.

The next ad had a former United States presidential candidate – I think it was Bob Dole – flogging Viagra.

Unimpressed, Teddi started channel surfing. There was a pseudo-doco about a high school love triangle that led to a shooting mass murder.

I blew my nose again. SneezBan, eh?

Through Fawn Skin and Big Bear City we were among tall mountain pines and pockets of snow that had so far survived the spring thaw. Then the landscape changed dramatically. A zigzagging twenty-mile descent through rocky cactus scrub left us in a dustbowl where occasional lone horses were corralled among scattered trailer homes and gutted cars.

Beyond a dusty town with the dismally inappropriate name of Lucerne Valley, we encountered a real-life Boulevard of Broken Dreams. A brand new divided road led to a subdivision of dead palms and fallen signs advertising a non-existent golf course. Then there was a 35-mile flat run along Highway 247 that featured bullet-riddled signs warning us that our speed was being monitored by aircraft. I'm glad to report we made it all the way to Barstow without being dive-ticketed by a flying sheriff.

Barstow could have been our first-night destination. I suggested it. The name popped out at me one night at home in Adelaide while I was looking at maps. It seemed familiar. Then I remembered. It was a literary connection: 'We were somewhere around Barstow when the drugs began to take hold.'

Yes indeed, Hunter S Thompson and his Samoan attorney had hurtled past Barstow at 90 miles an hour, 'in a horrible, slobbering sort of spastic stupor,' just before they terrorized an innocent Okie hitch-hiker en route to even more substantial *Fear and Loathing in Las Vegas*. There was obviously some acid-flashback part of my psyche that believed it would be cool to go there, too.

Barstow prides itself as being the gateway to the Mojave Desert, which I guess should have had me looking at the map a little closer. I would then have noted Barstow's close proximity to the aptly named Death Valley, and also to the area's multiple military purposes – which include the Marine Corps Air-Ground Combat Center, the Fort Irwin Military Reservation and the Inyokern Naval Ordnance Test Station. About the only part of the area that's not either restricted or dangerous or both is Barstow itself.

'You wanted to stay *here*?' Teddi demanded incredulously as we rolled down a long dusty hill into town and found ourselves near a strip of Motel 6 and Best Westerns that cater no doubt to military types in town for a bit of bombing practise and low flying – both in *and* out of aircraft, if you get my drift. I was happy to get back on the freeway.

For a hundred miles we dodged the maniacs on I-15 as they raced towards Las Vegas across the state line in Nevada, listening to some idiotically cheerful DJ describing the city's routine roadway carnage and seeing some too.

By osmotic agreement, we had no intention of stopping overnight in Las Vegas. We took a long easterly detour, down to where the Colorado River is dammed up to form Lake Mohave, on the edge of which the map showed a place called Cottonwood Cove.

It was a lovely drive, down into the rugged river valley, and the Cottonwood Cove motel looked big and clean and modern. It was booked solid, and the matron in the office had her ham-sized arms folded so firmly across her chest I knew there was no point hoping for a cancellation. I asked for alternatives.

'In Searchlight? Thirty-nine dollars plus tax'll get you a room at the El Rey. It's the only place in town.' She gave a mirthless chuckle. '*They'll* have a room.'

The screen door to the El Rey's office nearly fell off its track when I tried to open it, and I could smell the years of stale cigarette smoke long before I got there, but I forked out my Visa card and asked where a man could find a meal.

'Nuggets, son,' said the concierge, handing me a key. 'That's the casino. You got all-day breakfast, dinner or lunch, whatever. It's 24-seven.'

Like her office, the restaurant stank of smoke. The menu had food like beef liver and onions, chicken fried steak and fried catfish nuggets. We ate hungrily and watched half a dozen wizened oldies pumping quarters into slot machines. A younger woman scored a payout and a scrawny desperado in a bowling shirt materialized eagerly at her side. He scooped a pile of quarters into a paper Pepsi cup and headed for the bar. The bartender was even more wizened than the oldest of her patrons. She dragged on a cigarette and gazed across the gaming room with a look of vast indifference. I'm not sure what kind of small-town American heart beat inside her, but she looked like she could use a drink or it might just stop pumping.

Next morning we were on the road by seven. Our detour into the Nevada boondocks may have saved us from an overnight in Las Vegas, but unless we could walk or drive on water and magically get ourselves east of the Colorado River, we still had to navigate our way through the infamous Nevada drawcard. We cranked north with the early-morning big rigs on US-95 and got to Vegas with the commuters.

Just past Railroad Pass, a sweep of awful new subdivisions in which every house is identical, we got a panoramic view of the city. The downtown buildings were invisible. Incoming aircraft disappeared beneath a wide blanket of brown smog. Even the distant slopes of Mount Charleston were stained. We got on I-15 northbound and kept on going.

Teddi might be an American, but she was seeing everything with the same stranger's eyes as me. The desert landscape was just as awesome, the mysteries of the names and bizarre topographies just as compelling to speculate about, because so many of their names called out to us: would we be welcome in the Moapa River Indian Reservation? What about the Valley of Fire? There was the border town of Mesquite, much tidier than Vegas, with its casino resorts and riverside golf courses like linked oases in a wild world where, like us, every human is only passing through.

Maybe, just maybe, we would find a place that said to us: 'Stop. Don't go. Yes! Live here!'

We stayed on I-15 as it cut across the northwestern corner of Arizona, climbing through a spectacular lower gorge of the Virgin River towards Utah and the landscapes of Canyon Country. Just outside the little city of Saint George, Utah, we came to a Visitors Center, where a smiling elderly lady redolent of pioneering Mormons told us to be sure to visit Zion National Park and go for a drive along a 'Scenic Byway' with the romantic name of State Route 12. She did not add that we'd be wise either to have no fear of heights or a good stash of Valium, so we happily took her advice, feeling like we'd just been stuffed with home-made icecream and apple pie.

One way to get to Route 12 is to literally drive right *through* the Zion park, so that's the way we went, innocently starting out on what looked like a short run along the Zion–Mt Carmel Highway. The road was engineered in 1930, amid predictions the project would prove impossible. At first it was hard to tell what the fuss was about. We were travelling upstream along the now babbling Virgin River, past cottonwood copses and orchards and campgrounds and beguiling little towns with names like Springdale. But then the Zion Canyon walls started to close in, glowing like fire and brimstone above the road as it began a steep climb, leaving the boulder-strewn river far below, snaking perilously around sheer-sided walls with vertigo views, through a mile-long, unlit tunnel to a series of high plateaus where the mesas look like frozen flowing mud. Here we safely stopped to take a photo, knowing the frame had no hope of capturing the sheer, boggling grandeur of the vista – nor the winding terror of the narrow-track climb: 2750 feet in less than ten miles.

We were attracted to a tiny town called Glendale, where we found an even tinier room in a bed and breakfast full of antiques and genuine Navajo rugs called Historic Smith Hotel. It had hostesses named Rochelle and Bunny, and a back yard that ran clear to the beautiful sandstone cliffs of the Markagaunt Plateau.

The paint has peeled in Glendale, Utah – it was no postcard. But there was a beauty about it, because it was not far off being a ghost town and the little town was reverting to nature. There was a pick-up truck with a load of fruit-tree prunings that hadn't been driven for so long its tyres were flat. There was a country store that said it was open when it was clearly locked fast. There was an abandoned Sinclair Oil gas station with its green brontosaurus logo looming over the road like a fossil from the Museum of Modern Times. There was a car graveyard too, and most of Main Street was long ago boarded up.

But there was a fruit market there, too, ready to re-open for another season. Ranks of trees in the orchards set back from the road were set for bud-burst. The general store was busy with customers. The back roads off Main Street featured rows of tidy houses and pick-up trucks and yards with horses and hogs. Business may have been slow, but there was a community here. Rochelle and Bunny told us over a breakfast of French toast and maple syrup that there was a push from the local Chamber of Commerce to have Glendale go back to its original name of Berryville and everyone thereabouts would be happy with that. Whatever it amounted to, the spirit of survival surely seemed to be living on in Glendale: people had found their patch here. And, unlike Teddi and me, they weren't going away.

We were in a beautiful valley following a meandering northbound creek called the Sevier River, with neat farms in the floodplain, immaculate horse and cattle ranches on the slopes, plateau tops stretching to the horizon. We were in no hurry to leave. There was a furze of the Aboriginal horseman at the Melbourne Cup. A human horse whisperer was calling. For the first time on this serendipitous journey, we found ourselves saying to each other: 'You could *live* in a place like this!'

We followed the entire stretch of Utah's Route 12 that day. It was the most spectacular drive of our lives. At day's end we felt the same sort of sensory overload you might experience inside a major art gallery if you try to take in the pointillists and impressionists as well as Picasso's blue bits, all in one go.

Beyond the oddly named cow town of Tropic, which lies on a floodplain beneath the soaring ramparts of hills that hide the awesome

Bryce Canyon, we came to a state park with the even stranger name of Kodachrome Basin. It was full of the sort of impossible geography you see in the old Roadrunner cartoons, including rocks that looked like they'd successfully been taking Extenz for the past umpteen millennia and had the balls to prove it. Table Cliff Plateau was tiered like the layers of some enormous prehistoric wedding cake. We inched to the top of a frighteningly narrow ribbon of road called Hog's Back, teetering above Escalante Canyon on one side and Box Death Hollow on the other. At Boulder, which until 1940 received its mail by mule cart, we saw the excavated ruin of a ridge-top pueblo that housed about two hundred Anasazi for several generations back around 1000 AD.

Out of Boulder, a tiny town that bears absolutely no resemblance to its namesake in Colorado, we found ourselves in the Dixie National Forest. Climbing through 8000 feet, the pines gave way to a beautiful aspen forest that offered glimpses of deer. The forest stretched unbroken all the way to the summit of Boulder Mountain at 9400 feet. It's the highest forested range in the United States. It overlooks a mind-boggling hundred-mile view clear across the Escalante Staircase canyons and down, down, to where the Colorado River cuts towards the Grand Canyon. It's awesome, just bloody awesome. Go there if you can.

Route 12 ended near a little town called Torrey. We cut west on Highway 24 towards Hanksville. Still that Utah roadway kept turning up amazing sights: Capitol Reef National Park, hidden valleys with human stories inscrutably told in Indian rock art, buttes and mesas. There were mountainsides that looked like frozen flows of once-molten ash-coloured lava, picturesque improbabilities made stranger by the fact that some of the locals seemed to enjoy driving all-terrain vehicles up and down the muddy slopes like they were the sides of some prehistoric skateboard rink, their tracks like the graffiti of wild white Cavemen.

Next day, still queasily digesting last night's Redrock Restaurant and Campground 'Navajo taco' – a plate-sized thick crust pizza strewn with red kidney beans and molten bits of cheddar that even I couldn't finish – Teddi consulted our maps while I made some serious miles, crossing the San Rafael Desert to Interstate 70, then cranking east to Colorado. We still had one more night before we were due in Denver, so we stopped at the visitors' center at Grand Junction and loaded up on pamphlets.

I figured it was my turn to choose a stop. I picked the historic mining town of Leadville.

'That's in the *mountains*,' said Teddi, who had had quite enough of life-threatening narrow roads in the Zion Canyon and along Route 12. I conceded this was true. Indeed, we would have to climb up through Tennessee Pass (a mere 10,424 feet) to get there.

'There'll be *switchbacks*!'

'True again.'

'You're not to go over twenty!'

'Okay.'

No matter how slow you're going, to get to Leadville from I-70 you get onto Highway 24 at a place called Minturn. This is where Teddi attempted a last stand. 'It's pretty here.'

'It'll be prettier in Leadville.'

'You're tired.'

'There's a gas station. I'll get coffee and a candy bar.'

I went to make the purchase. Teddi disappeared inside an antiques store and showed no inclination to come out. This was dangerously close to *shopping*. I stayed outside and drank the coffee. Still she lingered. I relented and went inside, and found myself back in the Wild West, lost on a frontier of woodsmen and trailblazers and Indian tribes. It was wonderful. 'Wow!' she breathed. 'I could *live* here!'

In Leadville we got a room at the Timberline Motel, which is on the main street across from the Silver Dollar Saloon and just a few doors south of the so-called Hyman Block where 'Doc' Holliday shot his last man in 1890. In between is the Tabor Opera House, which opened in 1879 and next door is the Bonanza Trading Company where we met a lady who might have been able to help Teddi track down a history story of her own. Her name was Running Deer, but she also went by the name of Mary McVicar. Her business specialized in Native American art and craft and clothing. Teddi got a pair of Taos moccasins there and while the Visa machinery was humming, she and Running Deer got talking.

Teddi explained how her grandmother was one-quarter Indian but nobody in her family had ever wanted to talk about the background and by the time Teddi got interested in finding out more, there was no-one left to ask. Running Deer reckoned that various Indian tribes had growing databases of family trees. She showed us a huge book that listed the relevant groups to contact, but there was no point asking unless a searcher had a valid tribal starting point, for example a known reservation and some dates to work with the names.

I hoped the trail was not dead. Teddi decided to ask some questions in Denver.

I could have lingered longer in Leadville, checking out the old mine works and rummaging in the museums. It was a place of spectacular views, and a morning shop-walk revealed that the local newspaper was looking for a journo. I considered finding out what the package involved, but the office was locked up and there seemed to be nobody inside. And we could both have stayed for another of Quincy's Steak & Spirits' unbelievable $5.95 filet mignon dinners. But now we were due in Denver.

We wanted to get there early enough to check into La Quinta Inn at Cherry Creek, chosen because of its proximity to Tedd's place, do some much needed laundry, and get out to Denver International Airport in time to collect Wyeth, who was due in from Milwaukee at 5 pm.

Leadville's only a few hours from Denver, downhill from the 'rim of the Rockies' all the way, but suddenly we were in a hurry. On Channel 9's breakfast news, we saw the story of how one *entire* section of Interstate 25 near downtown Denver had been blocked when a huge crane toppled over and fell across every lane, squashing several cars in the process, miraculously with no serious injury. Live helicopter-based updates confirmed the accident was causing mayhem. We had to travel along I-25 on our way to La Quinta. Would we encounter the blockage? Should we allow extra hours?

As we drove down on Colorado Highway 91, past a ski area called Climax and three 14,000-foot crags called Mount Democrat, Mount Lincoln and Quandary Peak, looking for Interstate 70, we learned more from the radio. The company that crashed the crane was now suspended and under investigation. It might have been in deep shit, but *we* needn't have worried. Freeways are the lifeblood arterials of urban America. Authorities had the mess cleared up well before we got into traffic-clagged Denver.

Still, I could not relax. There was the unknown factor of the run to Denver International Airport to get Wyeth. The well-meaning clod at the La Quinta desk gave me directions that defied all cartographic logic. On my map, I could see what looked like far shorter routes. In the end, though, I followed the fool's flight plan, on the basis that it was local knowledge.

Had local knowledge prevented the crane collapse? For nearly two hours, for more than 20 miles, we were meshed in gnarling fender-to-fender traffic.

Had local knowledge produced a nice, user-friendly airport? Am I fond of rhetorical questions?

DIA looks like an enormous multi-peaked marquee covered by the world's largest piece of shade cloth. It covers 53 square miles of former prairie, and is one of the largest public works projects in recent United States history. It has an underground railway that takes 88,000 passengers *per day* from the terminal to the far-flung departure gates and back again. It has a parking lot so vast that you have to catch a shuttle bus to get to the terminal – if there is a shuttle bus. If there isn't, you walk a mile through an adjacent building site.

When we got to the terminal, there were five levels to choose from – none of them, apparently, set up as an arrivals hall. Pimple-faced kids in military fatigues patrolled the concourses with efficiently evil-looking assault rifles slung over their shoulders, and the tightened security resulting from Nine Eleven prevented us from taking the railway to meet the plane at its gate. Somebody told us to wait by a bank of elevators and escalators: 'Everybody comes in through there.'

Everybody except Wyeth, that is: flight after flight disgorged its human cargo. For an hour and a half we waited, way past Wyeth's flight arrival time. His airline had no information desk that we could see, but that wasn't necessarily Midwest Express's fault because neither did any other. There were 750 closed-circuit TV cameras monitoring the DIA premises, but it was an hour before I could find an arrivals screen. When I found it, it claimed with incontrovertible electronic logic that the plane had landed. The designated baggage carousel was stopped. The one remaining bag had a name and address in Sweat Circles, Nebraska.

When Wyeth eventually showed up, via an invisible arrivals aperture not unlike Platform Nine-and-three-quarters in the Harry Potter books, his luggage was lost and he was shittier than Teddi and me. Denver International Airport employs 23,000 people. *Nobody* wanted to help. Eventually he was given a phone number to call next morning.

Muttering darkly, we made across the concrete tundra for the car. I got us back into Denver *my* way.

For Teddi's family, all roads led to Denver that day. Wyeth's wife Jill and Teddi's sister Chris had taken two days to drive across from Wisconsin through Iowa and Nebraska. Chris's son Jeff had flown in earlier and spent the day just walking the streets 'like a homeless guy.' Teddi's younger sister, Julie, had also flown in with husband Steve and daughter Ava.

Next day we pulled the big 80th birthday surprise on Tedd and it worked a treat. It was one of those easy-going well-oiled days where lots of people flow around each other, indoors and out, in the kitchen, by the barbecue, passing beers from the cooler by the back door, in and out of conversations, everybody loose and relaxed and happy to be together. There was a fantastic dinner of prime rib and sensational salads and cake and cards and family tomfoolery to wind it up. Tedd the deejay played his old vinyl jazz records, drumming the rhythms of the evening with his vast supply of witticisms and yarns from fun family days gone by.

But if there were clues to be had about Teddi's Native American ancestry, neither Tedd nor her sisters had any recollection – only that the sisters' long-dead grandmother was of half – or perhaps quarter-blood. They knew of no tribal name; the speculation was Chippewa. But as for a reservation, in which she may have grown up, the trail was cold.

Chapter 26

Crawdad dreaming

We had six days to get back to Los Angeles, no rush at all, plenty of time to see if the westward-ho portion of our journey would cough up some places as potentially habitable as Glendale, Utah.

The early going was rather strange: we sought a town that was marked on the map but didn't exist. Then we found a place that existed, but wasn't marked. It was a sort of hog and cattle-farm crossroads, the accommodations for animals and humans alike hewn from now-scarce local timber and paintlessly delapidating in the cold cloudless sunshine. We passed a highway town featuring a welcoming gas station and a less-than-savory diner advertising 'Beef, Beets 'n Beans.' We followed lonely side-roads with names like Owl Canyon Road, often dirt-gluey with snowmelt, all the way to the distant mountains. Then it was north and west across a high rolling veldt decorated by long irregular ranks of snow fences, into Wyoming, where we found it is quite legal to buy large quantities of fireworks, because there is a huge blockhouse offering bargains right on the border.

In Wyoming the names of the towns, Cheyenne, Laramie, Sundance, Buffalo and Cody, just *drip* with the wild and lawless romance of the frontier. Our route took us through Laramie, but it seemed now to resemble a college town for lumberjacks and forest rangers, where everyone drives powerful pickup trucks.

We kept going, along a windswept hundred-mile stretch of US-287, which used to be the main interstate highway until I-80 came through and turned tiny towns like Bosler, Rock River and Medicine Bow into hamlet-sized ghost towns.

Medicine Bow, which looks far less romantic than the name suggests, remains just alive thanks to the Virginian Hotel, built in 1911 to capitalize on the fame brought to the area by Owen Wister's famous western novel, *The Virginian*.

I had hoped we might stay there, and a lady serving a couple of thirsty cowboys in the bar gave us a key to take a look for ourselves. The rooms smelled like they hadn't been opened for months.

We hit the road and ended up in Saratoga, about 7000 feet up near the headwaters of the North Platte River and other famous trout streams that flow out of the surrounding Medicine Bow Mountains and the Snowy Range of the Sierra Madre. Galleries and restaurants and heritage buildings jumble in the centre of town, unspoiled by the usual sprawl of ugly motels, gas stations and fast food joints. Apart from the local ranchers, it caters to skiers, anglers, rafters and – of course – hunters. We went into a gas station to buy a phone card and Teddi found a far more useful item: the 2002 Black Bear Hunting Regulations. It's a pretty wild place. We went for a walk across the bridge, the river running fast with snowmelt, in company with two honking Canadian geese. Upstream near the hot springs for which the town was founded in 1878, we were transfixed as a family of deer sniffed timidly out from the riverside undergrowth onto a spit of rock, sipped a drink of the cold water, sniffed some more, then crossed through the water and up the bank straight towards us, aware of us but quite unafraid.

We were instantly charmed, by the deer, by the unhurried pace of the place, by the well-maintained historic buildings, by its cheek-by-jowl proximity to the beautiful surrounding ranchlands ribboned downstream along the river, and the wildernesses that reached their green tentacles into all the surrounding streams. We ate Tex-Mex tucker in a friendly restaurant and raved about our serendipitous discovery. On the way back to the historic Wolf Hotel to get some kip after a long day's driving, we found that Saratoga too had a newspaper with an opening for a reporter/photographer: there was a poster, yet again, in the window of a locked office. I filed the fact away for possible future reference.

Not long before my cancer was diagnosed, Teddi and I actually made the first tentative moves towards Saratoga as a place to live and work. Teddi looked up a local realtor in the internet. He obliged by sending photos and details for several pretty and affordable properties. He also sent the email address of the Saratoga Sun, the newspaper edited by a gentleman with the wonderfully approachable name of Coy Hobbs.

So I wrote Coy an expression of interest. He wrote back saying the opening was currently filled but would likely come up again because the money was crap, justified only by Saratoga's wonderful outdoors lifestyle. We left it at that, for the time being, but Teddi always hankered for Saratoga, and I sometimes wish I had just dropped everything and taken her back, then and there.

In the morning we motored on. I looked out over a white ranch house surrounded by still leafless tall trees, the Platte River cliffs and a meandering valley fringed with cottonwood. A great wave of yearning washed over me. All I could do was put some Crosby, Stills, Nash and Young on the CD, crank it up, and head on up the highway with prayers for happiness and freedom in our hearts.

Wyoming is a wild and sparsely settled state. Of more than 300 cities, towns and places on our map, only 96 are mentioned as actually having people living in them. Lost Springs has four, and Van Tassel eight inhabitants. Saratoga is a metropolis with its 1969, and Cheyenne and Casper are dueling Babylons with 50,008 and 46,742 respectively. It has 3.1 million acres of wilderness areas and it boasts seven National Parks including Bighorn, Flaming Gorge, Grand Teton and Yellowstone.

We felt its loneliness as we followed I-80 west towards Flaming Gorge. Keen to see some wild horses, Teddi had noted on the map a lonely and isolated place called Red Desert Basin, where we were told we might get lucky.

So we got off at Red Desert (population one trucker trying to tie down a load of timber and one recently collapsed building) and followed the main track out of 'town' for several miles. We encountered a lot of wandering groups of grazing antelope, which obligingly posed for us, but we saw no horses. I detoured briefly to take a photo of an abandoned corral, and we were surprised by the sudden approach of a shiny new pickup truck, with two guys inside wearing ties and black suits. They pulled over and seemed to expect me to do the same. I wound down the window and explained we were just taking photos; were they from the oil company?

'No,' said the driver. 'We're Jehovah's Witnesses. We've just been visiting some folks we know back there.' There was a dusty brown trailer not far away. To my untrained eye it had looked deserted.

We wished them good day and I took my photos. As we drove off, I noticed a new-filled grave at the edge of the track to the trailer. It had fresh flowers.

Vernal is a good name, though our destination for that night could just as easily be called Equinox or Bland. It is so *nice*. It has a family restaurant in which a waitress named Chelsea serves table-sized plates of ribs, and the honey comes in Yogi Bear squeeze bottles. It also has fossils like Hanksville, but in Vernal they're above the ground as well. It has Latter Day Saints (LDS) churches and people outside who look like Whistler's Mother and the old codger with the pitchfork. It has sheriffs who cruise the streets to make sure nobody's speeding too fast to get to church, or maybe to make sure that's where they're going.

We rolled through Salt Lake City. It looked as solid and upstanding as any Rock-founded metropolis should. Have the scandals of Olympic bribery been forgotten here? Little towns live on their memories. In cities they get swept away like a clean white snowfall that can't be allowed to block the blustering behemoth of commerce.

West of Salt Lake City the country flattens out into hundreds of miles of flat, scorched, sand-and-salt-blasted wasteland, with far outcrops obscured by vast eddies of dust. The salt beds glitter and glare. The road flies arrow straight and disappears on a horizon of mirage and strange possibility. We followed it past the famous Bonneville Salt Flats into northern Nevada and the town of Elko, 109 miles further on.

Next day we reeled in the miles, clear across Nevada through Battle Mountain (which has a sign saying Prison Zone, No Hitchhiking) to Winnemucca and the 'biggest little city in the world,' Reno, which was far more attractive than Las Vegas. We kept going, though, because we were aiming for California and a visitors' centre that might give us some ideas about where to stay. This might sound stupid, considering the famous resort of Lake Tahoe was so close, but the weather had turned foul and a blizzard was blowing in the adjacent mountains. Driving in snow seemed risky, so we aimed for Truckee, the railway town just inside California, the snow thickening and the traffic almost suicidal in its collective defiance of the need to cut speed.

Suddenly we came to a place where the eastbound freeway lanes were completely blocked by an enormous multi-vehicle pile-up. (We found out on the TV news that night, there were 21 vehicles involved, including six 'big rigs.' Miraculously, no one was killed.) We were grateful to get to Truckee in one piece.

There was no visitor centre, so we went into a café that sold firewood on the side and ordered a burger for me, and an egg salad sandwich for Teddi who looked like she could use a triple Scotch to wash it down. While the food was cooking, she browsed a magazine featuring articles and photos on unusual places around the state and came upon an area on the Monterey River between Sacramento and San Francisco, called the Delta. We had a destination. We just had to get there.

We got to Sacramento by pointing the car downhill from Truckee and simply steering for the next hour or so – the Taurus cruising with gravity from up around 9000 feet to less than one thousand, leaving the snowy alps behind and entering the fecund spring of northern California.

We worked our way through Sacramento's freeway interchanges and there it was, Highway 160. What an immediate transformation we encountered. From traffic clogged roads and urban congestion we were suddenly in a late-afternoon rural idyll, the road running high along a levee bank, with the broad river on our right, glinting in the setting sun, and immaculately manicured vineyards and fruit trees stretching away on the fertile floodplain to the left. As the river meandered so did the road. We crossed three drawbridges and passed homes the editors of *House and Garden* would drool over.

We'd driven 485 miles that day – at 776 kilometres easily the journey's record – and I was stuffed. At last we came upon the township of Isleton, and a neon sign advertising the Del Rio Hotel glowing in the dusk. I planted my foot on the brake and we charged inside to ask for a room. Some film crew had booked out every room in town, for the entire week. But nobody was sure when the crew was turning up, so the owners took a risk and let us have number 35. I would have taken the roof!

We ate in a restaurant where the Italian chef who married a Chinese wife cooked Mexican because that's what most of the farm workers wanted. After dinner we walked along the streets of the old Chinatown and among the kitsch little workers' houses and the big white weatherboards that faced the river We were heading for Los Angeles but I nearly said, 'Teddi, LA can wait.'

But, of course, LA didn't wait. I'm actually *glad* it didn't. We stayed two nights in Tinsel Town, and I finally got to find things I like about the place. I declared a freeway-free day, and you may be astonished to learn that it was successful, all the way from our airport motel to Venice Beach, along Ocean Boulevard to the Pacific Coast Highway, up into the Hollywood hills along Sunset Boulevard through Pacific Palisades, Bel Air and Beverly Hills, onto Rodeo Drive for window shopping and lunch at Prego, back up to Sunset Strip, up again to Hollywood Boulevard and all the way back, we never once drove on an LA freeway.

We gave the Taurus back on a Thursday morning. A lady with a computer on her belt gave me a Visa docket and we were on the courtesy shuttle to LAX as easy as that. The kids with the M-16s were still hanging about. Qantas allocated us four seats across so we could stretch out on the flight home.

We got some sushi and watched Colorado Avalanche beat LA in game one of the hockey play-offs. CNN had a live cross to the LA District Attorney, announcing that the actor Robert Blake was being charged with killing his wife. There was trouble in Israel. Still. With the addition of the intense new sabre-rattling over Iraq, the outlook for world peace seemed as usual poor.

We thought about writing postcards. But no: thanks to Nine Eleven, LAX had not one single postbox.

Chapter 27

The wake-up call

I had taken so many holidays over the past few years that I *owed* time to the ABC, my employer. I proceeded to make it up, as usual producing the 7 pm TV news, observing the farce of Australian politics and the unsuccessful search for Osama bin Laden in the aftermath of the US-led war in Afghanistan. I found myself looking for good news. If it wasn't available on weekdays, we could try to make some of our own on weekends.

One Saturday, Teddi and I drove up to the National Motor Museum at Birdwood in the Adelaide Hills, where the tourism business that is the Arkaroola Wilderness Sanctuary and Resort was holding a media launch: 'As Year of the Outback celebrations enter the awe-inspiring mountain landscape of Arkaroola,' said the pamphlet, 'they will become a tribute to the Legends of Outback Transport.'

The most famous Legend was undoubtedly Tom Kruse, then 87 years old, who for nearly 30 post-war years delivered vital supplies and mail from Marree in far northern South Australia to far-flung cattle stations along the Birdsville Track to Birdsville itself, in a Leyland Badger truck which has since been beautifully restored and was to be on display up at Arkaroola along with Tom.

Tom was by no means the only attraction. There was to be a spectacular antique air show, plus vintage car and motorcycle rallies, camel treks and a Sequins and Sandshoes Outback Ball: 'You'll be flat out like a lizard drinking meeting such Aussie trailblazers as Griselda Sprigg, Dick Smith, Professor Ian Plimer, Captain Tony Schwerdt, Chris Sperou and Cliff Coulthard.'

Arkaroola's marketing people were optimistic that the event, set for 4–7 July, would attract big numbers of tourists on their annual escape from the southern winter – perhaps 800, even a thousand per night.

As you know, my personal favourite Aussie trailblazer is Griselda Sprigg. The events of 5 July were to include 'Outback yarns by Griselda Sprigg, with *Dune is a four letter word* book signings.'

No disrespect to the other Legends, but the idea of all those people potentially buying *my* book was an exciting one. I wanted to be there, maybe sign a few books myself.

'The village is booked solid,' we were told. 'We might be able to find you a tent.' Ah, there's nothing like being in demand.

Feeling more than a little deflated, Teddi and I took a consoling drive in the Barossa Valley. Along the way, we decided we'd give Arkaroola a miss this year.

But then in June – just back from the USA and just past the solstice, we received an invitation in the mail: 'Please find an entry pass included herewith. In the spirit of this great outdoors event, we have reserved a Deluxe Tent for you, which will be fully erected with linen provided.'

It was a *deluxe* tent. We were wanted after all! I scrounged an extra couple of days off work.

It rained non-stop all the way to Clare, where we stopped to buy Myra (who naturally insisted on coming) some day-night cold and flu capsules. Beyond, she slumbered as a heavy fog fell across the landscape, punctuated by the sudden alarm of oncoming headlights. We were well beyond Laura by the time the cloud lifted, just high enough to shroud the upper hills and the central Flinders Ranges all the way past Parachilna where, at last, the sky cleared and the clouds were tumbleweeds, somersaulting away to the east. Arkaroola was a deep and dusty blue.

Before the creek crossing, there was a big stop sign and a queue of incoming vehicles, the drivers having their credentials checked by kids with clipboards and lists. It was like a border crossing. Our names were on the list. We were given a big white envelope and instructions: 'Just go left here and past the village, there'll be a man with a walkie-talkie. He'll direct you up to the tents.'

There'd be no fancy room in Mawson Lodge. This time we were going to the caravan park, and we were looking forward to it. The man with the walkie-talkie said: 'Follow that water cart to the top of the hill and you'll see the tents.'

The water cart was there to keep the dust down, because there was plenty of it. We followed in its slippery wake and circumnavigated the campground. Its facilities were augmented by a pair of demountable shower blocks and a scattering of portable dunnies, three of which were perched at the fringe of a tent city. There were forty or fifty two-man tents spaced with military precision along a graded knoll overlooking Wywhyana Creek and the village itself, half a kilometre away.

Another man with a walkie-talkie consulted his clipboard and assigned us tent number 22, unzipping its 'door' with a rasping, ratchet sound that sounded like a huge marlin had taken the bait and started stripping line from a heavy game-fishing reel. It was a sound we were to hear about 13,000 times over the next three nights as our neighbours stumbled, muttered, cursed and caroused their way by torch and starlight through this hazardous zone of guy ropes, awnings and hidden pegs.

It's a good thing it was a Deluxe Tent and not a regular one, is all I can say. The floor space was the size of a double bed. The stony ground below was covered by a lumpy square of blue carpet. There were two aluminium fold-up camp beds the width of the stretchers they use to get concussed footballers quickly off the turf. With a third bed imported for Myra, there was no way we'd have room for our luggage.

This was a reality we decided not to confront immediately. It was getting close to sundown. We could hear the sound of bagpipes in the village. Myra rummaged inside the big white envelope and found a 'What's on' schedule. The pipers were 'heralding the start of Legends of Outback Transport' right then. It was time to go and say g'day.

On previous visits to Arkaroola, even the intense few days of the book launch festivities in 2001, we had always been able to enjoy time with the Sprigg clan, Griselda and her offspring Doug and Marg. This time, it was immediately obvious that the size of Arkaroola's promotional venture was going to preclude the lazy intimacies of years gone by. 'Oh, hi, glad you made it!' was about as close as we got to the inner circle, pre-occupied as it was with making sure that legends like Dick Smith and Tom Kruse, the rampaging geologist Ian Plimer and the soft-spoken conservationist Warren Bonython, the champion aerobatic pilot Chris Sperou and the humble Darwin-to-Adelaide walker Ainsley Rowe were adequately lime-lit and introduced to the paying customers.

Griselda was nowhere to be seen. Marg said she was keeping things quiet for her, until the legend's dinner and all the formal speech-making that was soon to commence.

This was a function we had not been invited to. The wrist tags contained in the big white envelope *did* entitle us to a Welcome Barbecue, so we said we'd catch up later and joined dozens of tourists and ravenous Country Fire Service volunteers in the queue for steak and snags with bread and potato salad and half a dozen other salads, our ears assaulted for the first time that long weekend by the strains of a bush band called Tradewinds, which right then was attempting a tortured version of Men at Work's 'Down Under.'

Teddi and I decided to make one more attempt to greet Griselda. I guess she must have tired, though. She was gone. So we decided we'd catch up again next day, and retired to our tent, leaving Myra to party with a collection of likely lads, stumbling across the creek and up the unlit hillside pathway with the aid of our kitchen torch and the indifferent starlight. Away from the fires, the cold was numbing. Fully clothed, we climbed into our cots and shivered ourselves to sleep.

I was in a shitty mood all the next day, which began before dawn with a frozen-fingered rummage through our suitcase – still in the boot of the car, parked adjacent to the portable dunnies – for clean clothes and toiletries. Breakfast got brutishly dispensed from the tucker box in the car's back seat as I consulted the 'What's on' listings for evidence of Griselda's 'Outback yarns and book signing'.

It did not appear. Instead, a bloke called Terry Krieg was getting Warren Bonython to launch *his* book about walking around Lake Eyre. I took a raincheck on that one.

I might as well also have dipped-out on the day's main event – a cavalcade of restored World War II-vintage Jeeps and half-tracks and assorted legends, led from the village to the caravan park by old Tom Kruse and his Leyland Badger. When it got there, all the tourists hovered around getting photos of the legends and the Leyland. Griselda was there too, seated next to Tom and the others, surrounded by tourists and a little gang of media types.

I waited my chance, then ventured in to say hello.

She didn't seem to recognize me. Disconcerted, I said she looked busy, and offered to catch up later. 'That's nice, dear,' she said, and looked away. She didn't know me. I felt like a part of my life had suddenly vanished.

In fact, it had. I never saw Griselda again. She died the following March.

Saturday dawned a degree or so above freezing, the sun coming up in a still and cloudless blue sky. 'It's a good day for an air show,' I told my journal, sitting in the car and rubbing circulation into near-numb hands as the women slumbered on in the tent. 'Was I dreaming?' I asked the diary. 'Myra didn't get back to the tent until about 1 am, escorted up here by one of the flyboys with whom she seems to have become a hit. I seem to recall she told Teddi she's flying today from Balcanoona Airstrip as a passenger in a Chipmunk.'

'Yeah!' said Myra, when conscious and queried further. 'There are three of them here for the air show. Chipmunks, I mean. We're flying formation!'

We, it then transpired, referred to Jim Whalley, Mike Hannel and Mark Mitchell. This trio had turned up at sundown the previous evening in their fur-lined leather jackets (Whalley badged with the insignia of a man who has flown Australia's top-line combat aircraft, the FA-18), nonchalantly acknowledging their own prowess in landing safely despite hurricane-force cross winds, restless natives, and a herd of 3000 wildebeest on the runway.

Their aircraft were deHavilland Chipmunks, used by the British,

Australian and Canadian air forces to train fighter pilots in the dire days of World War Two. Swaggering into the Arkaroola village just in time for a 'pilots' briefing', they had proceeded immediately to the bar to drink away the traumas of their flight.

And there, temporarily forgetting the demand for chivalry among existentially imperiled fighter pilots and those they seek to impress, Mr Mitchell suggested Myra might not have the ticker to risk a flight with him at the controls.

'Bullshit!' she appears to have said. 'Try me!'

Balcanoona Station, once the district's biggest sheep station and now headquarters to the rangers who keep watch over the Gammon Ranges National Park, is a 35 kilometre drive south of Arkaroola.

Thanks to the National Park, the airstrip was recently upgraded to all-weather status, and its apron area was the temporary home of dozens of interesting aircraft. Among them were Chris Sperou's Pitts Special, a Russian Yak biplane, the three Chipmunks with their roll-back Perspex canopies and wartime insignia, Dick Smith's big Cessna jet, Doug Sprigg's ancient Oster monoplane and a Tiger Moth streamlined for aerobatics. The Royal Flying Doctor Service air ambulance up from its base at Port Augusta, came complete with smiling nurse and a fundraising plea so planes like this one could continue to serve the sparsely populated reaches of a vast continent.

Hundreds of people came to see the air show, which was a big success. Sperou's genuinely death-defying aerobatics were worth the drive alone. The Chipmunks were sedate by comparison, but the pilots' skills, maintaining tight formation in bumpy winds, were also admirable.

Myra had to wait until after the show before she got her ride, but soon I was snapping photos as she was strapped in and shown controls she should never touch unless she also wanted a ride with the Flying Doctor.

It later transpired that Mark Mitchell never said anything to Myra about taking off in formation, but that's what he now did, in company with one of the other Chipmunks. They droned off together towards the bone dry salt pan of Lake Frome, returning about fifteen minutes later, Myra flushed and elated at the extraordinary experience of seeing another plane only three or four metres off her own wingtip. Teddi was just glad to have her daughter back in one piece, but I was jealous as buggery and said so.

Mitchell shook his head. 'I'd give you a ride, but *you're* not young and gorgeous.'

Back in Adelaide on Sunday morning, 13 October 2002, I got up early to do some work on what was then just the first draft of this book. I was delving back to 1984 and two weeks in Bali. But I wasn't making much progress. My memory, I realized, needed some prompting if the things that happened during that trip were going to form a chapter in these pages.

Then I recalled that – along with a 29th birthday Seiko watch I had promptly lost in the sand at Lovina Beach – Teddi had given me the present of a red-covered trip diary. I'd recorded everything we'd done. It was stashed in a box of memorabilia, somewhere in the garage, stored there when we'd made the abortive move to Alice Springs. I'd just wander out and find it.

It was nearly 7.45 am. Ian McNamara was pausing from his radio show *Australia All Over* to throw to the ABC radio news, so I paused to catch the headlines. Then, in horror and disbelief, I listened to the lead story.

Details were still sketchy, but an unknown number of Australians were among the victims of an overnight series of bomb blasts in Bali's Kuta Beach district. Two popular nightspots, the Sari Club and Paddy's Bar, had been destroyed in the subsequent fires. The death toll, said the newsreader in a dead-voiced monotone, was in the thirties but expected to climb. There were large numbers of people unaccounted for.

The diary forgotten, I hurried outside to pick up the Sunday paper and brewed a quick cup of tea to take to Teddi, to wake her with the news. I turned on the TV, to see if the other media had managed any coverage. Nothing. I got on the internet but so far there was nothing new there, either. In frustration, we stayed glued to the radio. On the next bulletin, there was a grab from Australia's Foreign Affairs Minister warning us all to expect a major loss of lives.

Then there was a phoned-in report from the scene of the bombing, from my colleague at the ABC in Adelaide, Alan Atkinson, also in Bali with his family on a two-week holiday:

I'm standing outside Paddy's or what's left of it in the normally bustling Legian Street in the middle of Kuta. Where the footpaths would normally be jam-packed with shoppers and Balinese offering taxi rides, there's debris, glass and bodies. I've counted 50 bodies covered in white sheets lined up on the footpath as rescue workers toil through the ruins of the two nightspots. They're still bringing bodies out. Both clubs, on opposite sides of the street, were packed at around 11 o'clock last night when the bombs went off. The force of the blasts was so great that for about a kilometre around the scene, plate glass windows of shops and big stores were shattered. And the normally smiling Balinese, who would usually be offering to sell you their goods, are standing outside their shops or watching the rescue effort in stunned disbelief.

The phone rang. It was Myra. She had sat up with Teddi and me, watching the coverage on CNN, that ghastly night of 11 September 2001. Now, one year, one month and one day later, she had called to share further terrible news: she had friends connected with the Sturt Football Club. Sturt won the South Australian National Football League's major title in 2002. She celebrated with them, kissed their premiership medallions, and wished them a 'wicked' time during their end-of-season trip to Bali. She had just received a call on her mobile phone. Two of the team members were missing. A third had suffered terrible burns.

I asked her if it was okay if I called the ABC newsroom with this information. She said it was. I called it in and, for what it's worth, the ABC had itself a scoop.

All day the death toll climbed. Six members of a single Perth footy club were missing feared dead. Terrible stories of young lives wrecked surfaced from other cities and towns. Sturt's chief executive held a news conference to confirm that their missing were the club's veteran baggage master Bob Marshall, and the young up-and-comer Josh Deegan. The player most badly burned was premiership player Julian Burton.

Work next day was bedlam. After the bulletin I went outside and puked.

The burns victims were first to come home. The Royal Adelaide Hospital's burns unit was full of them, as were hospitals across the country. The reality of terrorism was there for everyone to see on Aussie TV screens, as the incoming military aircraft handed blanket shrouded shattered bodies to the retrieval experts at airports and chopper pads in every capital city. Their work was heroic.

Then I saw the video our crews shot when the surviving Sturt footballers came home. Their unashamed tears of relief to be away from the horror were gut-wrenching to witness. I cried too. I couldn't help it. My veil of journalistic objectivity was shot through with a million holes.

Alan Atkinson was seconded to the ABC's foreign desk to help cover the multitude of story angles in Bali. One morning he went on radio and touchingly told of how his holiday literally went to hell. A sketcher and a keeper of journals like me, he too loved Bali. It was his family's second visit.

A day or so later Alan called the newsroom and I happened to answer the phone. He was coming home soon, to catch up with his family who had already been repatriated. I asked him if he would be having some kind of debriefing session, to help him handle everything he saw.

'Not in Australia,' he said. 'Nobody can comprehend it who hasn't seen it with their own eyes. I'll be doing my debriefing here.'

In the event, Alan wrote a book, *Three Weeks in Bali*. As he winds up his story, he recalls looking out the windows at Denpasar airport, preparing to fly home. 'I can see a line of big Garuda jets gleaming in the terminal lights. Many of these planes have spent the past week helping to ferry the injured out instead of bringing tourists in. One day, I'm sure, they'll be full of holidaymakers again.'

Soon afterwards, ABC radio's Phillip Satchell asked me if I'd join him and Channel 7's experienced reporter Mike Smithson, live on air, to talk about how we handled these abysmally depressing news stories, day after day.

Mike, always the professional, managed to sound convincing when he said it was a journo's lot to report the yarn objectively, not get embroiled in it.

I confessed I could no longer do this. I confessed my tears and vomiting. I drove home feeling cleansed.

For several months, as the Bali outrage continued to dominate the news, along with sabre rattling against Iraq, I had been getting stitch-like aches and pains in my chest and upper abdomen. An earlier x-ray had indicated some sort of pleurisy-like inflammation in my left lung. I'd taken two courses of antibiotics, but this was a red herring. The symptoms and the pain were getting worse.

On 7 January 2003, I was asked to go and see my doctor to discuss the results of a CT scan I'd had the previous day. I turned up at the doctor's office, waited the obligatory 24 minutes and 30 seconds, and was guided to his rooms.

When he came in, he gave me a reassuring pat on the back, but his words were frightening: 'We're in trouble, my boy.'

You know the rest: The CT scan had identified tumours in my lungs (two), liver (two) and spine (one). The spine was the worst; there was evidence of major damage. I am aware that the disease has not simply gone away. One day, it's going to get me.

Chapter 28

Red Centre express

The train left Adelaide's Keswick terminus at its scheduled departure time of 5.15 pm. This time Teddi and I were bound for Alice Springs, 1335 kilometres of 'the legendary journey into the heart of Australia' aboard the famous Ghan.

It was still midwinter 2003, just a month after our jaunt to Perth on the Indian Pacific. But there was no rain to bother Sylvie and Jason as they gazed into our cabin from the platform, huddled with heavily coated arms around each other, waving goodbye.

This ride on the Ghan was not just another 'first' for us to savour and enjoy before my disease catches up with me and precludes future travel. Far more important than that was the reward at the end of the line: we'd have a three-day visit with our friends Ken and Fiona Newman.

When we arrived in the lounge car there were few empty seats and the place was already a raucous din as the passengers got to meet each other over a few coldies, no doubt intent on partying on this one-night-stand of a journey.

Dinner was the same. It was impossible to hear our companions unless they raised their voices to compete with the human racket.

After dinner, it was almost a repeat of our first night aboard the Indian Pacific. We twined our legs together, and pillowed ourselves up against the walls, facing each other, Teddi reading with her glasses balanced on her nose, me attempting a note in my journal, eyes drooping from a surfeit of good South Aussie plonk, the plonk that might help me sleep – in case my painkillers didn't.

From my journal: The Bunker, Semaphore Park, Thursday 3 July 2003

Much has happened since our return from Perth. They started happening pretty much as soon as we got back:

- *My old schoolmate Bruce Robbins came down from Maleny in the hills behind the Sunshine Coast to visit one weekend. (We'd hit the Barossa Valley in foul weather but scored a wonderful winter lunch at a terrific restaurant in Tanunda called 1918.)*
- *My Mum, brother Jamie and sister Andy, flew down the following week, to celebrate my birthday, and, to their surprise, Sylvie's pregnancy to boyfriend Jason.*

- *Jan from Poochera and Marty turned up as a surprise, Marty armed with a short story screenplay he's written me as a birthday gift.*
- *Wakefield Press has sought a revision of Wallaby, and an afterword for a new third edition of the Griselda Sprigg book, marking her death in March.*

During all of this time I have been irritable and mean spirited. Because of it, I failed to enjoy the Indian Pacific and Perth as much as I could, and the fractiousness of my own negativity can create the same in Teddi. More recently I have flown off the handle at Sylvie for reasons that do not justify anger.

Teddi picked up my narky behaviour way before I did. She contacted the SA Anti-Cancer Council and got names of psychotherapists and psychologists. Among them was a Doctor S. He was listed as specializing in 'resolving psychological pain associated with cancer patients'.

I am seeking clues about anger management, and how to let go and (eventually) trust Teddi and the kids to survive successfully after I'm gone.

We had a get-to-know-you session, and Dr S gave me a lot of reading ideas – stuff like existential psychotherapy stories, A Zen way to martial arts, *and another book called* Choose to be happy. *The real work is yet to start.*

Tomorrow, meantime, I have a session with RAH oncologist Dr B. I plan, for the third month in a row, to hold out on chemotherapy. Once again, I am feeling okay and am in no real need of chemical intervention beyond the painkilling drugs I'm already prescribed, (plus the 'private use' of marijuana, which I do find therapeutic in helping my attitude and my striving to remain creative through the pain).

The days do go fast. I feel the need to get cracking on the writing again. It's good that I have my projects.

But I also have my goal: as I told Dr S, I want to maximize my quality of life REALLY – not just talking about it, but by separating myself from anger, so that my fears and frustrations don't negatively and hurtfully impact on Teddi and the girls.

As well as marketing the Ghan as 'legendary' in every ad and public announcement, the train's new owners exuberantly declare the famous service is actively 'tracing the footsteps of the Afghan cameleers'.

The *original* Ghan certainly did that. In its earliest days, starting in the late 1920s, the track to Australia's Red Centre meandered north towards the desert wastes from Port Augusta via towns like Marree, where the Afghans who drove camel caravans to supply the cattle runs and far-flung telegraph stations *began* their long-range ramble to the Alice during the late 19th century. The tracks ran east of the wastes of salty Lake Eyre, then zigzagged northwest through Oodnadatta and into the Northern Territory. Next stop, the Alice.

These days the Ghan's route is more direct and modern, with millions of concrete sleepers replacing the hardwood lumps that used to be eaten out by white ants within a single season, or get swept away by flash flooding. One train was held up for weeks, the passengers surviving on kangaroos and wild goats, shot and butchered by the multi-skilled steam locomotive drivers.

In the morning the glaring bloodshot sun climbed over red dirt country, now and then crossing a dry watercourse faithfully ribboned by river gums. Beyond the distant mesa tops were ancient remnants of geological upheaval on the oldest land on the planet. Despite this desert appearance there was enough green to support a scattering of cattle, and we passed several sidings set up to take cattle onto or off the freight trains that share the line with the Ghan.

We sipped an idle coffee in the lounge and watched as the train passed the unspectacular divide between South Australia and the Northern Territory. The carriage filled with people waiting for a shot of the so-called Iron Man, about which there is much written in the on-board information sheets: 'The Iron Man is a unique monument marking the site of the one millionth concrete sleeper laid on the stretch of railway line between Tarcoola and Alice Springs (the new route, completed in 1980).'

Well, the other punters on board missed the shot. The Man was so little to see, I got one by accident alone. There's a blackish gravel hump as a base for the 'statue', with the symbolic steelworker hefting a real concrete sleeper. As art it was barely worth having the photo developed, but considering the conditions in which the fettlers were working in those days, it would be churlish to criticise their effort.

Soon we crossed a long bridge, spanning the wide bed of the ancient Finke River. The last time Teddi and I saw the Finke, at Glen Helen in the Wet of 2000–01, there was water everywhere, gurgling from pool-to-pool along the river, and soon it would flood. Now the scene looked more typical, a long meandering bone-dry sandy swathe belted decoratively by beautiful red river gums, the riverside grasses turning desert blonde in the drought of the Dry. Far, far away to the east, we saw the hazy desert mesa of Chambers Pillar, remote as rejection.

The Ghan was running late, but still had us into the Alice around midday, and there on the platform, ready to take us to the comfort of their Red Centre home, were Ken and Fiona.

From my journal: 17 July 2003

A question for Doctor S:

First tell him the story of the American bloke who picked me up when I was hitching down to Brisbane from the Sunshine Coast when I was just a young fool, long before I met Teddi. It later turned out he was house leader for a Children of God house in the inner northern suburbs.

We got to the house. He asked me in for coffee and told me his story. He had been travelling alone in Mexico. He got sick, either by drug overdose or food poisoning. He was hitchhiking towards home when the people he thought to be his benefactors set on him. He was bashed and robbed and left to die by the side of the road. He told me he spent days in a delirium, doomed. He was about to die when he had a vision. He saw God, accepted God, and was healed.

Then he told me it was his mission – and God's – to see that as many lost souls like him could be saved. He asked me to stay. I think I could have been a diplomat. I told the bloke I had no problem accepting his faith in his own scenario, but it was not my *scenario. I had to find my own. He didn't put up a fuss. I thanked him for the coffee and left.*

The point of all this? I want to ask the Doc, politely, if he's peddling another magic bullet, like the Children of God.

(When we next met, I told Dr S the story and implied my way to the question. He replied, along these lines: 'In my garden I have two lime trees. Both were planted in the same soil and at the same time, and they grew uniformly. But before one tree was old enough to bear fruit it was damaged, one bough almost completely severed. But there was another bough, so we kept the tree. Today it too bears fruit, not as bountifully as its partner, but surviving quite well all the same.'

Typical bloody Zen! But this time the common sense was so obvious I think even I get the point.)

I've known Fiona Newman since she was a Robbins, a year my junior at Griffith Primary School in Canberra, where her brother Bruce and I were best mates. Ken's a Canadian who's called Australia home since the days the pair of them met and wed, at Yuendumu in the Northern Territory's Tanami Desert back in the early 1980s if memory serves me right.

When we lived in Darwin, they lived in Katherine, not far away by Territory standards, and we'd pay each other regular visits. We went to Bali together, kids and all. When we moved to Alice in 2000, they'd been there for years. We shared Christmas and a million memories.

When my bowel burst earlier this year, and I was just emerging from the terrors of nearly dying, completely immersed in myself, Ken and Fiona were there for Teddi and the girls, along with my sister Andy. Day after day, they came by with books, stationery, cards, Boost Juices, fancy Italian coffees, sweets and treats, *being* there unwavering and concerned only for Teddi and me. Of the dozens and dozens of people – old mates, work colleagues, current competitors – who sent us their best wishes at a time we could have crumbled and given up, Fiona and Ken were complete magicians – for myself and my deeply suffering wife.

Stepping off the train, we were pleasantly enveloped by the warm dry air of winter in central Australia. Ken was firing away with his camera, hauling our gear into the back of his twin-cab Toyota, and taking us a roundabout way home, through the Canberra-like suburban streets and crescents of Alice Springs.

There's a hill behind their place. I've no idea what it's called, but after a good night's sleep I was determined to climb it just as the sun was establishing full daylight.

It was a still, perfect morning. From the top of the hill – a boulder-strewn mulch of layered volcanic stones and sediments – I could see a motionless pool of blue-grey woodsmoke hanging in the settled areas along the Todd River valley far below. Beyond, the suburbs spread sparsely through an artifice of bushland, the houses invisible behind a bird-rustled belt of parks and shrubby hills like mine. To the south there was another mighty view – the line of the dawn-red MacDonnell Ranges.

I was reminded why Teddi and I had liked the landscape so much and how we were drawn to live here.

I watched my footing, all the way down.

From my journal: On a plane from Adelaide to Brisbane, Sunday 3 August 2003

Now the journey takes us to Brisbane and a celebration of two birthdays, Jamie's Barbara today and our Mum Barbara Norman tomorrow. There's to be a combined celebration tonight at Mum and 'Pod's' place at Kallangur, which is where we will stay tonight.

Teddi and I had been fighting, again. She almost hadn't come with me to Brisbane. I am undergoing therapy in the hope that I can somehow overcome my anger towards Teddi. I seem to scapegoat her for everything. I get angry at her for getting angry at me. But at least she can acknowledge her anger and be guiltless about having a rage. I'm just fucked up.

I am really losing the plot.

I am not in control and I am not handling my illness as well as I pretend to be.

Yesterday Teddi asked me not to pretend to my family. I got furious because I thought she was accusing me of being a charlatan and a liar. I am a charlatan and a liar, and making all these confessions about it won't change the fact of it.

In the book I'm reading, it talks about 'hungry ghosts' in Buddhist psychology, who are trying to reach back and get fulfillment from something in the past – a craving that is impossible to gratify until it is acknowledged as illusory. I am a hungry ghost, in my present phase, or mindset. I am miserable and depressed and haunted by some sense of dissatisfaction, and alienation from everyone and everything.

It seems the more I know about my behaviour, the worse it seems to get. The more I know myself, the less I like myself.

Ignorance was bliss.

Now I cannot turn back. There is a new fork in the road. One fork leads through knowledge to ignorance. The other wheels, in circle, through Samsara, up and down the roller-coaster, no way to get off, endlessly out of balance, constantly reacting to the buffeting of this ghastly life.

I promised Teddi and the girls I would not do anything to harm myself. I lied. I do it to myself every day.

Sunday morning, Ken and Fiona took us into town to scout the Todd Mall markets for gifts to take home to the 'girls' and their laddies.

Purchases made, we left the mall and found seats in a cool arcade, in a coffee shop that had been popular with one of my bosses at Imparja. We'd go there so he could have a smoke and let fly with his ideas, me the fella who was supposed to turn them into realities. He liked the coffee shop because it was right behind Imparja's back fence; he could slip back if drama flared.

I left the others and went to the rear of the arcade, stepped out into a parking lot, and there it was, the building with its impressive edifice and back yard full of satellite dishes and company four-wheel-drives. My own Subaru Forester was there: Imparja National News. Somehow I expected a feeling of failure and lost opportunity to descend on me. Nothing happened. I guess I was learning to move along in life.

So has Catherine Liddle. She was the colleague I was farewelling, on the day that also turned out to be my last day of work at the ABC. I had seen to it that the ABC poached her from Imparja for her news presenting skills and rapidly improving reporting skills. Now the ABC had poached her home again to the Alice. She was pregnant again, and chuffed about a yarn she'd just done for ABC TV News, the Territory's *Stateline* program and the nationally broadcast program *Lateline*.

The story was about an Aboriginal community, built and set up with a new school, only to have its generator never turn up. The place was dependent on this power and there appeared to be no money to find a replacement – one of the never-ending fuck-ups that regularly occur when government money is involved.

How ironic that a failure in Aboriginal self-development becomes a triumph for a journo whose bosses will say, '*Good* yarn!'

From my journal: 20 August 2003

I have chosen an auspicious day to enter something in my journal.

Wyeth and Jill arrived today from Milwaukee, on a two-week visit. I don't know how to describe the feeling of completeness I have been getting today, welcoming Jill, who joins Sylvie as an expectant mother in 2004, and seeing Teddi with all three of her kids.

Yes, Myra came over with Crowelly, Sylvie with Jason – just a few nights into the occupation of their brand new split-level rental apartment in swish old Collinswood, home of the ABC.

If being always content in the company of Teddi, who I dread to leave or be separated from, is not sufficient reason to clasp onto every day this life can squeeze out, all this fecundity gives a bloke two good reasons to hang around and become a grandfather.

Today, with this wonderful reunion, I feel it's okay to say to folks so dear to me that I thank them from the depths of my being. Without them, and all the friends who have surrounded my family in awfully uncertain times, I don't think I'd have lasted long enough to write these words.

Don't get me wrong. I am having no thoughts or fears of impending doom. I just want to say my thanks now – in case I get hit by a bus.

We could have been hit by a bus at Standley Chasm – there were so many of them, ferrying tourists into the stunning gorge for the few moments at midday when the sun is directly overhead and the chasm is filled with glowing red light.

So we contented ourselves with a walk along the rocky creekbed track, dodging the oncoming hordes (there must have been 400 people waiting for the midday photo), and getting away before midday – back towards town and Simpsons Gap, where we hoped the tourists had already been.

Our hopes were fulfilled. We had the wide riverbed that led upstream to the rocky gap itself to ourselves – apart from a Frenchman delivering a loud lecture on something important to his two children and silent wife.

It was soporifically warm on the sand. Teddi found a conveniently flood-tipped river gum and sunned herself peacefully while I stalked about looking for good camera shots – of which there were plenty. I wandered for ages, stopping now and then just to savour the calmness of the place, and to listen to the parrots – which mercifully had taken over the commentary from the Frenchman. Standing among the lower rocks of the Gap's outwash I looked across the beach-blonde riverbed at Teddi, my partner in this happy and varied life. She looked so quiet and contented, though maybe she was still worrying: about me, about what she would do when my hospitalization came, always alert, always ready for the horrible moment. She had a hundred contingency plans.

As for what she will do when I'm gone, she has never looked me in the eye and said, 'Don't worry about me, Charlie.' This is what I *encourage* her to say. As for the *reality* of what she will do, I realised, that is her business, not mine. I was suddenly clear on this, like it was the voice of inner command. Trust Teddi to do what is right for herself. Trust the kids to help her, and each other. They will. I know.

God, what a woman. She has stuck by me. I owe her my life, and what I have grown into, too.

We stayed a while at Simpson's Gap, and wandered peacefully back to the Newman's in time for Teddi to turn on a brilliant French Onion soup for our hosts when they got home from their Monday labours.

From my journal: 9 September 2003

That was one horrible night. Thank God it's over.

In fact yesterday wasn't much fun either. I was bothered by pain from the new trouble zone on my spine. It's at L3 level, around my hips, lower back, whereas the tumour that caused all the trouble earlier in the year is higher up at T7. But the pain is the same: it's nerve pain caused by pressure from the tumour mass, and it's radiating all over that level of my body. And it's possible there's new action in my bowel. Or maybe the tumours in the liver are starting to act up. I'm not sure, but there seems a constant pain in my lower right side that's separate from the L3 shit. I have dubbed it the jellybean tumour.

Yes, it bothered me all day. I wrote nothing, feeling so lethargic from the extra dose of morphine I gave myself, for no result. The feeling of chronic mid-level pain is bearable but so frustrating. I have been learning deep relaxation and meditation techniques from Dr S. Several times I tried but failed to do a 'spot' meditation to visualize the pain away. I recall now I had also failed to ease the pain when I started the day, with my regular morning meditation. It's bothering me now, as I write. Last night it had me in tears of powerlessness to stop it.

Tomorrow I'm going to see the radiologist who treated me during my hospitalization last January. The head of Royal Adelaide's Palliative Care Department, who looks after my pain control, has referred me back to radiology in the hope I'll get some relief from the new tumour as I did from T7 after five zaps of radiotherapy. I got the hiccups and lost a lot of hair and had to take steroids, but (for a while at least) it made my T7 tumour smaller. I am prepared to accept that technique because it's not systemic, like the chemo drugs such as the proposed Dacarbazine that can wreck your immune system.

Of course, the doctor may say I'm a lost cause. Most likely, he'll order a series of new tests—MRI or CT scans, maybe a bone scan. Then we'll know one way or another. But if that happens, I'll have to go back to the palliative care boss and see about some stronger drugs. Already she's tripled my methadone. (Yes, I have become quite the legal junkie!) Fingers crossed for the possibilities of radiotherapy.

And of course I shall continue with my meditations. For several months now, with the guidance of Dr S, I've evolved from some cognitive therapy anger management techniques to an exploration of hypnotism and deep meditation as a method for psychological and physical pain reduction – and hopefully healing.

The operative word there is 'hope' and it is something I still possess in great abundance.

Teddi told me the other day that I was now eight full months past my initial diagnosis of multiple metastatic melanomas, and two months past the 4–6 months average life span for a person like me who has stage 4 melanoma.

I was surprised. Not that I had made it, but that – somewhere along the trail of these recent weeks of writing – I had stopped counting the days. I do not think this is because I'm getting blasé. My chronic pains remind me that I am still a person in palliative care, which (never forget) means to alleviate disease without curing *it.*

I am not one of the handfull who go into what the doctors call 'spontaneous remission'. But while there's a chance to put my hand up for one day being in that lucky little category of survivors, count me in.

14 September 2003

It has not been good start to the day for either of us, which is a pity because yesterday despite its rocky start, turned out to be a good day – once I had sufficient painkillers sustaining me.

Teddi and I had lunch at the Port Adelaide footy club. We had a lazy afternoon reading and I did a second meditation, using an excellent CD. Later, Myra came over and we enjoyed dinner together, then the Port Power v Essendon footy final, which the Power to our triple happiness won by 39 points.

I crashed early, as usual, and slept like a log until 3 am, when I woke in a sweat and in pain. It was the usual culprits: the belt of pain on my lower back, the jellybean, plus I noticed as I got up to take a hit of morphine that the numbness is spreading from my little toe all the way to the back near the ankle. There are new pains in my left leg too. This has to be due to the tumour impinging on the spinal cord. I'll report it to Dr R tomorrow. While I'm listing symptoms, I'll also mention the numbness around my bum and testicles, which really haven't felt the same since Wyeth and Jason and I got drenched at the footy two weeks ago. I'm not sure if further radiotherapy will be able to help here or not. It may depend on whether these things are caused by the tumour at T7, which I thought was stable, or the new activity at L3. Whatever, it all hurts, and I need better palliation than I'm getting at the moment. I shall seek it tomorrow.

It cannot be good to be forced to improvise as I did during my sleepless two hours this morning. As well as the little dose of liquid morphine I took a slow-

release morphine tablet, saved up for just this type of emergency from a defunct prescription. There must be a new level of medication that can 'cover' me adequately.

I will confess it now: I'm scared. I know my body is entering a new phase, and my mind – turning inwards as it is – is going there too. This business with the numbness in my nuts and left foot is the proof of what the doctors at RAH have forewarned about. This is a stage that could lead to paralysis, from the waist down, possibly worse. I don't know what's happening yet; I am not in control. Tomorrow is so long to wait. Often I'm in tears of frustration that the pain is so chronic. My meditations are good, and I understand why I should welcome pain in the sense it's proof the body is trying to help, but it is so fucking difficult to endure when it's constantly THERE, niggling, sometimes sharply – as with a dig from one of the devil's pitch-forked helpers.

Teddi, when she woke to find what a horrible night I'd endured, immediately felt awful herself. Soon she was having a panic attack, and sympathetic pains. This is the roller coaster. We're on it.

I am no suicide. But how I'd love to be free from pain.

Courtesy of the ever-thoughtful Fiona, Teddi and I got a massage each to send us on our way Tuesday morning – from the professionally qualified daughter of the Territory's Attorney-General. Teddi virtually *sashayed* onto the Virgin Blue 737.

I love take-offs and landings at Alice Springs. The sky is so brilliantly blue and the extraordinary folds and washouts of the surrounding range country are superb to view at any time of day.

Strangely, Virgin did not yet have a service direct to Adelaide. We were zigging to Sydney first, then zagging all the way back to Adelaide later in the day. At 39,000 feet the Simpson Desert dunes stretched to infinity, fleecy balls of rain-free cloud the only break in the lines of elongated dunes, red-brown and apparently barren far below. The clouds threw grey shadows, replicas of the glaring white originals far above. Earlier I had seen a single snaking dirt track crawling along a dune corridor, heading north-northwest towards the ranges. Then there was nothing. Just dunes. Thousands of them, from Andado Station to Birdsville. I was reminded of the magnitude of crossing this awful place on the ground, as the Sprigg clan had in 1962.

Next I saw the elongated salt lakes that mark the Simpson's south-eastern fringes. These were the ones Griselda and company crossed and nearly got bogged in. Reg later had one of the biggest saltpans officially named Lake Griselda. Griselda had taken two weeks to cross this wasteland. Teddi and I and the chattering holidaymakers around us were doing it less than half an hour.

Away from the Simpson, dry watercourses meandered across the now grey-brown desert wastes. The cloud was thickening, soon the view would be gone altogether.

So soon we were going home. Where, we knew it, the journey would continue.

The Bunker, Monday 15 September 2003

Now there's an occasional strong pain shooting up my left leg. Today I see the radiographer. I fear that soon I will have to spend so much time being treated or resting, that there'll be nothing left for writing.

As far as Wallaby*'s concerned, that's okay, because now my journal has drawn level with and gone ahead of the story, in terms of time, whatever that is.*

I guess that means the yarn is told.

Thank you Teddi. Thank you Wyeth and Myra and Sylvie. Thank you Ken and Fiona and Jonathan Bear and all our wonderful friends. Thank you Jamie and Andy and Mum and Pod. And Dad, thank you too, even if you did have the temerity to die on me like that, before I said goodbye. If the preachers got it right, I'll be seeing you soon, anyway.

Somewhere in samsara, within which lies the pure white light of home.